Praise fc
Agile Transformation

"*Agile Transformation* is a wonderful, very readable, and very important book. What makes virtually all other books on transformation, leadership, and business so inadequate is their partial, incomplete, and non-inclusive character. This is exactly the inadequacy handled by *Agile Transformation* through the use of Integral metatheory, a systemic framework built to be as comprehensive as possible. Thus, *Agile Transformation* is as inclusive as can be, and that is what makes this book so incredibly important. So if you are engaged in a transformation, I strongly recommend that you not continue to be fractured and broken in your own approach, but step up to the wholeness and completeness of *Agile Transformation*."

—Ken Wilber, *The Integral Vision*

"This book does not pull its punches. From the first page to the last, the Agile Transformation operating system works the simple and core truth about transforming an organization—it depends on you being transformed. There will be no Agile organizational transformation otherwise. There is much in this book that will help you learn about how to implement a successful Agile Transformation, but it is all for naught if you don't embody and lead the change. You are the vessel. It won't change unless you do. If you're serious about having your Agile Transformation succeed, read this book."

—Bob Anderson, chairman, The Leadership Circle

"It's difficult to keep your focus sharp while broadening your perspective, but that is what Michele and Michael have pulled off in their new book on leading Agile Transformation. Impressively succinct, they provide straightforward tools and essential advice that will be useful for all leaders of transformation initiatives. So how did they do it? Well, for one thing, rather than positioning traditional and Agile-inspired management viewpoints as locked in combat, as many of their predecessors have done, they show how they are equally important, complementary features of a single unifying framework. Just as important, they know what is imperative, what to simplify, and what to ignore, the kind of knowledge that can only be distilled from decades of experience."

—Charlie Rudd, chairman and CEO, SolutionsIQ, an Accenture company

"This is a must-read for any leader embarking on or in the midst of an Agile Transformation. Michele Madore and Michael Spayd's integral approach provides organizations with tremendous insights into how to overcome the pitfalls of process-centric transformations that are all too common. They have done a brilliant job of making clear, relatable, and actionable what many see as the most nebulous aspects of leading transformation."

—Shannon Ewan, managing director, ICAgile

"Michele and Michael have written a beautiful book about change, intertwining their in-depth knowledge and vast experience with Agile Transformations. It gave me a vocabulary and understanding of the change territory, so now I have a way to navigate, too, and at the same time, it has nudged me gently to start exploring the same and go for my own development journey."

—Zvonimir Durcevic, enterprise Agile coach

AGILE TRANSFORMATION

AGILE TRANSFORMATION

USING THE INTEGRAL AGILE TRANSFORMATION FRAMEWORK™
TO THINK AND LEAD DIFFERENTLY

Michael K. Spayd

Michele Madore

♦♦Addison-Wesley

Boston · Columbus · New York · San Francisco · Amsterdam · Cape Town
Dubai · London · Madrid · Milan · Munich · Paris · Montreal · Toronto · Delhi · Mexico City
São Paulo · Sydney · Hong Kong · Seoul · Singapore · Taipei · Tokyo

For information about buying this title in bulk quantities, or for special sales opportunities (which may include electronic versions; custom cover designs; and content particular to your business, training goals, marketing focus, or branding interests), please contact our corporate sales department at corpsales@pearsoned.com or (800) 382-3419.

For government sales inquiries, please contact governmentsales@pearsoned.com.

For questions about sales outside the U.S., please contact intlcs@pearson.com.

Visit us on the Web: informit.com/aw

Library of Congress Control Number: 2020946163

Cover image: Juha Sompinmaeki/Shutterstock
Page 14, Figure 1.1: A Brief History of Everything, Ken Wilber 1996 © Shambhala Publications, Inc.
Pages 27, 28: Photo of dog courtesy of Michael K. Spayd.
Page 27: Microscope illustration by Alemon cz/Shutterstock.
Page 28: Silhouette of dog by Naddya/Shutterstock.
Page 31, Figures 2.3 and 2.4: About Integral Theory. All Quadrants: The Basic Dimension-Perspectives. Integralacademy.eu/about/about-integral-theory/all-quadrants-the-basic-dimension-perspectives. Integral Academy © 2002.

ISBN-13: 978-0-321-88531-9
ISBN-10: 0-321-88531-7

1 2020

Contents

Preface

In today's business world, "Agile Transformations" have become the norm. The journey from Agile as a means of software development to thinking of Agile as a means to achieve organizational agility has been trodden by many who have influenced and shaped the thinking in this space over the last two decades. The challenges, resistance, failures, and successes of many individuals and organizations have all contributed to the way in which we continue to learn and adjust course. When we come to recognize that we all play a part in making true agility possible for organizations, it is then that we will have a shared unified vision of a reimagined organization—we will truly "see," in the deepest way, where we are, where we want to go, and what is missing. This book is written from that deepest place within us: from our experiences, our passion and sometimes our loss of passion, our successes and our failures, our joys in achieving our purpose and our pain when that purpose is not realized, and, ultimately, our understanding of and "seeing" what is missing and what we believe is possible.

We "see" that how leaders respond to transformation defines the results their organizations will get. Three primary responses of leaders lead to very different results—the status quo versus real transformation:

- Not seeing (or acknowledging) that anything needs transforming and, therefore, not changing the way they operate—that is, staying on autopilot. This view may lead to ignoring the problem, throwing more money at the problem, using the same techniques to solve problems, and so on. This then maintains the status quo results (and potentially something worse).

- Recognizing that something is broken—hearing a wake-up call—and knowing that a transformation is needed, but failing to recognize their own contributions and instead pointing to the "other" as the problem. This results in an "us versus them" mentality throughout the organization. "If only Information Technology would adopt these Agile practices more effectively." "If only the 'business' would do their part." "If only leaders would get it." But achieving agility requires all of us to operate differently. Indeed, if we don't own our part and don't see our interconnectedness in organizational transformation, then we will actually make the situation worse. When we point fingers at each other, we move further apart, rather than closer together. This second response also leads to status quo, unpredictable, or mixed results.

- Realizing there is a problem, and more importantly, that the leaders themselves are part of that problem. These folks have an understanding that if they want their organization's thinking and behavior to change, they have to change theirs first. When leaders model the change in this way, the rest of the organization starts to "see" and begins to assume accountability and take ownership of their part, becoming truly enrolled in the transformation. Collectively, the leaders realize that they must move together to span boundaries that have become borders, limiting innovation and their ability to create the future that wants to happen through their organization. This third response is what leads to transformational results, and it is the mark of transformational leadership.

If you are reading this book, we envision you as leading an Agile Transformation. You may be in the role of an Agile leader within your organization, an internal or external Agile coach, a consultant, or some other variation of these roles. We use the term "leader" to mean all of the aforementioned roles; a leader, in our parlance, is anyone who is part of leading and guiding an Agile Transformation.

Our experience in working with many transformation efforts—and several thousand Agile coaches—is that the stories and dilemmas are largely the same: "Management just doesn't get it; we can't change our culture; we don't have meaningful customer involvement" or "Agile works fine, but our organizational processes and systems—finance, performance management, sales, production support, staffing, HR policies, governance, etc.—don't align with our new Agile way of working." You may have thought that an Agile scaling approach would solve this dilemma, only to find that your organization was still the same company after implementing the framework as it was before.

A sobering realization—that this requires more of you and your organization than you ever realized when you took this on—becomes painfully evident when these new problems are embedded within a full organizational context, an enterprise. Organizations are complex phenomena. The job we undertake in an Agile Transformation—helping that complicated and complex nexus of people, personalities, culture, structures, policies, and systems of all kinds to *transform* into something very different—well, that is a huge challenge that we must approach with a serious understanding and a scientifically based method for addressing the human and business dynamics of organizational change.

A leader's level of complexity in making sense of these complex contexts is the single most important determining factor influencing the leader's impact and performance. Our intention is to inspire you to think differently, to see more clearly, to have a fresh perspective on how to approach transformation, using an Integral or "holistic" approach that incorporates all perspectives required for transformational change. The framework presented is intended to help you see more clearly, so that you can act more effectively.

If we have done our job—and you do yours, in reading with an open mind and heart—the lessons in this book will deepen your relationships, help you understand things that were previously obscured, and give you an altogether new way of thinking about and acting in the world.

Our deepest hope is to inspire you to use this book to begin your personal transformation and to take that new way of being into beginning your organization's transformation. Enjoy the journey!

Register your copy of *Agile Transformation* on the InformIT site for convenient access to updates and/or corrections as they become available. To start the registration process, go to informit.com/register and log in or create an account. Enter the product ISBN (9780321885319) and click Submit. Look on the Registered Products tab for an Access Bonus Content link next to this product, and follow that link to access any available bonus materials. If you would like to be notified of exclusive offers on new editions and updates, please check the box to receive email from us.

Acknowledgments

As we complete the writing of this book, we feel deeply grateful to the many special people on our life's journey who have played a role in our personal and professional development. We acknowledge and appreciate so many of you: teachers, students, colleagues, and friends who have helped us to evolve our ideas and thinking and cheered us on to bring this book to life.

We especially want to acknowledge and thank the three most important thought leaders who influenced and inspired us in the writing of this book: Ken Wilber, Bob Anderson, and Bill Adams.

Ken, you not only generously gave us your time for an interview, but for 30 years you have masterfully articulated what it means for a person to wake up, grow up, show up, and clean up. This book fully relies on your lifelong work.

Bob, thank you for bringing your brilliant mind to the creation of The Leadership Circle and the pioneering work you have done in service to being a steward of the planet and applying human development to organizational leadership. We are grateful for the time you spent with us as we thought through our conceptualization of Integral leadership. Thank you for your friendship, inspiration, and partnership in our lives.

Bill, thank you for the example and inspiration you offer as a leader and as a human, in doing this work of evolving the consciousness of people and organizations. We are deeply grateful for your friendship and partnership in this work.

About the Authors

Michael K. Spayd's career in Agile began in 2001 as one of the leaders of a very large-scale adoption of Agile XP. Subsequently, Michael led and coached Agile Transformations in a wide variety of contexts. As part of his practice, speaking, and teaching, he has endeavored to bring in key disciplines from fields external to Agile, such as professional coaching, systemic management, organizational development (OD), organizational culture and change, and approaches to develop more effective sensemaking in leaders. In 2010, Michael cofounded the Agile Coaching Institute, where he trained several thousand Agile coaches. In 2016, he cofounded Trans4mation, and in 2020 he and colleagues launched the Collective Edge (www.the-collective-edge.com) to help expand consciousness at the critical edge of our collective needs.

Michele Madore is the principal and cofounder of Trans4mation (www.trans4mation.coach). She is passionately devoted to the development of Agile coaches, leaders, and organizations across the globe. Her entire work life of nearly 30 years—whether as an organizational leader, consultant, coach, or employee—has been guided by an inner desire for positive change, with a focus on humanity in the workplace. She has spent the last 15 years helping organizations of all sizes on their journey to agility, and she has coached and trained hundreds of Agile coaches. Michele is a Professional Integral Coach, using a coaching method that has helped her to bring the Integral Agile Transformation Framework more alive in its practical use for organizations and in the development of leaders. Mostly, she feels incredibly blessed to share her voice, to be of service to those seeking to find their way in their work, through the gift they give in the making of it, but most especially in the feeling of it.

Integral: "Possessing everything essential or significant; complete; whole."

An integral approach (whether to medicine, education, ecology, or leadership) incorporates all of the essential perspectives, schools of thought, and methods into a unified, comprehensive, inclusive, and empirically accurate framework.
—Brett Thomas, AQAL Elements Applied to Leadership

Introduction: Why an Integral Perspective?

The power of Integral is profoundly valuable to us in how we *are* with our world. Integral is natively systemic; it's intentionally multilevel—from individuals up to organizations; and it's inherently both feeling oriented (heart-centered) and objectively oriented (data-driven), joining our hearts and our minds. Integral recognizes the realities of how we go about creating our future together, every single day—through our relationships, conversations, actions, and decisions, which are shaped by our thinking, assumptions, and all the biases we hold. It looks with compassion at the different and conflicting worldviews of real people, and offers us clarity and new ways of understanding both each other and our own inner world.

Ken Wilber is an American philosopher and interdisciplinary researcher who developed the Integral framework (or operating system) as a way to pull together hundreds of different systems of thought he had studied over many years. We will return to various aspects of Integral theory throughout the book; at this point, we note that the theory is *integral* in that it combines many different aspects and perspectives, without taking any one perspective as primary or final. Thus, perspective-taking is fundamental to thinking in this new way. Wilber has a large canon of work, some highlights of which include *A Theory of Everything* (2000a), *Integral Psychology* (2000b), *Integral Spirituality* (2006), and *Sex, Ecology, Spirituality* (1995).

In the world in which we find ourselves, leaders are being called to a higher way of leading both our organizations and our world. Unfortunately, what we see on the ground is that most organizations continue to utilize management thinking tied to Newtonian science—still acting as if we can predict the world and make a plan to fit that prediction. Of course, in the world in which we live, that is not possible. To be fair, in the past this approach worked pretty well, in both simple and complicated environments. But regrettably it doesn't work in an emergent complex world, in a world of pandemics, in our world. Leaders are being asked to peer into a future that has never been seen before, a future changing with the speed and complexity we now face. They are being asked to reshape and rethink their organizations, to create organizations that excel at change. This undertaking of a multilayered and complex journey toward such agility—with its myriad of enterprise variables and constantly expanding Agile and organizational approaches to choose from—is shining the light on the need to upgrade our way of understanding and approaching our situation. In essence, we are being asked to upgrade the thinking behind our thinking. When we do, we begin to "see" with a fresh set of eyes the need to go about this in a fundamentally different manner: We recognize that unless we adopt a holistic approach that includes a way to work with the embeddedness of culture and mindset, we will not change our organization into be what it needs to be. This type of holistic approach is an integral approach; it is our approach.

To share that approach, we will provide you with both a map and a compass. We believe you will see that this map truly does justice to the complexity of an organizational transformation. It is a map that can serve as a universal translator—like the Rosetta Stone—to help us meaningfully understand the context when we run into obstacles; a map that helps us sort out the territory, and enables us to find our way when faced with all the obstacles that you will confront; a map with a built-in compass that provides both directionality and destination. The map is built on the Integral Model, also known as the Integral Operating System (IOS).

The Integral Operating System

Michael's Take

On a trip to London a few years ago, I was hoping to take in a few sights before teaching a class the next day. I carefully preloaded my Google map, knowing I would not have Internet access but that I would get a GPS signal, setting out for Shakespeare's Globe Theatre (coincidentally, I had arrived on the quadricentennial of the Bard of Avon's passing). The path seemed straightforward, and I felt confident I knew where I was going. I had a lovely walk through London, seeing pubs and very old buildings (I am an American, after all, so easily impressed with age), until I passed the Wall of London and decided to check it out. Well, a brief step off the path, then continuing on in the direction I believed I was going, quickly had me lost. When I referred back to the map—noting my actual location per the moving dot—I found I was considerably off track. Without frequent reference to the map—and feedback from the GPS signal, my compass—the course I had actually taken versus the one I intended diverged wildly. I needed both a map *and* a compass!

Now suppose we extend this story a bit: Imagine we were in Italy rather than England, and the map was in Italian instead of English, a language we don't speak. Now we need an extra feature—that of a universal translator on top of our map. A bit like the ancient Egyptian Rosetta Stone that provided the key to translating hieroglyphics into a common language, this book provides a fundamental and powerful framework to translate the many complexities in organizational transformation work into one system, one map. In this framework, all the elements of organizational life—including leadership mindset, culture, organization structure, financial models, team dynamics, adoption patterns, personality conflicts, and the Agile process itself—have a clear place.

This Rosetta Stone includes two components: the *Integral Operating System* (developed over the past 25 years by Wilber and thousands of Integral practitioners around the world) and the *Integral Agile Transformation Framework* (developed by Michael initially, then since 2016 in collaboration with Michele). The Integral Agile Transformation Framework (IATF) is *built on top of* the Integral Operating System (IOS), and is designed specifically for use by transformational leaders, change leaders, and enterprise Agile coaches engaged in the Agile Transformation work that is the focus of this book. Part I of the book is designed to help you "download" the IOS and all its components and fundamental building blocks that will give you the understanding you need to work with the IATF. The IATF is specifically customized to support your thinking in major organizational transformations, particularly Agile ones.

Both the general IOS and the specific IATF can be seen as organizational **operating systems** because they share some essential properties of operating systems—namely, providing basic functions, a context within which "applications" have a place to operate, and services to help those applications work together. "Applications" in this metaphor are really anything that shows up in organizations—leadership development models (e.g., The Leadership Circle), scaled Agile frameworks (e.g., LeSS, SAFe, SOS), Agile practices (e.g., Scrum or Kanban), human relationship development techniques, and so on. These applications are contextualized within the IATF in a way that helps the transformation leader and the whole organization see what each application *does* within the overall scheme of their complex organization, *when* each might be suitable and when it will *not* be, and which *other* applications might be needed to support the original app and keep it functioning well, plus how each application impacts, interacts, or conflicts with the other apps.

Most importantly, the Integral map that is the IATF does not attempt to *replace* any other models or apps; rather, it gives them all a clear place within an understandable *meta-framework*, one that provides a sort of universal address. Said another way, the IATF does not supersede the "applications" (such as scaled frameworks or leadership models) by attempting to take their place; instead, it provides a map or *addressing system* within which all these applications have a place, and a clear relationship to all other applications, whether current or emerging. The IATF reveals each application's inherent strengths, as well as its limitations. It is neutral in the sense that it's not biased to one approach, but accommodates—and maps—all equally. This is not to say that all apps are seen as "equally fit for purpose" for a given situation. In fact, the IATF will help make clear when a given app is unlikely to work in a given situation. It is a framework that helps you *see more clearly so that you can act more effectively*.

How This Book Can Change Your Perspective

The deepest purpose we have in writing this book is to truly be helpful to you in your role as transformational leader—helpful beyond giving you some good ideas, a new theory, or more things to think about. This book is designed, on a fundamental level, to *change your perspective*, in part by giving you new perspectives—on your work, on your organization, on your world, and on yourself.

For that is what the Integral Model is truly about, the ability to take more and more perspectives. If you genuinely embrace these new perspectives, that openness can radically change the way you relate to your challenges, both personally and professionally, and be the catalyst that shifts your way of being as a transformational leader.

We have established that we need to upgrade our thinking and our approaches for transformation, and we know Integral is a tool that will do just that—upgrade your thinking and bring awareness and a deeper way of "seeing" both the many complex challenges you are facing and the new possibilities for working with those challenges. First and foremost among these new ways of seeing is recognizing how we ourselves are the instrument of the transformation. By exploring this framework, you will discover ways in which your own limitations are likely blocking the organization from realizing its full potential, how you must start with yourself, and what that really means. Thankfully, there is a proven way to address your leadership limitations and your organizational transformation in a systematic and science-based way of working.

The IATF (and underlying IOS) have huge lifting power, helping us make sense of the complex issues we face in organizations, enabling us to develop a strategy for this complexity, making clear why previous strategies did not work well, and helping us be clearer as to how and where to take action now.

This book goes beyond theory by arming you with proven, practical ways to take a ground-breaking approach to Agile Transformations. It takes a deep dive into our framework, how it is designed, how it works, and how you can use and apply it in your own unique organizational context. Integral is not a static or prescriptive framework; rather, it is a living, "tetra-arising" model that will develop your systems thinking in ways other tools simply cannot do.

How This Book Is Organized

There are three parts to the book, described next.

Part I, Agile Transformation: An Integral Approach

Part I provides the underlying conceptual model upon which the book, and future extensions, is built.

- In Chapter 1, we explore holons. We explore how they relate at the individual, team, and organizational levels and how we see them both as parts and as wholes of our organizational system. More importantly, we consider how they matter when we are aiming for enterprise-level agility.

- In Chapter 2, we take a full tour of the four quadrant perspectives (Intentional, Behavioral, Systems, Cultural), examining how they are all equally necessary to include in our Agile Transformation strategy.

- Chapter 3 is an exploration of altitudes, which provides a map of the evolution that happens within each quadrant perspective, from less to more complex. These altitudes are important in the development of organizations to effectively work with more complexity.

- In Chapter 4, we dive into the developmental lines within each quadrant, and how organizations may need to develop further in a particular developmental line to achieve their goals. Each quadrant will have a set of developmental lines, which may be expressed at different altitudes, because just as we human beings might be good at one thing and not so good at another, so organizations work much the same way. Therefore, organizations may require building capability in one line more than another, so as to evolve into an organization with more agility.

Overall, these Integral components provide a unifying mapping system for everything that goes on in the world, including in organizations, from individual people to structural and cultural systems, from command and control to emergent leadership. Integral refers to its overall way of seeing as an AQAL map: All Quadrants, All Levels, All Lines (Figure I.1). We can view this AQAL map from the various holon levels that we will describe in Chapter 1.

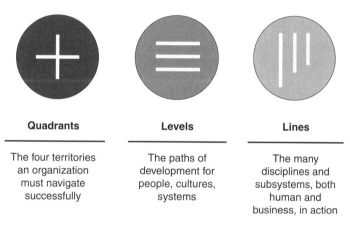

Quadrants	Levels	Lines
The four territories an organization must navigate successfully	The paths of development for people, cultures, systems	The many disciplines and subsystems, both human and business, in action

Figure I.1
The components of the AQAL model

Part II, Transformational Leadership: Upgrading the Leader's Operating System

In Part I, we laid the foundational building blocks of Integral, the operating system on which we have built our IATF model. In Part II, we switch the focus to the operating system of the transformational leader and the personal upgrade needed to successfully lead transformational change. To fully realize the promise that agility offers, organizations must come to a deeper understanding that it is the leadership's level of consciousness that imposes a ceiling on the scope and effectiveness of the change that's possible. So rather than first focusing on Agile frameworks, systems, scaling models, dev-ops, or other external factors, we address the shift in consciousness in the transformational leader as the first order of business. This shift entails upgrading the leader's operating system (LOS), consisting of both how the leader makes meaning of the world and the tools the leader needs to accomplish transformation. It is a bit like a primer based on Gandhi's famous quote, "Be the change you wish to see in the world."

Part II covers this internal change, including what we mean by transformational leadership (Chapter 5); how the LOS works at the three major levels with which almost all leaders in organizations engage (Chapter 6); and the developmental path from one level to the next, both for developing ourselves and for developing others (Chapter 7).

Part III, Organizational Transformation: Putting the Integral Compass to Work

Having laid the groundwork for using an Integral approach to Agile Transformations in Part I, and the transformational leadership needed to guide an organization through the journey to agility in Part II, we are now ready to put the full Integral compass—the IATF—to work in Part III. The IATF (built on the Integral Model) is the underlying *organizational operating system* for Agile Transformations, creating a place to "locate" any given state of affairs encountered in the organizational change effort, plus a way for the transformational leader to think about—and operate—on that state of affairs in an intelligible, effective, and relevant manner.

- In Chapter 8, we provide a complete overview of the IATF, taking you on a tour of the quadrants. We then address each holon level, including how they are specifically applied in the context of an Agile Transformation.

- Chapter 9 details the specific five *Integral Disciplines* that we have developed, mapping them to a number of developmental lines we have identified as a way to focus on the overall objective of achieving greater levels of agility, and considering them from that quadrant's viewpoint and from an overall change discipline.

- The book concludes with Chapter 10, which provides a set of competencies for transformational leaders, and an extended look at some practical ways for an enterprise coach or transformational leader to begin leading an Agile Transformation using an Integral change framework.

Questions Addressed by This Book

- What is really meant by an *Agile Transformation*, and what is realistically required to accomplish one (in terms of leadership commitment, organizational focus and persistence, and the scope of changes needed)?

- How can I use a change approach that includes the elements to attend to, and comprehensively addresses both the human and organizational aspects of change?

- What kind of leadership is required to effect such a transformation?

- How can I work with the leaders in my organization to help them see and understand the importance of modeling the behaviors of the culture and mindset aligned with the Agile philosophy?

- Can I realistically change my organization's culture to be more consistent with the notion of agility, self-empowerment, and customer responsiveness?

- As an enterprise coach or Agile Transformation leader, how do I work with my organization, and its current reality, in a way that inspires change and evokes curiosity for the possible?

Our Perspective (and Biases)

Perhaps our most fundamental belief and value is that you, as an individual, are the primary instrument for leading a transformation—not the books you've read, the skills you've been taught, or even the experiences you've had. Your inner development, more than anything, will make a difference in—or be the limiting factor for—the transformation you are responsible for leading. In short, to be successful, you need to work on yourself first. When you have gone through that process of change for yourself, you will then have the experience and understanding of how to help someone else go through it. We want you, the reader, to understand the deep interconnection between the tangible side of organizational life (metrics, business results, processes, systems) and the intangible side (beliefs, thinking patterns, mental models, shared values, our humanness); further, we want you to see that they are inextricably intertwined and always arise together, such that changing one side will help change the other side.

We attempted to rigorously take an Integral view of ourselves and our work when writing this book. For us, that means seeing different value systems across organizations—and within the same organization—as having their time and place; it means honoring each, while also clearly recognizing their limitations. At the same time, we see clearly that not all value systems can get us where we want to go in today's complex world of global challenges: Leadership and organizations must evolve to get us through the problems we have created out of our current ways of thinking and acting.

Regarding ourselves, we know that we are limited by our own biases, upbringing, training, and socialization. We attempt to counteract these limitations by soliciting feedback, and by systematically adopting different, even foreign, perspectives on what we do. We are both inveterate lifelong learners.

We intentionally call out those perspectives and biases now, as we are about to begin Part I, because using an Integral approach is fundamentally tied to perspectives and to evolving our ability to see *more* perspectives, in real time, and to see how our biases shape and limit our ability to see the perspectives of others. We invite you to open your heart, mind, and will and to see and relate to your work through a fresh set of lenses.

PART I

AGILE TRANSFORMATION: AN INTEGRAL APPROACH

To establish a common language and understanding, we are writing from the viewpoint that Agile Transformations are intended to help organizations achieve a greater level of agility. The first part of this book describes a fundamentally different approach to Agile Transformations, based on Integral thinking. It is a comprehensive approach that, over the course of the book, we expand into an intentionally designed meta-framework that can serve as a new organizational operating system for Agile Transformations (Part III). In this first part, we lay out the main elements of Integral thinking—namely, holons, quadrants, altitudes, and developmental lines—and give examples of how each can be used in Agile Transformation work. These elements incorporate both the human and business aspects of transformational change and provide a means for us to consciously work with the internal and external dynamics that are at play in every organizational transformation.

1

The Holon: Fundamental Building Block of the Integral Framework

We begin the book by focusing on the building block of everything in Integral theory, the *holon*. This will allow us to see more clearly the relationships among individuals, teams, groupings like organizational departments, and the whole enterprise. We will also look at the universal patterns that each of these holons follows in the course of its existence. We start with the complex context within which holons exist.

Organizational Complexity

In an Agile Transformation environment, complexity shows up in at least four different configurations: individuals (leaders, team members, clients), teams (delivery teams, management teams, quality teams, production teams), programs (products, departments, value streams), and organizations.

Looking first at the level of the *individual*, all individuals have their own needs and values, opinions based on their experiences, and unique professional and personal goals and aspirations. This individual meaning-making is why we encounter some people who are aligned with the Agile approach and others who have not bought into the change.

As for *teams*, research shows a "real" team will form only when there is a single overriding, clearly articulated performance challenge (e.g., winning a championship or creating an industry-changing e-commerce site) that demands cohesive team behavior to succeed. With all the overlapping and conflicting goals and initiatives within any organization, it's difficult for anyone to articulate a purpose. If they do, then everyone on the team must find themselves in alignment with that purpose and with each other! Add in the team's relationship to their manager, and things get really interesting!

Looking at the *program* level, the complexity increases further, as we add the dimension of how members of Team A feel about Team B (and Teams C and D, and vice versa), how their leaders coordinate with each other, how clearly each team's goals fit into the overall program goals, and the political issues between each of the leaders and the teams and other stakeholders. Yikes!

Bringing in the *organizational* context, the complexity reaches new heights. This is where the organizational impediments become transparent. At the team and portfolio levels, these problems can't be resolved alone. There are *policies* that thwart the transformation (e.g., performance management systems that optimize individual contribution, not team collaboration), *metrics* that drive conflict between departments (e.g., facilities are driven to minimize cost per square foot of office space, not maximize team collaboration), *traditional management thinking* that creates a confusing context (e.g., maximizing resource utilization instead of maximizing value flow), and that most devilish constraint of all, *culture* (e.g., we can't become a truly Agile culture because our traditional thinking has us stuck in valuing achievement over creating value for customers).

Putting all this complexity together, we see that systems are ubiquitous: our spouse and kids, which are part of an extended family; the department we work in, which overlaps with the team we're on (or the multiple teams we're on); our company, plus all the companies in our industry; our social or spiritual organizations . . . you get the picture. Barry Oshry (1995) describes systems from a combination of these perspectives in his seminal and poetic book *Seeing Systems*:

> We humans are systems creatures. Our consciousness—how we experience ourselves, others, our systems, and other systems—is shaped by the structure and processes of the systems we are in. As a single example, when Tops are involved in turf warfare, this is less likely to be a personal issue—much as it may seem like that to the participants—than a systemic one, a vulnerability that develops with remarkable regularity in the Top world; therefore, to deal with turf issues as a personal issue is to miss the point entirely. This is true of many of the other "personal" issues in organizational life as well. (p. xiv)

Failure to see these systemic processes and consequences (to take it personally when it is not) leads to what Oshry calls *system blindness*. In subsequent chapters, we will explore systemic seeing, thinking, and even systemic consciousness in greater depth. An even greater level of complication arises when different levels—individuals, teams, organizations—start to interact with each other.

If we are to transform the entire organization to achieve agility, it stands to reason that we have to go beyond the delivery team level to include all levels of the organization. And, to be effective at working at different holon levels, we must use a variety of approaches, including boundary-spanning practices (covered in Part II), to help us eliminate borders to collaboration across programs, across cultures, and within ourselves. So, what must shift is our thinking about transformation to create a perspective that incorporates all parts of the entire system (individuals, teams, programs, organizations), the logic of each level and its interactions with the others, and the methods that help span the various boundaries. Achieving this goal requires us to think about all parts of the system and the different perspectives they bring to create the entire product, and that each perspective is needed and equally important. Each has its own logic, its own utility. In this chapter we look at how we see "from" the different holon levels—individual, team, program, and organization. So, what exactly do we mean by this odd term *holon*?

Holons

For thousands of years, people (largely those whom we now call *philosophers*) have debated how the universe is constructed and specifically what its fundamental parts are. Their answers have ranged from one big *object* (with many constituent objects), to a series of *processes* or *events*, to an all-encompassing statement of "the mind of God." Long arguments ensued (*atomists* versus *holists*) about which was more real: the whole or the part? Is the universe composed of fundamental building blocks that are all *parts* (like atoms or bosons)? Or is it one big *whole* (like a system of systems, Gaia, the process of history, or the mind of God)?

The Integral perspective is that, if we simply look directly and practically, what we see are both wholes *and* parts. For instance, *individuals* are parts of *teams*, which are parts of *programs*, which are parts of *organizations*. On the one hand, each can reasonably be seen as part of a larger whole; on the other hand, they are wholes in and of themselves.

Let's take a really simple thing like a dog as an example. A dog is clearly a whole thing—perhaps one is near you right now if you're reading at home. Pretty simple, right? Looking closely, we observe the dog is a whole composed of parts. For instance, the body systems (e.g., circulatory, respiratory) are parts of the dog, as are the cells in the dog's body. A dog is a whole made up of cells and body systems as its parts.

Continuing to look (in a "downward" direction), we note the dog's cells are also wholes that in turn have their own parts. The cell's parts include molecules—millions of them per cell—each with its own complexity. Each of these molecules has its own parts (like atoms, made up of electrons and protons and bosons). Thus, all of these items—dogs, circulatory systems, cells, molecules, atoms— are both wholes and parts, or holons.

Looking the other way ("upward"), our dog may be part of a larger whole, such as a dog pack. (If you have only one dog, perhaps your pet has joined your "human pack.") A dog pack is also a whole that has its own **structure** (e.g., based on dominance, who eats first, or something else) and constituent **parts** (the individual dogs). So far, so good. Switching now to people, we as individuals are clearly a type of whole, made up physically of cells and organ systems, and psychologically composed of beliefs and values and subpersonalities. At the same time, we are parts in larger collectives, like families and ancestor groups, tribes, professional groups, churches, social clubs, and so forth.

All the things in our world—whether physical, symbolic, conceptual, emotional, or systemic—are both wholes and parts. The technical term for these whole/parts is *holons*, a word coined by Arthur Koestler (Wilber, 1996). This much may seem straightforward or obvious, but its importance lies in the common patterns across all these whole/parts, and how they interact in a transformation. Moving now to the work context, the individual people are holons—whole in and of themselves—but they are also parts of teams, departments, business units, work functions, and enterprises (as well as the families and other systems that typically remain in the background). Moving up, we see that teams are not only wholes composed of individuals but also are parts of bigger programs or departments; and, in turn, programs are parts of organizations, like business units, which are parts of enterprises. Strictly speaking, the holons of team, program, and organization are not the same as atoms, molecules, and cells. The former, termed *social holons*, have a bit different structure than regular holons. For our purposes, we won't worry about this distinction but rather will treat them all as holons.[1]

You might ask how this analysis of whole/part relationships (holons) is useful to us in an Agile Transformation. Research shows that holonic frameworks have the characteristics and potential to significantly address and incorporate the many perspectives and aspects of organizational change. In Wilber's extensive studies (from physics to psychology to spirituality to social meaning-making), he found that holons all share certain fundamental characteristics, or patterns. There is a different logic for each level of holon: Working with an individual (a leader or team member) is *not* the same as working with a team; working with a team is *not* the same as working with a program; and so forth. As an example, we are used to thinking of our individual consciousness, but most of us do not typically think about systemic consciousness—for instance, the way a team develops certain ways of doing things that a given individual is not really at liberty to change. The logic of the consciousness of an individual and that of a team is different. By understanding the basic patterns across different holons, we develop insights into the underlying logic (and inherent sameness) of each level, from people to organizations, and across the many organizational boundaries and perspectives—such as culture, structures, and policies—that constitute an enterprise. This will eventually help us see patterns within our transformation. We'll focus now on four of these holon patterns.

Four Patterns of Holons

Wilber (1996) identified some 20 patterns (or tenets) of holons. For our purposes, we will focus on what we consider the four most fundamental ones: agency, communion, integration, and transcendence (Figure 1.1). The first two are opposing tendencies: On the one hand, a holon "strives" to maintain its own integrity (what Integral calls *agency*); on the other hand, it "desires" to associate itself with similar holons, to bond as part of a larger whole (called *communion*). Agency and communion represent the human needs for individuality and belonging, two forces or polarities that are always in dynamic tension. Agency and communion can be thought of as horizontal dimensions; the other two tendencies we address are vertical. *Integration* is the "downward" force of a holon to embrace and bind its constituent parts into an integrated whole. The opposite force, *transcendence*, reaches in an "upward" direction to seek a higher level of complexity or consciousness. We describe each further in the following subsections.

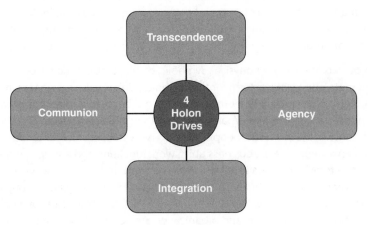

Figure 1.1
Four holon drives: vertical and horizontal. (Adapted from Wilber, 1996)

Agency

Agency is the tendency of a holon to maintain its own integrity, to be and act autonomously, to express its wholeness rather than its partness, to be an individual. A simple physical example is a hydrogen atom maintaining its own integrity as a hydrogen atom, whatever its environment is doing. A human example is when a person expresses his or her own unique values and perspectives, without being unduly impacted by the environment. However, agency can become pathological when it is rigid, alienating, repressing, or isolated. For example, an individual who is alienated or isolated does not have sufficient contact and bonding with friends or colleagues.

Agency "holds together" a holon's wholeness. Self-determination theory (Lavigne et al., 2011) says that people have a basic human desire for autonomy—to be relatively self-sufficient, to steer our own destiny, to have a sense of personal integrity and individuality. Research across cultures has shown that satisfying this need for autonomy is important to healthy development, motivation, and general well-being. We each have different needs in this regard. We may have varying thresholds for when we feel our agency has been violated, but we all feel it at some point. In an organizational context, we see agency violated when we begin Agile Transformations without addressing the current roles, responsibilities, performance reward systems, and career paths that will change in an Agile environment. When we value the human need of autonomy (agency), people will feel as if they have a choice in their destiny. When we impose change on people, we do not respect the affected individual's need for agency—which may invalidate that person as a contributor—by failing to manage it properly. In turn, that triggers resistance, which may show up in many unhealthy ways.

Sometimes pathological agency may occur, such as when functional leaders compete for their own project priorities and are unwilling to work across organizational boundaries to collaborate on a higher shared organizational goal. Too much agency can lead to an undermining of the senior holon; the team (or program) holon might dissolve and become a group of individual leaders, rather than a collective leadership team, or a set of disparate teams, rather than a unified program. In our experience, it is especially difficult to achieve this sense of wholeness at the program, department, or organizational level.

Communion

The opposite of agency ("pulling" against it in dynamic tension) is communion. **Communion** is the tendency of holons to join with other similar holons, to bond, to be part of a larger whole, to adapt to fit into their environment. A physical example is hydrogen atoms stably coexisting with other hydrogen atoms as part of a water molecule. A human example is when individuals continue to bond with other individuals to form a more cohesive team holon, such as by learning about each other's strengths and challenges and getting to know each other as people.

When communion becomes pathological, it may show up as fusion, a herd mentality, and hyper-communion. In a team context, hyper-communion happens when there is extreme groupthink and avoidance of healthy conflict, such that bonding is overly valued at the expense of diversity and some amount of autonomy.

Self-determination theory (Lavigne et al., 2011) states that to function optimally, we must address, at the core of our very existence, a basic psychological need to relate to and care for someone else. This need for belonging (communion) is so deeply rooted in our psyche that when we feel rejection, it looks similar in our body to the feelings we experience when we are in physical pain. In a far different context, those facilitating systemic constellations find the same fundamental need to belong, starting with our own family system, to be the source of much pain and dysfunction (see Bert Hellinger and colleagues' 1998 work). No wonder communion is so important! Quoting Wilber, a holon's "own existence depends upon its own capacity to fit into its environment, and this is true from atoms to molecules to animals to humans" (1996, p. 22). As individuals we have agency, but we are also part of larger holons, like teams, professions, and organizations. We each experience pulls to stay in connection, to be part of these systems (to be in communion), as well as pushes to maintain a separate identity, to do our own thing (agency).

Polarities (tensions) will likely underlie your organization's most troublesome challenges when enacting organizational change. Consider the following example of too much agency from a transformation experience and how this tension between agency and communion became problematic.

Example

Bob (whose name was changed to protect his identity) is a senior manager of corporate HR and is in charge of leadership development across the enterprise. Bob's perhaps overly strong need for agency was expressed in the way he overruled the preferences of Sue, the local HR leader who wished to bring in a leadership development program that had been experienced and preferred by her colleague-clients, who were members of several leadership teams. Bob's overly strong agency prevented a group of leaders from achieving greater communion by participating in a leadership cohort they believed would improve their collective effectiveness. Holon Principle 1a (described later in this chapter): **Too much agency from a given holon tends to undermine the holon above it.**

On the flip side, let's look at an example of too much communion (or the need to belong).

Michele's Take

I was asked to spend a day with a group of senior leaders, including the new CIO, to address culture change, since their Agile Transformation wasn't working. When we assessed their collective leadership culture, what we discovered was a group of leaders who were extremely high in complying–reactive style (i.e., overly strong in *communion*). They had a history of high customer satisfaction and had close relationships with their customers. What they valued most was the communion with each other and with their customers. When their firm was acquired by another company with a very different culture, things began to change.

This acquisition took place because of shifts in the marketplace that demanded they reinvent their organization or be left behind by the competition. Their high degree of communion became a barrier in their Agile Transformation and their ability to let go of their past traditions (which no longer served them), thus limiting their ability to reshape their organization. They couldn't get past the status-quo results due to this high need for communion. **Holon Principle 2b: Insufficient agency compromises the healthy functioning of the given holon, and eventually undermines the holons above, of which it is a part.**

Raising the level of communion on an organization-wide scale is critical in an Agile Transformation. Consider that individuals must give up some of their autonomy to join a team; this joining is critical in a transformation process, since in our experience strong teams (with both agency and communion) are a fundamental building block of a transformation. Strong teams can then (relatively easily) combine to form a strong program holon (ideally, centered on products and value streams), which in turn can form strong organizational holons. The transformational leader can consider how to raise this level of communion across the organization as a system-wide pattern.

Integration ("Agape")

Integration is the vertical drive of a higher holon to enfold, bind, and integrate its parts into a unified whole; it is the force of "Agape" love to embrace all of its parts. This concept can also be described as the downward movement of *immanence* to include junior levels of wholeness, complexity, and consciousness as part of its own wholeness. The tendency of integration does not seek to move beyond the current configuration. An example is a water molecule that "embraces" its hydrogen and oxygen atoms, not attempting to destroy or alter them, but rather keeping them as they are. Human examples include people who accept and embrace their various psychological parts, including the parts that make them unique, the parts that serve them, as well as their inner wounded parts, their wildly self-expressive parts, and so on, without attempting to "fix" them.

When integration becomes pathological, it leads to dissolution, regressing to its junior holons. At this point, it is the force of "Thanatos," the death instinct, which ends ultimately in insentient matter.

Following are examples of integration (both healthy and dysfunctional) at the holon levels of interest to us in Agile Transformations:

- Individuals display integration by incorporating their internal parts—subpersonalities, personal values that may be in conflict, beliefs, and so on—into a more coherent whole, where they feel they are able to bring their full selves to work. When integration is dysfunctional, individuals reject their parts and disown certain of their subpersonalities or values that they don't find comfortable.

- Teams evidence integration when the team (perhaps embodied by the team leader) encourages members both to share their different perspectives and to act with respect, so that all the members feel integrated into the whole. When teams are dysfunctional, they are missing the collective goals and team spirit that bind them together and, therefore, they behave as a group of individuals rather than an integrated "whole" team.

- Programs with good integration promote all of the teams and their functions by wrapping them together into a cohesive whole within a common organizational goal or vision. In an unhealthy scenario, programs do not foster the necessary meaningful connection between the parts (teams, individuals), but rather display the behavior of a bureaucratic collection of teams and functions with no true "whole."

- Organizations that seek integration have a strong sense of community, togetherness, and common mission. In contrast, those in an unhealthy organizational environment lack a sense of real identity and are more like collections of separate businesses with a common ownership structure but no real reason to be together.

In the HR example given earlier, the individual holon (HR senior leader) thwarted the desire for *communion* of the leadership team (the higher level) holon, resulting in undermining of the community and failure to become a more cohesive holon. In the example cited by Michele, when individual members of the leadership team wouldn't exercise their own *agency* by bringing their potentially controversial individual ideas and solutions to the group, the result was a lack of a leadership team holon. (They weren't really a team but rather a group of individuals, each managing their own functions.) Table 1.1 summarizes each holon with its associated holon drives.

Table 1.1   Four different holons, with examples of agency, communion, integration, and transcendence at each level

Holon Level	Agency	Communion	Integration	Transcendence
Individual	Making a decision or acting on my own; being aware of my own feelings and needs and acting on them; disagreeing with others when I have a different perspective.	Creating relationships; surrendering some of my autonomy to join with other individuals as part of a larger whole; playing by the team's or organization's rules.	Including and binding the parts of myself together into a coherent whole.	Reaching upward toward a higher level of self; seeking higher, deeper, and wider wholeness, complexity, and consciousness as an individual.
Team	Deciding as a team; not being overly dictated to by the larger whole (program or organization); resisting being disbanded when a project ends.	Surrendering some of the team's autonomy by participating with other teams in the larger whole of which we are a part (like a program or organization).	Binding the members to each other; embracing their unique contributions while maintaining the cohesiveness of the whole.	Becoming a highly cohesive team that embraces the current state, while also seeking to move past the limitations to develop greater capability as a team.
Program	Acting as an autonomous body implementing its mission, despite political or other organizational pressures.	Willingly surrendering some of the program's autonomy to participate in an organizational initiative.	Creating cohesion and integration between constituent holons (like teams and other functions in the program) to help them work better together and be honored for their uniqueness.	Embracing and appreciating the cohesive integration of teams and functions of the program, while recognizing their potential to move beyond their existing limitations and transcend to a higher functioning program.

Holon Level	Agency	Communion	Integration	Transcendence
Organization	Acts clearly on its own purpose and mission, without undue regard to industry trends, outsider preferences, or overly influential internal leaders or teams.	Participating in larger wholes like industry groups and trade associations with other organizations; acting as a global citizen.	Binding the parts of the organization—individuals, teams, departments—into a cohesive whole, balancing each junior holon's uniqueness with its need to be part of the community of the whole.	Honoring and appreciating the organizational whole and the value of each contributing part, while also reaching upward and seeking a higher, more developed wholeness capable of working with more complexity and with greater consciousness.

Transcendence ("Eros")

The fourth main holon drive, critical for vertical development and moving to greater levels of agility, is transcendence. **Transcendence** is a reaching upward toward a higher level; it is the force of "Eros" that seeks higher, deeper, and wider wholeness, complexity, and consciousness. The hydrogen atom acts to join with other hydrogen and oxygen atoms to transcend to a higher holon—the water molecule. A group of individuals—bonded with other individuals around a common objective—comes together to form a team holon, with needs and expressions of its own, beyond the individual holons that make it up.

When transcendence becomes pathological, it turns into fear ("Phobos"). It does not attempt to transcend the current configuration, but rather seeks to get away from it, repress it, and be free of it. As an example, when we as individuals seek "higher" levels of development, we may be afraid of the current characteristics and tendencies that make up our current level, wishing to get rid of them (repression) rather than including them as we reach higher.

When integration and transcendence are both healthy—as we transcend to a higher, more complex holon (Eros)—the useful parts of the lower holon are also included (Agape). Integral calls this "transcend and include," a term we will come back to again and again in the context of development. Note, however, that transcendence is concerned not only with the four holon drives but also with other aspects of the Integral map that we will continue to explore in subsequent chapters.

Transcendence into higher-level holons is an *emergent* property. For instance, individual persons can become a real team (transcendence); cohesive teams, in turn, can come together to form tribal programs, where there is both a strong sense of the team and a clear sense of being part of something even larger (again, transcendence). Programs may join together with strong teams and individuals to create a vibrant, integrated community (or organizational holon) organized around an overall common mission, with individuals and teams understanding their own place within that purpose.

The concept of transcendence is a core principle of Integral theory, which we will expound upon further in Chapter 3 when we explore altitudes. Transcendence is one of the core elements of growth, because it refers to transcending the limitations of the current environment while including the healthy or valuable aspects of it. In terms of holons, transcendence from one holon to the next is the ability to move beyond the current limitations of that holon to accomplish a particular goal.

Michele's Take

"Ben" is a very creative developer; he is an introvert, a deep thinker, and prefers to work alone to avoid distractions. He is also highly respected for his expertise in his technical craft. Ben is soon assigned to an Agile team for the first time in his career. The challenge for Ben is soon apparent with the lack of personal space, the noisy Agile team room, and the extraverts who continue to disrupt him wanting to "run something by him" or to help them think through something. Ben has a high need for autonomy, and this new Agile team and team space cater to people who prefer a high degree of communion.

Transcendence looks at this polarity of autonomy and belonging and asks you to discover the limitations of your current way and transcend those limitations (move beyond them). How can Ben transcend the limitations of operating as an individual with too much agency (autonomy)? How can other individuals on the team look at their high need for communion and transcend the limitations? And how can the organization look at the environment it has created (unconsciously) that attends to high communion and low autonomy?

Many organizations initially went about their Agile Transformations "unconsciously or unaware" of how those polarities would play out with the team focus. Later many of those organizations restructured their Agile team rooms/spaces to honor both agency and communion. They also began to consider their requirements for when, where, and how Agile teams worked, allowing individuals to self-manage to tap into their autonomy, creativity, flow, and productivity.

We must guard against the assumption that this transcendence will happen just because people are grouped together. If only individuals could routinely become highly cohesive teams, which in turn acted synergistically to create smoothly functioning and bonded product lines, which in turn realized amazing gains in market share and generated wildly enthusiastic customers, all leading to a fulfilled sense of mission as well as healthy profits! Alas, the reality on the ground appears a bit different. Thus, we must work on the communion that leads to transcendence at each level, while respecting each level's need for autonomy.

Holons and Agile Transformations

In an organizational context, highly effective leaders are effective partly because of their ability to manage the agency–communion tensions (polarities) in their purview. Likewise, high-performing organizations have designed their organization's systems, processes, and culture to manage these tensions well. To become a more effective transformational leader, we can focus on the boundary between holons, since these boundaries are the major "fault lines" where breakdowns may occur or opportunities may arise. We first seek to recognize the patterns of the underlying forces at work within and between levels—from individuals up to organizations—and then systematically apply the holon principles to mitigate the potential problems or take advantage of the opportunities.

In looking for patterns, the following questions can guide leaders and coaches in the transformation: At what level (people, team, program, organization) is there insufficient *agency*? Insufficient *communion*? A lack of *integration*? Assessing the holon fault lines is one key approach in an organizational transformation. Healthy holons at each level enable appropriate relationships between the levels.

So, what exactly do we mean by fault lines? In short, things tend to break down at the boundaries between holon levels. Fault lines are where agency becomes too strong, or communion too weak, or there is not enough integration from the senior holon, and things break down. The fault lines play out in both vertical and horizontal patterns:

- Horizontally, some patterns you might see are battles between holons at the same level: different departments competing for funding, resources, test environment access, . . . and the list goes on.

- Vertically, we pay attention to the patterns within each of the four holon levels: individuals, teams, programs, and organizations. An example of a holon pattern might be a poorly implemented Agile scaling framework that tends to enable too much agency at the program level at the expense of the team level. Thus, the teams don't have the necessary autonomy to make their own decisions within the confines of their backlogs and product owner.

Holon Principles for Transformation

Since these holon principles represent a new way of thinking for some people, here we summarize them in one place:

1. **a) Too much agency from a given holon tends to undermine the holon above.** For example, this principle becomes relevant when individuals don't play well with the team, when teams aren't willing to join with other teams in their program, and when leaders behave as individuals rather than as collective leadership teams and unduly resist efforts to create a common plan or achieve joint organizational goals. This undermines the cohesiveness and effectiveness of teams, programs, and organizations (failure to form the senior holon).

   b) Insufficient communion prevents transcendence and the formation of the holon above. This is logically related to Holon Principle 1a but may be visible in different circumstances. For example, a collection of teams may have strong team identity (agency at the team level, communion at the individual level), yet not acknowledge the importance of other teams and the critical work they do for the program or value stream; instead, teams are stuck reveling in their own "team-ness," rather than seeing themselves as part of a larger whole. Likewise, this principle is exhibited by team members who cannot sacrifice some of their own ego needs to join with other members to form a team entity (insufficient communion). Of note, people do not always easily identify with a large organization but rather need to connect with lower-level holons to create a meaningful sense of belonging (communion) to the organization. It is easier for this connection to take place with the people we work with on a day-to-day basis.

2. **a) Too much communion from a given holon tends to undermine that holon itself.** While appearing to reinforce the holon above, too much communion means loss of autonomy or integrity for the individual. For example, this principle is evident when individuals fail to have courageous conversations needed to solve conflict, when teams wish to get along with other teams and do not communicate their own viewpoints of their team's unique work (ultimately compromising the program), and when leaders don't engage in "out-of-the-box" thinking for fear they won't fit in with their colleagues. The result is a lack of creative ideas and solutions and potentially a decline in performance.

   b) Insufficient agency compromises the healthy functioning of the given holon and eventually undermines the holons above, of which it is a part. This is logically related to Holon Principle 2a, though it may be easier to see under the description presented here. For example, when individuals on a team do not have enough agency (e.g., speaking their mind when disagreeing about a technical approach), it is difficult to form a team holon. Imagine a group whose members all thought exactly alike or went along with one strong personality without each contributing their own perspective. This situation undermines the formation of the team holon, since a team is a synergy of individuals, not merely a heap of people who all think alike. In short, we cannot have relationship (communion) without boundaries (agency).

These holon principles help focus and prioritize our work with varying holon levels, including with boundary-spanning practices, developing a greater understanding of the logic of each holon (competencies as a team coach versus an individual coach), and developing our own inner complexity to more skillfully handle all these situations. Each holon has its own logic, its own techniques and methods, and its own way of being. One final use of holons is mentioned next to introduce a different perspective.

Scale Shifting

The classic Bette Midler song called "From a Distance" illustrates the idea of scale shifting:

> From a distance there is harmony,
> And it echoes through the land.
> From a distance we all have enough,
> And no one is in need.

From the right holon perspective, things are in harmony.

Scale shifting is a means of intentionally taking a different perspective to see things in a new way. When we focus on the individual holon, we may see a personal conflict between two members of a leadership team, say a vice president of finance and a vice president of R&D. This leads us to look for their personality characteristics, their emotional intelligence (EQ), or the historical source of the bad blood between them, as a means to understanding the conflict. If we shift a holon up—to the team level—we can observe this relationship from a different perspective, and we see new things. Understanding how teams work as holons, we can ask, What is the pattern being played out? What function does the conflict between the two individuals serve for the team as a whole? How are other members of the team subtly aligned with one or the other of the two in conflict, yet not acknowledging that allegiance? Further, if we shift to the level of the organization holon, we see things even more differently. We might look at the culture of the organization and the split between the way finance is perceived (lower risk, create safety for the whole organization), and the way R&D is perceived (higher risk, create big splashes and opportunities for the organization).

When this situation is viewed from the individual level, it looks like a personality conflict; from the team level, it could be a way of avoiding team conflict; and from the organizational level, it looks like a way to balance needed organizational polarities (manage risk for security versus take risks for innovation). In and of themselves, none of these is the "real" perspective, yet each is valid. To increase the ability to utilize a systems thinking perspective, try scale shifting for the various issues in your organization.

Summary

Observing holon patterns, followed by acting on holon principles intentionally, is the work of a transformational leader. Working at this level has a systemic and leveraged effect, because by implementing certain practices—such as boundary-spanning leadership and systemic consciousness—we can affect the entire organization at multiple levels. For instance, teaching leaders to use boundary-spanning practices that help bridge traditional borders between disparate groups can create a leverage point for increasing the level of communion everywhere. Next, we look at the four fundamental perspectives we can use to look at a given holon; this will provide us with even more leverage.

From Insight to Action

Questions for transformational leaders to ask themselves and/or their change team follow:

- As a transformational leader, how can you raise the level of communion across the organization as a system-wide pattern?

- At what level (people, team, program, or organization) is there insufficient agency? Insufficient communion? What is the overall organizational pattern?

- At each level of your organization, can you define what agency, communion, and integration even look like?

- If you are using a scaling framework, is there too much control (agency) at the program level at the expense of individual team autonomy?

- Agency and communion are polarities that can be managed but are never resolved. What practices can help create organizational skills in developing agency and communion at each level? For instance, mission and values statements, chartering, inquiry and advocacy conversational practice, having hard conversations constructively, and other means can be used to reinforce articulation of agency and/or communion at different levels.

- What scale shifting can we do to understand various issues from a different perspective?

Chapter Notes

1. The interested reader is referred to this Wikipedia article: https://en.wikipedia.org/wiki/Holon_(philosophy)

    Individual holon: An individual holon possesses a dominant monad; that is, it possesses a definable "I-ness." An individual holon is discrete, self-contained, and also demonstrates the quality of agency, or self-directed behavior.

    Social holon: A social holon does not possess a dominant monad; it possesses only a definable "we-ness," as it is a collective made up of individual holons. In addition, rather than possessing discrete agency, a social holon possesses what is defined as nexus agency.

2

The Quadrants: The Four Fundamental Perspectives

In the last chapter, we saw how we can see *from* different holon levels. When we look from the individual level, we see things the way people see them—things like my feelings, beliefs, how I behave, what I'm aspiring toward, what my goals are, what systems I belong to, and so on. However, when we look from the organizational holon, we see quite different things—organizational dynamics, systems, structures, workflows, the emergent patterns of multiple people's thinking (including both culture and structure), and so on.

Now that we have a good understanding of holons and the four tendencies (agency, communion, dissolution, and transcendence), let's consider how we can look *at* (rather than *from*) the various holons. The four *quadrants*, it turns out, are the four primary ways that we can look at anything; together, they create a map that has room for everything for us.

Deconstructing the Four Perspectives

We will come back to this point in much greater detail later in the chapter, but let's briefly address why these four fundamental perspectives are so important for us to understand in an Agile Transformation. In Integral theory, there are four basic irreducible (fundamental) dimension perspectives: subjective, intersubjective, objective, and interobjective. The quadrants represent the four fundamental ways people have looked at, and understood, the world and any of its fundamental issues and realities, throughout human history. At any given time, any situation possesses multiple dimensions of reality, which may be seen through these four distinct perspectives. Each perspective is valid but partial, so without all perspectives, our view can be only partial.

Generally speaking, each of us tends to have a primary quadrant from which we orient ourselves (i.e., a way of orienting)—in other words, a certain perspective from which we make sense of things and decide how to engage with people and the world around us. When we are selectively biased toward only one or two of the four fundamental perspectives, we lose out on the vital information and approaches contained within the other viewpoints that can help us resolve challenges in a complex, uncertain environment. A given profession or role often has social conventions and/or training that privileges a certain quadrant. For instance, traditional management thinking acts as if only the right-hand, objective quadrants are the "real story"; it deems the left-hand ones to be more or less irrelevant.

Of course, just because we orient ourselves from one or two quadrants, that doesn't mean we are necessarily highly developed or skilled in those quadrants. Rather, our tendency simply reflects our preferred way of looking at things, a type preference, similar to being introverted or extroverted. Further, when we systematically take all four perspectives, we increase our own systems thinking and overall leadership competency (the major focus of Part II), which requires a balanced, holistic approach. Likewise, it does the same for our leadership team.

With that rationale in place, let's return to our friend the dog. Recall that we talked about dogs in both the singular and the collective (i.e., in packs). Simple as it seems, those are two of the fundamental perspectives for addressing any holon: the *individual* and the *collective* views or perspectives. When I look at the individual level, I see certain types of things; when I look at the collective level, I see other things. In the Integral Operating System (IOS), we distinguish four perspectives; the other two are the perspectives from the *inside* and from the *outside*—that is, the interior, intangible view, and the exterior, tangible view, respectively.

Configuring these perspectives as a 2 × 2 diagram will make this clearer. Specifically, we place the individual view on top, the collective view on the bottom, the exterior view on the right, and the interior view on the left (Figure 2.1).

Using the individual dimension first, we can take either of two perspectives on a dog: from the inside and from the outside. We might also think of these as, respectively, the subjective (left) and objective (right) perspectives on the dog. When we look from the outside, we see the surfaces or *exteriors* of the dog, things that anyone can *observe*. From this external perspective, we can look in an objective way by measuring, examining, and so forth. We might, for instance, see that the dog's color is gray, one leg is slightly longer than the other, and so on. Examining the birth records, we might find the dog is five years old, or examining it with a microscope, we may find it has an infection. Even if we dissected the dog after it died to examine its "internal" parts, we will still be looking at surfaces or exteriors. This perspective on the individual dog from the exterior is certainly a useful one, from which we can learn a lot about the dog. But it's also not the whole story.

The left side of our matrix is about the interior, subjective side (or *depth)* of the holon in question. As an example, let's consider a dog Michael once had, Feine (pronounced "fen-eh"):

> I return home from a 10-day business trip. Feine goes crazy when she sees me, wagging her tail, knocking around from side to side, banging her tail against the door noisily, running here and there, bumping into things, looking up at me with a wistful but happy look. I don't know for sure, but I believe I can feel that Feine loves me, she seems so glad to see me.

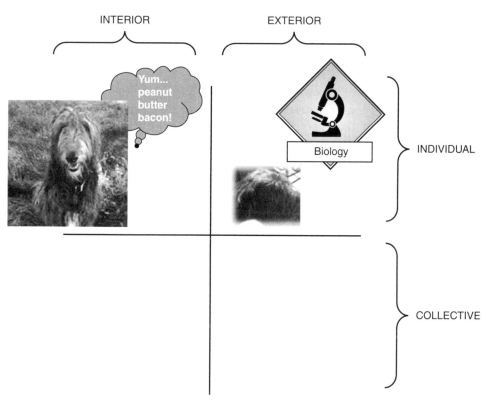

Figure 2.1
Quadrants: subjective and objective views at the individual level

The phrase "so glad to see me" is a description of the presumed internal state of Feine. Since she is not a human and we can't ask her, we can only make an educated guess. Regardless of whether that interpretation is correct, the perspective we are taking focuses on the interior of Feine. Figure 2.1 represents Feine's subjective state in the upper left quadrant (with a picture of her). The exterior view is shown in the upper right quadrant, with the image of a microscope used to represent the scientific way of knowing.

Looking from both the interior and exterior views, we get a fuller picture, though it is still incomplete. Another consideration is how the dog fits into a collective. As it turns out, Feine is a member of a small pack of three dogs (Griffin and Teddy are the other two members). Let's look at them in action as a group:

> After I have been home for a while, the pack is resting contentedly on the floor in the entryway and living room. Unexpectedly, Feine stirs, comes to see me, then goes and appears to rouse Teddy, who eventually gets up; suddenly the pack is ready to go outside. Feine appears to be the "instigator"; she gets the pack to take action, "flirts" with Teddy (which makes Griffin jealous), and then "leads" them all outside, even if from behind.

If you're tracking here, you can see this is the interior (*intersubjective*) view of the collective, a bit like their pack culture, including the interrelationships; therefore, we place it in the lower left quadrant of our matrix. Though it is difficult to do with a different species, one can get a sense of these dogs' "culture" as a group—how they are motivated, their relationships to each other, and so on. This process will become clearer and more familiar when we start looking at people.

We balance our interior perspective by looking at things from the lower right perspective, the exterior of the collective. We could, for instance, create experiments to examine how dog packs are organized: They generally have an alpha dog, exhibit certain behaviors that establish dominance and submission, have ritual ways of fighting that prevent serious injury, and have ways of sharing food, among other behaviors. We could even use such scientific approaches in observing Feine's pack, noting each dog's place in the pecking order, the dogs' behaviors in interactions over time, the relationships among the three dogs in terms of size and age, and how adding a fourth dog would emergently change the relationships. Figure 2.2 adds these interior and exterior views of the collective, with a picture of Feine's pack in the interior view, and a systems-oriented object meant to depict the scientific study of the dog pack from the exterior view.

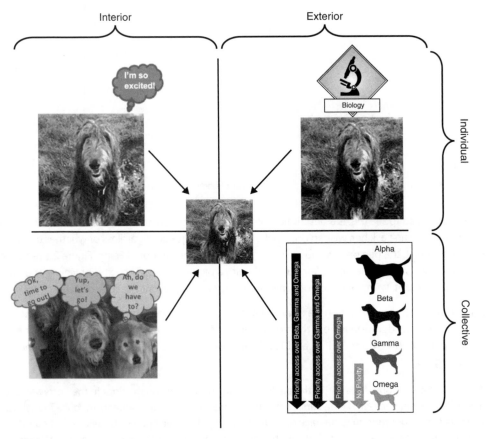

Figure 2.2
Quadrants: adding subjective and objective views at the collective level

How Each Quadrant Operates

With that brief orientation, we'll first summarize the four perspectives, and then examine how each works in more depth.

- The upper left (UL) quadrant is the view from the interior of an individual holon, whether that holon is a dog, a person, or an organization. It is generically labeled the "I" perspective, as it looks from a *first-person singular* viewpoint. When we look from the I quadrant, we see thoughts, beliefs, values, motivation, individual thinking patterns, assumptions, feelings, and other subjective and individual things. Some methods or techniques that are valid from an I quadrant perspective include introspection, meditation and prayer, reflection, journaling, and more generally an approach known as phenomenology. **Phenomenology** is defined as "denoting or relating to an approach that concentrates on the study of consciousness and the objects of direct experience" (*English Oxford Living Dictionaries*). Alternatively, we could say that it is a personal empirical method related to how things appear to us within our conscious- ness. In general, we are the only person with direct access to our own "I" perspective, and some of us are better at applying this approach than others, so it is a methodology that can be developed. Eastern spiritual traditions have concentrated on mastering these methods in meditation practices for more than 2500 years.

- The upper right (UR) quadrant—the exterior of the individual—is labeled "IT" because it rep- resents the *third-person singular* viewpoint. Looking from the IT quadrant, we see individuals' observable behaviors, their physical body including the brain, and their movements. We see people's skills and expertise, and the talents of people as well as their individual performance ratings and measurable results. Some methods or techniques that are valid from an IT per- spective include observation, empirical study, measurements of things in various ways, and the scientific method generally. IT also includes specific areas like neurobiology—that is, how the brain reacts to threat, anxiety, and trauma. The IT quadrant is described as objective, tan- gible, and attending to surfaces. People and organizations oriented toward action or measur- ing things, or who are more comfortable with concrete and observable ways of seeing things, often operate in the IT quadrant.

- The lower right (LR) quadrant is the exterior of the collective, labeled as "ITS." Note that the *third-person plural* viewpoint is ambiguous in English. In this ITS quadrant, we see things from an ecological, social, economic, political, structural, or systems theory viewpoint. Some valid methods for working in this quadrant are systems thinking, network theory, ethnology, struc- tural design, and other types of scientific interobjective analysis.

- The lower left (LL) quadrant is the interior of a collective, called the "WE" perspective and representing the *second-person plural* point of view. The WE quadrant sees intersubjective things, like shared beliefs, shared values, human relationships (the interior side or experience of them), mental models that drive what we do, cultural manifestations, and emotional fields. Some methods that are valid from a WE perspective are cultural views and worldviews; philo- sophical, religious, and political exploration; emotional–social intelligence; sensing the emo- tional field among a group's relationships; empathy; and relationship systems intelligence.

We often use simply I, WE, IT, and ITS as shorthand for the four quadrants and as a reminder of the point of view, or perspective (or epistemology), that they represent. Moreover, it is often helpful to add another characterization for each quadrant beyond merely I, WE, IT, and ITS. We can think of the I quadrant as *intentional* (or *mindset*), the IT quadrant as *behavioral*, the WE perspective as *cultural* (or *relationships*), and the ITS quadrant as a *systems* (or *structural*) view. These new labels do not replace I, WE, IT, and ITS, but rather add something to indicate the underlying perspective or **methodology** of that perspective (these will be further distinguished in Chapter 8, when we fully articulate the IATF).

Up to this point, we have been exploring the quadrants in a general way. In fact, we can use them in two different ways: as dimensions or as perspectives (Sean Esbjörn-Hargens, 2010). The perspective, or **quadrivium** method, entails examining a given situation—for instance, Michael's dogs—using each quadrant as a perspective (or methodology) *from which* to look at that situation (Wilber [2006] calls this taking the "view from" the quadrant perspective).

In contrast, when we use what Integral refers to as the **quadratic** approach, we could examine the dogs in terms of *how the dog sees the world*, using the lens of each quadrant from the dog's point of view (Wilber calls this the "view through" the quadrant). In Figure 2.2, notice that the arrows point inward, indicating that we are looking at the dog from each quadrant perspective. If we shifted to the quadratic approach, the dog would be in the middle with the arrows pointing out, as we would then be taking a viewpoint from each dog's quadrant lens or dimensions (assuming we could actually be in a dog's head and know it could do this).

As human beings, we can look at how we see and make sense of our world by using this same approach (Figure 2.3). In Figure 2.3, notice that the arrows point outward to the four quadrants. This indicates that the person is making meaning based on his or her own reality and experience. In this quadratic approach, the person applies his or her own embodied reality and ability to see the world using each of the dimensions of reality represented by the quadrants—experientially, behaviorally, culturally, and socially systemically.

Another use of the quadrants to look "at" a particular scenario or issue (the **quadrivia** approach) is depicted in Figure 2.4. In this example, the four quadrant perspectives are now directed "at" the scenario of "dying fish in a lake." The scenario is that hundreds of fish are dying in a lake, so what we are analyzing is the deaths of these fish. If you were using this quadrivia approach, you would likely seek to have experts from each quadrant's viewpoint involved in this analysis.

In the study and analysis of the dying fish, each quadrant represents the particular methodologies used:

- In the I (UL) quadrant, you study the emotions, self-identity, and beliefs of the people who live on the lake through psychological and phenomenological inquiries.

- In the IT (UR) quadrant, you explore the empirical, chemical, and biological factors contributing to the dying fish through behavior and physiological analysis.

- In the ITS (LR) quadrant, you investigate the environmental, political, educational, legal, and economic factors contributing to the issue of the dying fish through ecological and social assessments.

- In the WE (LL) quadrant, you seek to discover the philosophical, ethical, and religious factors involved through cultural and worldview investigations.

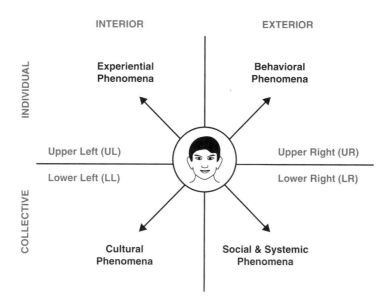

Figure 2.3

Quadratic approach: looking from their individual reality or experience. (Source: Integralacademy.eu/about/about-integral-theory/all-quadrants-the-basic-dimension-perspectives)

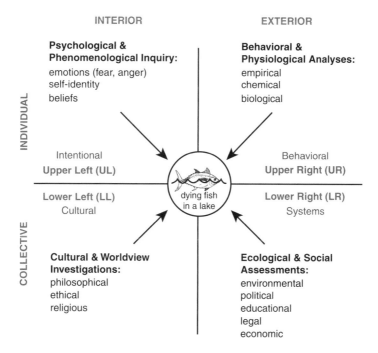

Figure 2.4

Quadrivia approach: looking "at" something (Source: Integralacademy.eu/about/about-integral-theory/all-quadrants-the-basic-dimension-perspectives)

By looking at all of these perspectives, we are attempting to discover the reality of all factors contributing to the issue. Without the data obtained from all four quadrant views, the complexity remains impenetrable—each view is only partial and may even hide the fact that the others are missing. Furthermore, we are unable to solve the problem without incorporating all factors into our solution.

From each quadrant's viewpoint, we see different types of "objects," reflecting the quadrant's underlying worldview, which in turn gives rise to a standard set of methods, assumptions, and beliefs that are considered valid from that perspective's worldview. Further, we see that each quadrant naturally has a limitation, or bias. We can say that each quadrant is "right" but represents only a partial perspective on reality. Some people get lost in the belief that there is one, single perspective that is correct, which is the "really real" thing. Scientific materialism, for instance, is the belief that all human psychology can be reduced to brain biology. Being in love, in this view, is merely a matter of neurotransmitter chemical reactions (due to the underlying belief that the IT quadrant is really real, while the other quadrants are somehow illusory).

From an Integral point of view, such a narrow focus misses something essential; only all four perspectives, taken together, can help us see the whole picture. Unfortunately, many modern organizations tend to be biased toward the right-hand quadrants, acting as if metrics, competencies, workflow, and organizational structures trump deeply held convictions, integrity, organizational culture, shared vision, and compassion. This sort of marginalization in organizations comes at quite a cost.

How to Be Integral

If we look closely at our own preferences or orientation (and consequent biases), we will likely see our preference for one or two of the quadrants. In fact, some people do not even recognize the other perspectives as being valid, believing instead that their perspectival bias is the one, true perspective. For a leader, this might take the form of overemphasizing objective measures, while glossing over having a shared vision with direct reports. For a different leader, it might involve creating great relationships (WE) but not focusing enough on achieving concrete business results (IT).

Michael's Take

My primary quadrant orientation is the WE quadrant. I am most at home in this place, orienting myself to how the group is feeling, how to be in relationship with others, and finding out what is most true for me by talking and listening to others. This is reflected in my background in psychology and coaching, especially in family systems therapy and systems coaching. This WE orientation then supports my secondary orientation, the I quadrant. I am fascinated by the ITS quadrant (and objective systems thinking), though I am not as naturally inclined to see the world that way—I have to work at it. Meanwhile, the IT quadrant is often practically hidden from me, receding out of my awareness unless I specifically focus on it.

Michele's Take

My primary quadrant orientation is the I quadrant, through accessing my inner place, my feelings, thoughts, and views—my internal experience is how I mostly make meaning of things. You can observe my primary orientation from this quadrant through my love for music. As a musician, I find this my most powerful vehicle to connect to my inner voice, as a spiritual expression, a universal language that brings people together. This primary way of orienting then serves as a way for me to connect to others, which is my secondary quadrant orientation (WE). Being in tune with my inner values also guides me in the actions I take (IT). In organizational life, it has been reflected in my pursuit of understanding organizational psychology and my own personal development (I), as well as mentoring others and leading culture change (WE). I had to consciously grow my capability in the ITS quadrant to lead organizations through complex change.

Here's the rub: When we become wedded to one or two quadrants, we lose track of the others, missing out on much of what goes on in a given situation. Returning to our question—whether there is one really true perspective—it should be evident that the answer is "No." In fact, when we examine a given situation, all four perspectives are already present and active in every moment; the only question is whether we are paying attention to that perspective, being informed by its wisdom.

Example

A person on an Agile team is being interviewed by one of the Agile coaches to determine how to be helpful to her. The coach might start by noticing her inner motivation and aspiration (I quadrant) and asking her powerful questions about these topics to formulate an "I" perspective understanding of her. In a later meeting, the coach might notice her behavior as seen from the outside (IT quadrant) and whether it complies with team norms or her own stated values. Is she adhering to the Agile practices? The coach might also examine the team member's context: What is her team's culture (WE) like, what are their shared values, and how do they influence her behavior (IT) and her motivation (I)? Finally, the coach could observe the social systems (ITS) that form her organizational environment, including the organization's structure, the policies that limit or empower what the team can do, the competitive environment of the company, and the influence of the performance management system on her and the team. Examining each perspective in turn, the coach can gain a fuller, more complete picture. (We will come back to this idea when we walk you through doing an *Integral systems analysis* of a given dilemma.)

Recall that none of these is the "real" perspective; rather, all are happening simultaneously (we say that they *tetra-arise*). Each is a lens through which to view the given situation—whether a dog, a person, a team, or an Agile organization. Taking a given view allows you to access certain information, certain ways of thinking, and certain types of approaches, while at the same time leaving out other important things. Systematically taking an all-quadrants perspective—taking a tour of all four quadrants with respect to a given situation—gives us a very complete, or Integral, view.[1]

Arguments Between Quadrants

The Integral view unites different approaches and different schools of thought into one comprehensive map; it helps us see the wisdom of each perspective, rather than choosing the "right" one. As Wilber points out, all four quadrants are relevant in any situation, so by ignoring one or more, we lose significant data. In fact, history is filled with arguments between the right side—which stresses empiricism, repeatability, objectivity, and the ability to perceive things with the senses (or extensions of the senses, like a microscope)—and the left side—which stresses meaning, values, and depth and which must be accessed through interpretation or *consciousness*. This argument goes by multiple names, such as scientific materialism versus humanism, objective versus subjective, or hard science versus social science.

The characteristic approaches between quadrants can be summarized in two fundamental ways: (1) Each quadrant has its preferred subject matter or *object of study*, and (2) each has its preferred methodology or *way of studying*. So, we can study motivations or consciousness or engagement level using an I methodology (e.g., introspection, journaling, meditation), or we can study observable behaviors from the outside using an IT methodology (e.g., empiricism, objective/structured observation, formal interviews).[2] Alternatively, we can be Integral and do both. Figure 2.5 summarizes a few of the preferred methods, objects of study, and so forth in each quadrant. (Note that the I quadrant has here been renamed *psychological*.)

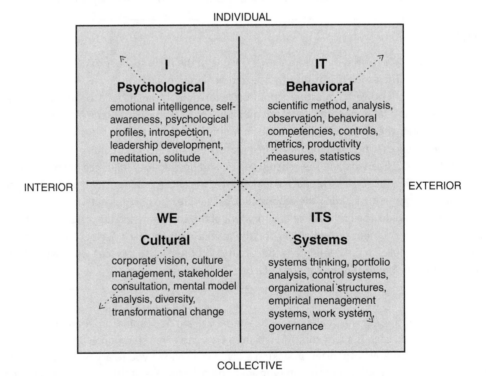

Figure 2.5
Preferred methods and thinking by quadrant

As Wilber puts it: "Surfaces can be seen, but depth must be interpreted" (1996, p. 90). Depth must be communicated and interpreted, whereas surfaces can be seen by all. The right hand asks, "What does it *do*?", whereas the left side asks, "What does it *mean*?" In the individual dimension, the key difference is between *intention* and *behavior*, whereas in the collective quadrants, the difference is between *cultural* and *social*. This bias between left- and right-hand perspectives plays out within the Agile community, with different schools of thought believing their way is best, to the exclusion of all others. The Integral perspective seeks to find the truth—and the utility—within each perspective.

As a leader, taking an Integral view of my organization creates both a holistic and a comprehensive understanding and basis for effective action. Such an approach helps me see all the implications of a strategy, what is missing, and how I can refocus or retool my own leadership to be more effective. Maybe I need to focus more on results (IT quadrant), for example, or maybe I should focus more on relationships and culture (WE quadrant).

One other point: Don't mistake "objective" for "true." The subjective, meaning-oriented perspectives on the left side have validity criteria just as the right-hand ones do, but they are quite different. For instance, there are clearly wrong interpretations of things, and there are ways to interpret well or poorly; the proper way to interpret a given something is generally defined by the community of practitioners who are engaged with the topic at hand. One criterion for judging the validity of the "I" perspective, for instance, is authenticity. When we hear a person stating an "I" perspective, we judge its "truth" by whether it seems to us to be (or not be) an authentic (genuine) expression.

The objective approaches have great power, but they also have great limits. For some people, they can be intellectually seductive because they seem to promise "objectivity" without those messy human emotions clouding the picture. Yet objective measurement succumbs to the limitation summed up in the following quote, which is often attributed to Einstein: "Not everything that can be counted, counts; and not everything that counts, can be counted."

This is akin to the story of the drunk looking for his lost keys underneath the streetlamp, even though he lost them in a dark alley, because "that's where the light is." Our scientific bent at times acts like that drunk: "Well, we couldn't find a way to actually measure the strength of relationships between people, so we settled for observing who spoke the most in the conversation, something an observer could be trained to do 'objectively.'"[3]

We are surely not implying there is no use for these measurements, as there certainly is. They provide a new view into human relationships and regularly offer new findings and perspectives. Moreover, we cannot reduce human relationships to things that can be objectively measured. We need the left-hand quadrants as well as the right-hand ones. We need to be Integral.

A further clarification is necessary concerning the lower, collective quadrants, since that perspective may be a little more foreign to many of us than the individual quadrants. Many models and frameworks are explicitly referred to as *systems thinking*; they focus on some definition of (or perspective on) the collective, the principles that govern system behavior, and the emergent properties (recall the characteristic of *transcendence* in holons) of systems. When we "see" at this level, from this perspective, we are starting to see from the whole (as Senge says), or we could say we are seeing from the next holon up.

Any focus on systems is always a focus on collectives, represented by the lower quadrants. Recalling how the quadrants are constructed, we find that systems have both an inside perspective (WE) and an outside one (ITS). This is a fundamental distinction for us—and a new one in the field of systems thinking, as far as we can determine.

The field of psychology and organization development (OD) has used the notion of systems orientation for at least 40 years. If we look at systems thinking in the Agile world, however, we notice a fundamentally different approach from that found in psychology, OD, and systems coaching.

The quadrants help us make a fundamental distinction between two types of systems thinking, or systems orientations. Some systems models and theories address concerns of the ITS quadrant. The systems dynamics school of Peter Senge (1990) and Donella Meadows (2008) is one example, and the theory of constraints is another (Goldratt, 1990). Other types of systems thinking focus on people and relationships (WE quadrant). The example of the tense energetic field in the meeting room is an example of this and is especially exemplified by CRR Global's Organization and Relationship Systems (ORSC) coaching school, as well as by systemic constellations.

Applying this distinction to Agile Transformations, the ITS quadrant variations are about the objective, exterior view of policies, feedback with delay cycles, numerical modeling, the effect of organizational structure, and the organizational environment. Frequently, this perspective is what is meant by the term "systems thinking" within the Agile community. The WE type of systems thinking—we call it *left-hand systems thinking*—is more about relationship systems, emotional fields, the culture or feel within a system, leadership culture, and systemic consciousness and constellations. WE systems thinking is just starting to be used by Agile practitioners but is less familiar. We will explore more traditional (right-hand) systems thinking and left-hand systems thinking in Part II of this book on the transformational leader.

Quadrants in Agile Transformations

If we now directly apply this quadrant thinking to an Agile Transformation context, there are two main questions to pay attention to:

- First, given the various approaches available for your Agile Transformation, how do all those different approaches map to the quadrants? Keeping in mind some need for quadrant balance, this will have implications for which approaches you might utilize as part of your change strategy at a given point in time, since taking an Integral approach implies paying attention to all four quadrants.

- Second, how do you use the quadrants to formulate your organizational change plan—for instance, to ask critical organizational questions that help assess your *change readiness*, or in designing the future state envisioned by your transformation (in all four quadrants), and finally to analyze and solve organizational impediments that arise along the way?

Summary

Systemic effects go up and down within an organization and around the four quadrants. One influences the other, for they are all merely views of the situation, windows on the truth, but not truly different things or places. We see them as different because of the nature of our mind and its preferences, biases, and natural abilities. Recall that the four quadrants tetra-arise—meaning all four are there at the same time.

The Integral injunction is to pay attention to all four, because they are all active in any situation: The only difference is whether you are proactively working with them or ignoring them. Agile Transformation uses quadrants and holons (as well as other components yet to be introduced) to thoroughly explore a large variety of topics, ranging from individuals to teams to programs to enterprises.

From Insight to Action

Think about your current approach to your Agile change effort. Here are a few questions (of many possible) to explore from each quadrant lens.

I Quadrant: Mindset

- Looking at the I quadrant, what are the attitudes, feelings, and beliefs about Agile held by team members? By middle managers? By senior leaders?
- What is the belief of individuals about why they are going through this Agile change?
- Do individuals have clarity about what they are supposed to be doing differently?

IT Quadrant: Behaviors

- Looking from IT, what are the common practices of teams? Of leaders? Of departments?
- Which collaboration practices are used to solve challenges?
- Do people have the skills needed for the new way of working?

ITS Quadrant: Systems

- What is your organization's structure—flat, hierarchical, matrix, or something else?
- Are the organization's current systems and structures set up for work to flow, or are there a lot of temporary workarounds and glitches?
- How does the organization's current structure support people's ability to adapt to emergent situations in the moment?

WE Quadrant: Culture

- How would you describe your organization's culture?

- What are relationships like in the organization between different team members? Between people in middle management? Between senior leaders? Across levels?

- Do people feel safe (i.e., psychologically safe) about trying something new, or is there a fear of failure in the culture?

Chapter Notes

1. Our quadrant preference carries over into how we think about systems. In the Agile community, we often think of organizational systems from an ITS point of view (think Kanban, Lean, theory of constraints, and other systems approaches), while also thinking of Agile teams from a WE perspective—their culture, human environment, shared values, and so on. We'll come back to this point in Chapter 3.

2. Wilber further says that we can think about each quadrant from the "inside" or from the "outside" (*Integral Spirituality* [the book]). So, we can meditate and introspect in the I quadrant (an inner perspective on the I quadrant), but we can also study meditation scientifically, from the outside. In either case, the focus of study is the interior individual perspective, the I quadrant. The inner and outer aspects of each quadrant are generally beyond the scope of this book, as this consideration gets complicated quickly and is not necessary for our work.

3. In parallel to the right-hand objective approaches that we associate with rigor, there is a long tradition in Western philosophical and Eastern spiritual traditions of the rigorous study of consciousness *from the inside* (I quadrant). No scientific inquiry is any more rigorous than, for instance, the phenomenological approaches adopted by Edmund Husserl, Martin Heidegger, and Jean-Paul Sartre in the Western traditions or the Buddhist study of abidharma—the microsecond-to-second analysis of consciousness as informed by very long-term meditation practice.

3

Integral Altitudes: The Evolution of Complexity

The four fundamental quadrant perspectives we just explored are a kind of horizontal way of seeing the full expanse of what there is; a way to "see things from a different perspective"; a way to help us move beyond the tendency of our minds to reduce the complexity we experience down into a simple pattern, which we then apply everywhere—our *quadrant orientation* or bias. When we push ourselves to look from all four perspectives instead—to act in an Integral way—we expand both our minds and our hearts into new territory. We enable ourselves to see things that we were previously blind to, that we previously shut out. We become both more insightful and more compassionate.

If we consider the quadrants as a kind of "horizontal" way of seeing, there is a "vertical" way to see as well. In Integral, we call this dimension **altitude**. Altitude has to do with the evolution of the complexity we experience, not just in the traditional biological sense, but really applying to everything, to all four quadrants; it is not just measured in centuries, like biological evolution, but may even be measured in months. As human beings, it is part of our nature to make meaning of our experiences and then to pursue what is meaningful to us. We are all born into the world at the same level of consciousness, into a given culture or altitude, and have opportunities to develop and grow throughout our lives.

If we reflect on our own lives and take a bit of a historical perspective, it becomes clear that we have evolved over time. As children, we may not have been able to fully grasp certain concepts, or we were not capable of tolerating certain emotions. Perhaps we were overwhelmed by a mathematical problem or by conflicting feelings within our family. As we got older, we matured, and our ability to handle relationships and feelings and thinking challenges grew. In turn, things that used to overwhelm us—whether cognitive or emotional—became more manageable.

Researchers have been studying how evolution happens in people, and in organizations, for many years. In turn, the Integral model takes full advantage of that fact.

If we can clearly articulate a salient and meaningful way to understand this evolution—the equivalent to the four key perspectives revealed by the quadrants—it will give us the other foundational element of our Rosetta Stone, helping us further decipher the many dimensions of our evolving enterprises. If this evolutionary model has applicability at both the individual and organizational levels—across all four quadrants, really—then we will have a very powerful map of organizational reality, one that will guide us like a good and wise friend, rather than like a dry textbook.

In sum, the quadrants are the horizontal dimension to our Integral map, and the altitudes are the vertical dimension. In the Integral model, this centrality is signified by an alternative name for the model: *All Quadrants, All Levels, All Lines* (AQAL). (Lines of development are covered in Chapter 4.)

Why Altitude Matters

The majority of this chapter summarizes research findings on the patterns of evolution. Anticipating that discussion a bit, let's consider for a moment why you should care about this background as a transformational leader. As we proceed through the chapter, it will come as no surprise to you to learn that Agile is an evolutionarily advanced phenomenon, which primarily becomes real in organizations as a set of practices (IT quadrant). By comparison, the underlying beliefs (I) and philosophy (WE) of Agile are quite secondary in the on-the-ground reality in many organizations, despite the recommendations of Agile coaches and other Agile evangelists. If you as a transformational leader use complex Agile practices (IT) as the centerpiece of your transformation, what will happen if your organization's leadership mindset (I), organizational culture (WE), and organizational structure (ITS) are not a good evolutionary match for those practices?

As Robert Kegan (1994), the famed Harvard researcher in human development, puts it, we are "in over our heads" when the complexity demands of the world we live in are simply too great for our current level of development. And that is where we believe you may find yourself right now: in over your head.

It's fair to say that Agile methods (as typically espoused) give their due to the importance of relationships, culture, and leadership, though they do so primarily by asserting those methods' own importance. Agile points to the WE viewpoint—a type of culture, a set of shared values, and the need for common vision; and it emphasizes the importance of values and mindsets (I quadrant.) The trouble is that there is generally no corresponding set of methodologies or practices for helping a culture or leadership evolve to the matching level of complexity.

Consider the relative effectiveness of the Agile community members in implementing practices (IT) versus their effectiveness and understanding of how an organization actually matures its leadership (I) or changes its culture (WE). It is not so much that these items are dismissed as "soft skills" or mere "nice to haves," but rather that we just don't know how to get there. The concept of altitudes provides us with a way to understand *what* is actually going on in such situations and where evolution needs to happen to achieve our desired result. Part II of the book addresses in greater detail *how* to get there. This more complete and more articulate Integral map, incorporating first altitudes and then developmental lines, will help us understand our current limitations to transformation and begin to see our way through.

The Integral Concept of Altitude

The Integral concept of *altitude* is a synthesis of many lines of scientific research. Indeed, it predates the idea of science, with a history stretching back to when meditative introspection in various Eastern wisdom traditions explored, in microscopic detail, the *phenomenology*, or directly lived experience, of the mind. More recently, research traditions have arisen within psychology, sociology, anthropology, biology, history, and other fields that focus on various perspectives on human development or evolution. These include research on the development of the brain (biology and neuroscience); the human social sphere (cultural anthropology); the cognitive, ethical, and sense-of-self aspects of psychology; the maturing of leadership (coaching and education); the progression in human and organizational culture (organization development, psychology, and anthropology); and others. Together, these form the foundation for the altitude dimension of the Integral Operating System. Altitude reveals how things evolve in complexity, complementing and completing the quadrant perspective.

The concept of altitude helps us complete the comprehensive map that accommodates the actual complexity of your organization, spanning from individual motivation to interdepartmental rivalries, from leadership culture maturity to workflow visibility, and from technical practices to organizational culture. Recall the fourth principle of the holons, *transcendence*: Altitude is transcendence in action.

Before proceeding, we offer up a major caveat: As Alfred Korzybski famously warned, "the map is not the territory." No model is perfect. Even so, the Integral Model is the best map we have seen to help the traveler not get lost along the way and not expect things that, given the circumstances, simply will not happen. This Integral map will help us recognize when we need to scale a mountain, navigate a body of water, or simply avoid dead ends. Altitude reveals these traps in an unparalleled way. Perhaps most importantly, it serves to guide us in increasing our own internal complexity, so that we can truly be of use to the organizations we lead or coach, helping them reach their full potential. We begin by laying out some of the research that describes altitude within organizations, then look more broadly across the quadrants at how altitude manifests in the various *lines of development* (capabilities) seen through that quadrant lens.

How Altitudes Show Up in Organizations

Throughout this book, we will return again and again to a recent piece of research on organization development: Frederic Laloux's *Reinventing Organizations* (2014). Laloux's research is remarkable in that it provides an in-depth study of cutting-edge organizations that have evolved to a new level of consciousness and functioning, affecting everything from management to personnel to culture to organizational structure to work practices. Laloux provides a summary of the various altitudes that show up within organizations today. His work will help frame our discussion on the feasibility of implementing evolutionarily advanced Agile practices in organizations that generally operate from a lower-level altitude, especially in their leadership and culture.

What You Need to Know about Stage Development Models

First, it is important to understand a few key points about what a *stage developmental* model is and does, since this is frequently misunderstood and underlies the research behind altitudes.

- The levels detailed throughout this chapter, such as Conformist-Amber, Achievement-Orange, or self-authoring mind, are *not* a typology (like Introvert–Extrovert, DiSC, Thomas Kilman Conflict Modes, and so on). They are not preferences or styles, and they are *not* "all equal, just different."

- Instead, they are a set of sequential *stages* or *waves* through which individuals (or organizations) develop. In that sense, they are organically hierarchical. Individuals at a "higher" stage have more capability than those at "lower" stages, because they have already gone through the "lower" stage. They're not better people, just more capable.

- A stage developmental model is similar to a computer game, wherein individuals move up in the levels only after mastering the skills of the previous level. As they progress, they do not lose what they have learned but instead are more capable and more complex. We say they "transcend and include" the lower level.

- Evolution through the levels is a cyclical progression, as we go through phases within one level before transitioning to the next. At first, we are able to identify with it from a "head" view (knowledge, awareness, and "talking the talk"). Then we become more competent, more solid, and more present in the level ("walking the walk"). Eventually, we begin to outgrow that level, as our new awareness takes us to the next level. This progression represents both a horizontal and a vertical development within the altitudes: We are not only transcending and including new capabilities that take us to another level but also developing to a healthy state within the current level. As we work with organizations, we sometimes find that the needed work is to get healthy right where they are.

- Another way to say this is that altitudes are holons: Achievement-Orange includes (and transcends) Conformist-Amber, since it is the next holon up evolutionarily.

- Just as we would never consider that an infant who had not developed language was "not as good" as an older child who had done so, so we do not say that people at a lower stage are lesser people, or of less worth, than those at higher stages. Higher stages indicate greater complexity and typically greater capability. Development adds greater complexity in the right-hand quadrants (e.g., new repertoires of behaviors or more adaptive structures) as well as greater consciousness in the left-hand quadrants (e.g., the ability to emotionally and cognitively handle greater complexity and to take more and more different perspectives).

- It is helpful to think of people as "lighting up" a given altitude, because it is active for them at that moment and perhaps even routinely in their lives. *People are not the same as their altitude.* We don't say that a person "is" Pluralistic-Green, for example, though the individual might light up that altitude with respect to work. In reality, that person might light up a different altitude with respect to spirituality or religion and have a different altitude from one work context to the next. Most people have a *center of gravity* from which they operate most of the time, as do organizations.

- One's *life circumstances* (e.g., problems, opportunities, challenges, worries, peak experiences, failures) are paired with particular altitudes (see Graves, 2005). Certain adaptations work well for a given set of life (or organizational) circumstances, while others don't. There is evolutionary momentum when current adaptations don't work and when the system (individual, team, or organization) is open to change.

- There is no difference between people centered at different levels in terms of most personality characteristics, including IQ. For instance, Graves (2005) used a variety of psychological tests on group members to determine their personality characteristics. He found that many attributes (e.g., intelligence) remained consistent between members of a given level and the population at large. In contrast, for a few attributes (e.g., dogmatism), he found that there were characteristic ways the attribute varied between the stages of development.

- The level of development (altitude) provides a *boundary condition* (limitation) on the level of complexity that can be effectively realized by the person or system (e.g., team or organization).

- Agile thinking was born out of relatively higher altitudes (Pluralistic-Green and Evolutionary-Teal). When Agile is introduced into organizations (or teams) that primarily light up lower altitudes (like Conformist-Amber or Achievement-Orange), those Agile ideas will tend to be either rejected outright or "watered down" into the corresponding Amber or Orange way of thinking (as Laloux's and Graves's research would predict).

- We could say that organizations below a certain altitude are "in over their heads," given the complexity of the modern world. This can represent either a positive developmental challenge or a disaster.

Transcend and Include

It is important to emphasize the *transcend and include* elements of development as we talk about altitudes. As pointed out earlier, altitudes are organically hierarchical in that they are levels that we move through and are depicted as moving up. The concept of transcending and including in Integral theory actually encompasses four components: transcend, include, negate, and destroy. That is, in this progression we *transcend* the limitations (of that altitude), *include* the healthy, valuable, or partially true aspects of that altitude, *negate* the unhealthy (no longer valuable) aspects, and *destroy* (break down or move beyond) the boundaries that limit our thinking. As we evolve through altitude levels in life, we eventually discover the next set of limitations, boundaries, and the healthy and unhealthy aspects of that altitude. In turn, the process of evolution begins again.

Michele's Take

As professional Integral coaches, we use the transcend and include method in working with people to develop capabilities toward a specific developmental goal. In the Integral method, we create metaphors, using *transcend and include* thinking so that the metaphors represent and include what is valuable and honoring about their current way, as well as how the current way closes down (limits) them in adopting the new, a more desirable way of being. The mistake people make, when this is not understood, is to completely overlook the good in what exists currently, what should be kept and appreciated, and what still serves them.

While the Integral Model is hierarchical in form, it is not meant to be used that way. It is a *natural* hierarchy rather than a *dominator* hierarchy. In other words, higher levels are levels with greater capability that can handle greater complexity, not a higher human status or privilege per se. At the end of this chapter, we will further explore how we evolve through the altitudes using a transcend and include approach.

Now we're ready to dig more deeply into altitudes, first as described by Laloux, and later by Graves and others. The following descriptions have the clearest relevance in the I and WE quadrants, but they also illuminate the IT and ITS quadrants. These descriptions are largely based on Laloux's work with cutting-edge organizations. However, Laloux's research itself is mostly based on (and embellished from) the research of Graves (2005), Beck and Cowan (1996), Kegan (1994), and Wilber. Further, the analysis of altitude is based on our own experiences in Agile Transformations applying these concepts over the past 18 years, and in that sense it is more tailored to the Agile Transformation context than the basic Integral Model.

Conformist-Amber Altitude

Conformist-Amber organizations are very process-focused, believing there is one right way to do things. They seek order, control, and predictability and do not like competition. They tend to be arranged in a fixed hierarchy with formal job titles: Planning happens at the top, execution at the bottom. The underlying worldview is that workers need direction because they are unable to make decisions for themselves. People become strongly identified with their role and tend to distance themselves from their genuine feelings and even from their uniqueness, valuing *social belonging* above *self-expression*, and strongly internalizing group norms (what Kegan calls the *socialized mind*, as we will see later). Identification with the group and its values is the beginning of strong ethno-centrism, the belief that one's cultural group is superior to others. It also begins the donning of the *social mask*, as we internalize behaviors associated with people of our rank and in our role. The ben-efit is a strong sense of being part of the group (*communion*), while the downside is being alienated from our own feelings and individual perspective.

Graves (2005) found that people with this orientation want clear lines of authority and role expecta-tions. When studying work groups of people in the midst of the Conformist-Amber stage, he found that they naturally organized themselves into two or more hierarchies or pyramids, with people at lower levels in one of the hierarchies talking only to people at the same level in the other hierarchy and never to people at higher levels.

In Laloux's organizational research, the Conformist-Amber altitude manifests as strong siloes based on business function, where workers follow the rules, and where innovation and critical thinking are generally not wanted. Managers rely on command and control and emphasize following the rules. Relationships between functional silos are often filled with distrust, blame, and suspicion (e.g., Graves found the most extreme conflict was between hierarchies in Conformist-Amber groups).

As opposed to the Impulsive-Red altitude, where power is in the hands of a specific person, power in the Conformist-Amber altitude is vested in a given role, like that of a general in an army. Even if a given incumbent is weak in his or her particular role, the overall hierarchy holds things together.

The rules and the hierarchy define right and wrong for everyone in the organization; taken to the extreme, this can become a bit like the Borg on *Star Trek: The Next Generation*.

Whether a given organization operates largely from a Conformist-Amber orientation or not, the traces of this belief system are deeply buried within our collective memory and often assert themselves unpredictably. Lest we are tempted to dismiss the Amber stage as outdated, we need to realize what a dramatic progression it was over the previous stage (Impulsive-Red) and the monumental achievements it enabled (the building of the pyramids, for instance). Moreover, a healthy Conformist-Amber structure is still appropriate and effective for simpler work environments and in those in which order is essential (e.g., the military). Further, there is a deep vein of honor, duty, and service in the Amber altitude that ennobles the human spirit and is the very foundation of civilized society. Without structures like regulating bodies, and rules and laws, social discourse and commerce become impossible. Having some amount of Conformist-Amber structures (and thinking) in your organization—particularly in areas like finance and regulatory issues—is essential to staying in business and even to having a civilized society. That's why businesses look for this level of thinking in foreign markets before investing in a less developed country: Amber is the foundation of a civilized society.

Achievement-Orange Altitude

Contrasting the Achievement-Orange altitude with the Amber altitude, Laloux (2014) says we see the world "no longer as a fixed universe governed by immutable laws, but as a complex clockwork, whose inner workings and natural laws can be investigated and understood" (pp. 23–24). This description points to the fact that Achievement-Orange organizations are based on a leap in cognitive development (to what Piaget called the *formal operations* stage, which enables more complex logic operations in the brain), superseding the notion that the universe is based on fixed, unchanging laws, and leading individuals to question authority and the status quo. The *scientific method* and discovering what is most effective replace the focus on morals and doing things right. This orientation also leads to viewing the organization as a machine and seeing management from an engineering perspective. In the process, it identifies only with solidly materialistic things that can be seen and touched (privileging the right-hand quadrants) and rejects any form of spirituality and transcendence (marginalizing the left-hand ones).

The Achievement-Orange altitude is very appropriate (and adaptive) in a complicated world, where analysis and discovery can lead to remarkable achievements. Orange loves innovation (having invented R&D and product management departments), accountability, and meritocracy. The premium on rationality can make people in Achievement-Orange organizations "hide emotions, doubts, and dreams" behind a professional mask, lest they be vulnerable. (Note the use of a professional, rather than social, mask at this level.) Our identity is no longer fused with our rank and title (as in the Amber stage) but rather with our need to be seen as competent and successful, ready for advancement as a professional.

Where an Amber organization is driven by process, the Orange organization is driven by both process and projects, focusing ultimately on *outcomes*. It retains the Amber hierarchy as its organizational structure but then "drills holes into it" with project and other cross-functional structures (since customers tend to buy the outputs of projects). *Command and control* (Amber) becomes *predict and control* as the organization seeks to achieve its desired outcomes. Management exercises its control by setting goals, then has these goals cascaded down over the hierarchy (*management by objectives*). Management relinquishes some control over how things are done (so long as goals are achieved) in an attempt to tap into the intelligence of people across the organization—though that effort typically falls short of the full empowerment found in the Pluralistic-Green altitude). Strategic planning, yearly budgeting, key performance indicators, performance appraisals, bonuses, and stock options are all signs of Achievement-Orange thinking. For most people, this is just what they call "business reality." This illustrates how Achievement-Orange thinking is the water we swim in as a culture, it is the lens we look through; for most of us, it is the subject we look through, not the object we look at (see Chapter 7 on subject–object relationships).

Graves (2005, pp. 116–117) found that work groups whose members were all centered in the Achievement-Orange altitude had aggressive fights for leadership. When one person got control of the group, that individual worked hard to stay in charge, tending to micromanage members' actions. In fact, reading Graves's research, one is struck that Conformist-Amber managers tend to exercise control via the hierarchy and an impersonal sense of role, whereas Achievement-Orange managers exercise control more personally, by wresting that control from others. The result is a bit like the law of the jungle, albeit not enforced by physical power but rather by political and performance-oriented power.

Laloux (2014) notes how the Achievement-Orange orientation asserts that decisions should be pushed down the hierarchy to foster innovation and motivation, but "in practice, leaders' fear [of giving] up control trumps their ability to trust, and they keep making decisions high up that would be better left in the hands of people lower in the hierarchy" (p. 27). In this way, we start to see where an inherently Pluralistic-Green meme (like team empowerment) or even an Evolutionary-Teal one (such as self-organized teams) may be of interest to people operating out of a lower level (i.e., Achievement-Orange) because it taps into some of Orange's values: being more efficient and effective, making greater profits, succeeding, and so on. However, other portions of the Achievement-Orange paradigm—for example, controlling others once one is in power and protecting one's position—get in the way of fully implementing the idea. The thinking that created the idea is at a higher altitude of complexity than the leaders and organization implementing that same idea. This is fundamentally relevant to the transformational leader in an Agile transition, as we will see in Part II; this conflict between Agile values and the underlying organizational culture can be a source of deep frustration and misalignment.

The Achievement-Orange altitude values *freedom*, which allows individuals to pursue their goals in life, and *meritocracy*, an environment where the best can make it to the top. In its healthy expression, this can lead to a culture that inspires innovation and achievement in a constructively competitive but fair environment. People still embrace their social roles, leading to social climbing (especially in less developed individuals). The darker expression of the Achievement-Orange orientation may manifest as pervasive greed, scheming to fabricate "needs" that do not really exist (through clever marketing), and pursuing growth for growth's sake. The Orange altitude also relies on externalities—not having to pay for all of the consequences of its production, such as pollution and consumption of resources.

The United States was founded by a very cutting-edge (at that time) group of Achievement-Orange thinkers. Achievement-Orange is the dominant worldview of business and political leaders today, though evolution in all the quadrants has started to pass this thinking by, limiting its effectiveness. Realistically, the modern world is a complex meme stack of Amber, Orange, and Green ideas, with a center of gravity in Achievement-Orange.

When considering what an Agile enterprise would look like in an Achievement-Orange–oriented organization (a theme we will return to throughout this book), we would do well to focus on igniting innovation, removing obstacles to accountability, and creating structures that lead to a genuine meritocracy. These three core innovations that Laloux identifies from the Achievement-Orange thinking organization are resonant with the values held by such an organization; this creates the kind of alignment that leads to successful implementations. In other words, we will be going with the flow if we work within such Achievement-Orange themes.

Pluralistic-Green Altitude

The Achievement-Orange orientation can take us only so far in our complex, interconnected, diverse postmodern world. It tends to drive toward a materialistic view of the world, where success matters more than people, where getting ahead trumps relationships with colleagues, and where reason is often judged superior to feeling, instead of being complementary to it. As Laloux states, "Pluralistic-Green is highly sensitive to people's feelings. It insists that all perspectives deserve equal respect," regardless of their source. The Pluralistic-Green orientation searches for belonging and inclusion over success per se. It is people-oriented and relationship-driven rather than goal-driven. Those of us strongly drawn to Agile will start to find many ideas we resonate with contained in the Pluralistic-Green altitude (and beyond).

Whereas the Achievement-Orange orientation makes decisions in a top-down manner and because they pragmatically work, the Pluralistic-Green orientation prefers bottom-up processes, getting input from everyone and striving to come to consensus, along the way validating different ways of thinking from different types of people and fostering feelings of inclusion. Pluralistic-Green prioritizes relationships over short-term outcomes, which can make it less efficient but more personal and humane. In Graves's study of student work groups, he found these folks had difficulty getting started with a project due to their strong need to hear from everyone and get everyone in agreement before proceeding; further, no one wanted to exercise leadership for fear of offending or being presumptuous. The result was often a fragmentation of the group into smaller interest groups and inefficiency in completing tasks. We can certainly see this in Agile environments.

Where the Achievement-Orange orientation values leaders who take charge and make decisions, the Pluralistic-Green orientation believes leaders should serve those they lead (hence the resonance with servant leadership). In an Orange organization, strategy and execution are paramount, whereas the Pluralistic-Green organization focuses on company culture. The Pluralistic-Green organization also expands the notion of stakeholders far beyond shareholders to include employees, customers, suppliers, society, and the environment. Pluralistic-Green thinking originated the idea of corporate social responsibility. Where the Achievement-Orange metaphor for the organization is a machine, the Pluralistic-Green metaphor is of a family.

On the one hand, Pluralistic-Green individuals are generally uncomfortable with power and hierarchy, sometimes leading to extreme egalitarianism and the possibility of becoming deadlocked during execution. On the other hand, Pluralistic-Green thinking birthed the ideal of worker empowerment, pushing decisions down to frontline workers, who are believed able to make better decisions than experts could from far away. This requires managers to give up control, which goes against the grain of our Achievement-Orange–centered corporate society. Laloux (2014, p. 32) establishes how ingrained this control-oriented leadership is, noting how Pluralistic-Green organizations spend a disproportionate percentage of their training budgets on helping new leaders adopt the mindset and skills of a servant leader.

A second innovation of the Pluralistic-Green altitude is the *values-driven culture.* Laloux points out that while such a culture can drive a truly vibrant organization in a Pluralistic-Green environment, in the hands of Achievement-Orange organizations, such "values statements" can often fall flat and be seen as nongenuine. Some research, however, suggests that values-driven cultures outperform their peers (e.g., Kotter & Heskett, 1992).

A third innovation identified by Laloux from the Pluralistic-Green paradigm is the *multiple stakeholder perspective,* wherein shareholders are not the only (nor even the most important) stakeholders; that is, stakeholders are also defined as including employees, customers, suppliers, local communities, and the environment. In nonprofit organizations, this has become known as the *triple bottom line* (people, planet, profits) way of managing.

Other ideas from Green thinking include 360-degree feedback, inspiring vision statements, the manager pool, and leaders as teachers supporting workers. Of note in our Agile work are two points. First, the connection to Lean thinking—and in particular the work of W. Edwards Deming[1]—seems quite clear; much of Agile thinking begins to take shape (and to truly make sense) when we are able to think in a Pluralistic-Green way. Second, when ideas such as empowerment and vision statements are picked up and implemented by Achievement-Orange managers (ever practical and looking to gain an edge), the results often fall flat or are nonexistent. This reveals the lack of the appropriate underlying mindset (e.g., the I quadrant ability to genuinely value others' perspective and feedback), which leads to mere mimicry rather than a genuine embrace. Clearly, this happens in quite a few Agile Transformations and is the source of frustration among enterprise Agile coaches.

The Pluralistic-Green orientation is particularly prevalent in nonprofit organizations but is not widespread in the for-profit world (with notable exceptions like Southwest Airlines, Ben & Jerry's, and The Container Store). Later in this chapter, we will examine Clare Graves's finding that people centered in the Pluralistic-Green level have a hard time getting started with their projects, waiting for everyone to be heard and agree. As Laloux (2014) notes, "Green is powerful as a paradigm for breaking down old structures, but often less effective at formulating practical alternatives" (p. 31).

Evolutionary-Teal Altitude

Those who had a psychology course in college will perhaps remember Abraham Maslow and his famous hierarchy of needs. The fifth need Maslow identified was that of *self-actualization.* Self-actualization can happen only when more basic needs for safety, security, esteem, and belonging have been met. When they have, human beings naturally evolve into the place of becoming their unique selves, of moving from a socialized mind to a self-authoring mind (which we'll cover later in this chapter). This is the place of finding one's calling in life, one's unique purpose in the world.

Laloux terms the type of thinking that emerges in this state Evolutionary-Teal, the first second-tier altitude. It is referred to as second tier (a distinction first made by Clare Graves) because people or organizations thinking in this way begin to recognize the validity of *all* altitudes and the perspectives they represent, from Amber up to Teal.[2]

The shift to the Evolutionary-Teal orientation happens as we begin to dis-identify with our own ego and "make room to listen to the wisdom of other, deeper parts of ourselves" (Laloux, 2014, p. 44). The locus of judging whether our actions are right shifts to an internal measure: We ask whether we have an *inner sense of rightness* about a given action, whether we are *being true to ourselves*, acting out of our *calling*, and *serving the world*—what the Greek philosopher Socrates called the voice of his inner daemon. This turns Achievement-Orange success motivation on its head, judging the world by a very different standard.

Note that this is quite different than trying to be successful per se. "Success" is generally defined in a social or professional context, in alignment with the social and professional mask referenced in the Conformist-Amber and Achievement-Orange altitudes. We could call this *outer success*. In the Evolutionary-Teal altitude, we focus on *inner success*: fulfillment as defined by the deepest, most unique part of us, the place where our "calling" comes from, where we can literally "be true to ourselves." The catch is that until we have found this place within, achieved a level of outer success, and met our basic needs (per Maslow), we won't be ready to grow into the Evolutionary-Teal level, since we will be ruled by our ego's needs. We will examine this inner development process at some length in Part II as we help you grow into a transformational leader.

According to Laloux (2014, p. 44):

> With fewer ego-fears, we are able to make decisions that might seem risky, where we haven't weighed all possible outcomes, but that resonate with deep inner convictions. We develop a sensitivity for situations that don't feel quite right, situations that demand that we speak up and take action, even in the face of opposition or with seemingly low odds of success, out of a sense of integrity and authenticity.

Laloux calls this innovation at the Evolutionary-Teal level *inner rightness as compass*. In Teal thinking, making decisions based on this inner compass is a perfectly valid approach, whereas in an Achievement-Orange world it would be seen as fuzzy-headed.

As we will see, operating from this altitude requires individual development into what Kegan terms the *self-authoring mind*, where we literally "author" our own experience, rather than being dependent on the opinions and values of others to determine how we judge ourselves.[3] Laloux (2014) characterizes this fundamental mind shift as follows: "instead of setting goals for our life, dictating what direction it should take, we learn to let go and listen to the life that wants to be lived through us" (p. 45). To the prevailing Achievement-Orange mindset, this will sound at best like some type of mysticism or at worst like airy-fairy hogwash. In contrast, the Pluralistic-Green paradigm might well find this attitude inspiring, though people acting from a Green perspective may be limited if they worry about whether others will agree with their actions, whereas acting from boldness and courage is often a requirement to fulfill one's calling.

A related (and second) innovation of the Evolutionary-Teal altitude is the idea of *wisdom beyond rationality*. In the Achievement-Orange altitude, rationality is king. However, any source of insight beyond concrete facts and logical reasoning is considered to be irrational and is typically discounted. Wisdom beyond rationality moves past this limitation to consider all data sources. Laloux points to another limitation of the Achievement-Orange orientation: Even when taking a hard data approach, sometimes that data is incongruous with our worldview or with a future state (like a goal) to which our ego has grown attached. Thus, when we adopt the Achievement-Orange perspective, we can be blind to the reality that we don't wish to see. In that sense, it is actually not fully rational, not truly "inspecting and adapting."

However, when we have grown to the point where our ego's needs don't have such a strong grip on us, we are less subject to missing data that is actually there. Further, we are open not only to analytical approaches, but also to emotional reactions that inform us on a different level, and to intuitive insights. All three approaches—utilizing the "brain" in the head, the heart, and the gut—can be developed and honed through practice and feedback. This is what we mean by wisdom that includes—but transcends—rationality.

The two previous Evolutionary-Teal innovations set the stage for the third, *striving for wholeness*. Laloux points out how the term "work–life balance" suggests there is not that much "life" left in our work. To truly act from inner purpose (in concert with the organization's purpose), and to trust the wisdom beyond rationality, requires tapping into the entirety of one's being, including one's experience, one's intuition, one's emotions, one's analytical brain, and even one's soul or inner voice. This means creating a culture at work where all those elements of being can be expressed. It's not that work becomes like an encounter group or psychotherapy, but rather that we don't hide our fundamental humanness when we go to work; we bring it with us and engage its gifts. We are whole human beings, even (especially) at work; we no longer need to "check our soul at the door" when we come to work (one of the "gifts" of the COVID-19 pandemic is this reminder).

The deep self-trust that comes from growing into the self-authoring mind leads to an ability to let go of our many judgments about others. In earlier stages, when we disagree with people, we simply judge that they are wrong and we are right. We then prepare to convince, teach, fix, or utterly dismiss them. When we have evolved to the place where we can trust and rely on ourselves fully, we don't feel the need to convince others to justify our own stance. Rather than needing to dismiss others, we are motivated to "create a shared space safe from judgment, where our deep listening helps others to find their voice and their truth, just as they help us find ours. . . . Now we have a chance to recreate community on new grounding, where we listen each other into selfhood and wholeness" (Laloux, 2014, p. 49). The "whole" we now include involves all aspects of ourselves, the community of people with whom we work, the community in which we live and offer our services, and even out to nature and the planet.

When Graves (2005) studied student work groups consisting of Evolutionary-Teal members, he found what we would call *emergent leadership*—not based on place in the hierarchy or previous success in goal achievement per se but rather reliant on a strong debate of ideas (not personalities)— and the idea that struck the group as most appropriate prevailed. Organization was around ideas, rather than personalities, and tended to revolve from individual to individual based on task (Laloux, 2014, p. 137).

The Evolutionary-Teal altitude of development is not merely nice in some esoteric respect but has significant business ramifications. Substantial research evidence shows that leaders who grow into the higher altitudes are more effective (Anderson & Adams, 2016; Graves, 2005; Laloux, 2014; Rooke & Torbert, 2005), both from an Achievement-Orange perspective (meeting goals, achieving success) and from a Pluralistic-Green one (including all stakeholders, treating people as people). Further, evidence indicates that the developmental stage of the CEO determines the success of large-scale organizational transformation programs (Rooke & Torbert, 2005). In fact, Laloux says he has seen no instance where an organization has evolved to the Evolutionary-Teal level without the CEO, and the board of directors, personally operating from that level.

Citing Graves, Laloux (2014, p. 50) describes a corresponding effect: "Clare Graves came to a similar conclusion with a different approach. He put together groups of people based on the paradigm they most often operated from [altitude] and gave them complex tasks to perform." Laloux then quotes from Graves (2005, p. 371):

> I took a group of people who thought the same way, and I put them in situations . . . where they were required to solve problems with multiple answers . . . and lo and behold, when the results started to come in I found this most peculiar phenomenon: the [Teals] find unbelievably more solutions than the [Red] plus the [Amber] plus the [Orange] plus the [Green]. I found that the quality of their solutions to problems was amazingly better. . . . I found that the average time it took the [Teal] group to arrive at a solution was amazingly shorter than it took any of the other groups.

The theme of finding one's calling, one's deep purpose, extends out (or up) from the individual holon to the organizational holon level. Rather than a machine metaphor (Orange) or a family one (Green), the Evolutionary-Teal notion is that the organization is a living organism. In fact, the organization itself can be said to have a purpose of its own. It is as if the Teal organization calls individuals to itself, ones who resonate with its purpose, and helps to mutually fulfill their overlapped purposes. Its purpose is not—as in the Achievement-Orange level—merely to continue to grow sales and profits forever (to be essentially immortal). Instead, it has a purpose that could be fulfilled at some point, and then the organization would naturally dissolve (i.e., "die"). This type of thinking is completely foreign to lower altitudes.

Teal organizations have learned to self-manage, largely based on peer relationships without the need for either hierarchies or consensus. There is a sense that the living system of the organization has a life and sense of direction of its own and that we can serve and collaborate with that purpose. Laloux speculates that people will increasingly affiliate themselves only with organizations that have a clear and noble purpose that aligns with those individuals' own purposes and that profitability, growth, and market share will recede in importance.

Teal practices, as researched and documented by Laloux, interestingly enough came from organizations not implementing Agile methods (Laloux, personal communication); nevertheless, the list reads like one most Agilists would find very appealing! Example Teal practices include self-managed teams that have coaches with no management authority, projects without project managers that are self-staffed, people with no job titles, a focus on team performance and peer appraisals (rather than management-led ones), and interviews by fellow team members who make their own decisions on hiring (Laloux, 2014). Let's reiterate: This research was not done on organizations implementing Agile! These findings are striking because they corroborate how Agile thinking largely sits on the cutting edge of human consciousness. That's the encouraging news. The more challenging news is that your organization has likely not evolved to this altitude—at least not yet.

Corroborating Research on Altitude

As we have mentioned, many research lines come together in the material summarized thus far, as well as in the cross-quadrant work outlined in the next section. To ground our understanding, we'll show how Laloux's organizational work corresponds to other researchers in closely related fields. Table 3.1 maps Laloux's altitude names (using his notes) to the altitude names and concepts used by other developmental researchers. These researchers were picked due to their centrality in their field and/or because we have seen them used in Agile Transformation work (e.g., Torbert, whose student was Bill Joiner, Spiral Dynamics, and so on) and wanted to provide a mapping. While there is certainly not complete unanimity among these research lines, they share a sufficient degree of correspondence that allows us to describe "orienting generalizations" about development (to use Wilber's term). We clearly see the general trend of human development—from less complex to more complex, and moving from lower to higher without skipping levels—even if one researcher measures those levels (metaphorically) in Fahrenheit while another uses Celsius. There's no disputing the evolutionary vector and where it's going—only what we decide to note as the milestones we find along the way.

Table 3.1   Mapping of altitude names across researchers (Adapted from Laloux, 2014, pp. 333–336)

Laloux's Altitude Name	Inspiration for Laloux's Name	Corresponding Name (Mapped from Various Researchers)
Evolutionary-Teal	Gebser: Integral	Cook-Greuter: Construct Aware
	Loevinger: Integrated	Kegan: Inter-individual (Self-Transforming)
		Torbert: Strategist and Alchemist
		Graves: A'-N'
		Spiral Dynamics: Yellow
		Maslow: Self-Actualization
		Wade: Authentic
Pluralistic-Green	N/A	Loevinger and Cook-Greuter: Individualistic
		Torbert: Individualist
		Wade: Affiliative
		Graves: F-S
		Spiral Dynamics: Green
		Generically: "Postmodernity"

Laloux's Altitude Name	Inspiration for Laloux's Name	Corresponding Name (Mapped from Various Researchers)
Achievement-Orange	Wade: Achievement '	Gebser: Mental
		Loevinger and Cook-Greuter: Self-Aware and Conscientious
		Kegan: Institutional (Self-Authoring)
		Torbert: Achiever
		Piaget: Formal Operational
		Graves: E-R
		Spiral Dynamics: Orange
		Generically: "Modernity"
Conformist-Amber	Loevinger, Cook-Greuter, and Wade: Conformist	Gebser: Mythical
		Graves: D-Q
		Spiral Dynamics: Blue
		Kegan: Interpersonal (Socialized Mind)
		Torbert: Diplomat and Expert
		Piaget: Concrete Operational
Impulsive-Red	N/A	Loevinger and Cook-Greuter: Self-Protective
		Kegan: Imperial
		Torbert: Opportunistic
		Graves: C-P
		Spiral Dynamics: Red
		Piaget: Preoperational
		Wade: Egocentric

Clare Graves's Research

One researcher stands out as especially important in the development of the notion of altitudes: Clare Graves from Union College.

Haunted by a student's question regarding which personality theory was correct, Graves entered into a 9-year research project, followed by 12 additional years of naturalistic observation and library research. The basic research topic for his (largely adult) students[4]—over a 15-week class—was asking them to define their own conception of "what constituted the mature adult personality." Students spent weeks conceiving, then additional weeks contemplating critiques and other questions, then finally revising or defending their position in writing. Graves then submitted the written conceptions to independent judges to categorize them into as few categories as possible, assuming categorization was possible. Each year, Graves retained a new set of 7–9 judges, who did not know the students or Graves's research aim. The results are striking.

Graves's Developmental Levels and Organizational Implications

To Graves's real surprise, the task was surprisingly easy and consistent for the judges, as the majority of students' conceptions could be unanimously placed into one category; virtually all remaining students' conceptions were put into two adjacent categories.[5] This happened the first year, which was remarkable enough, with its seven to nine judges. What we find truly stunning is that this same result happened in each of nine consecutive years, with a different set of judges each year![6] It would be extremely hard to conclude this was a fluke result.

Graves saw two high-level patterns emerge: Conceptions of the mature person tended to be oriented toward "expressing the self" (similar to *agency*) or toward "sacrificing the self" (similar to *communion*). There were three different varieties of express-self conceptions, but only two sacrifice-self types (for a total of five categories). Briefly, here are our[7] characterizations of the names Graves labeled each conception:

- Express myself, regardless of the consequences to others (since I do not want to feel ashamed about not dominating others)

- Sacrifice myself now, since I know I'll get a reward later

- Express myself in a strategic way, without much worry or guilt

- Sacrifice myself now in a way that gets me a reward now

- Express myself, but not in a way that hurts other people

Graves eventually referred to these conceptions as either *levels* or *stages* of development, as do other researchers in the field of adult development, including Robert Kegan, Susanne Cook-Greuter, Bill Torbert, Lawrence Kohlberg, and many others. This is the same basic distinction we make in the Integral Model with the concept of altitude, although for us it applies across all four quadrants, rather than being focused mainly on the I (or WE) quadrant.

Eventually, Graves constructed an additional three levels of development, making a total of eight. The original five are key, since they represent the stages where people found in modern organizations are primarily centered. The five levels originally identified by Graves were later labeled with quasi-arbitrary colors as a memory aid.[8] See *The Never Ending Quest* for Graves's fuller descriptions (Graves, 2005, p. 92).

After struggling for years to make sense of the data, Graves concluded that each category (level) represented a *personality system* in miniature: internally consistent systems that help us understand the purpose of life and guide our behavior (they would later be called *value memes* in Spiral Dynamics). In retrospect, Graves realized the categorization systems the judges developed were based not on what the person thought, but rather on *how* they thought (2005, p. 135).

Graves concluded that a person centered at a given level of development prefers specific types of approaches to all manner of things, from education to management to coaching and other forms of support. In addition, that person is strongly inclined to reject approaches *from a different level of development* than his or her own. Graves incorporated *cybernetics* and *systems theory* to address the failure of one-size-fits-all management theories that got great results in one environment with one type of people but failed miserably in another environment. (Schneider [1994] made a parallel discovery with his idea of core cultures and the fit of given management approaches to one type of culture but not to others.) *This is a wakeup call for us as transformational leaders.* Think about the challenges we face when we implement a Pluralistic-Green or Evolutionary-Teal management approach like Agile into an Achievement-Orange or Conformist-Amber organization and expect it to work.

In a talk given at an organizational conference in 1971, the YMCA Management Forum, Graves articulated the finding that people who are in what he termed an *open*, growing state prefer to be managed using the management style of the altitude *above* the one they are at. So, for instance, an open individual centered in the Conformist-Amber level prefers to be led in a *consultative* way (an Achievement-Orange approach), whereas a closed individual (one stopped at a particular level, who does not appear to be moving on) at the same stage prefers to be led in the style natural to that level, namely, a *paternalistic* approach. Likewise, open individuals at the Achievement-Orange level prefer to be managed in a *participative* way, those at the Pluralistic-Green level prefer *facilitative* management, and those at the Evolutionary-Teal level want to be led in a *systemic* manner.

Wow! What a shock to our Agile sensibilities! People centered in the Conformist-Amber level, even if they are growing, do not want to be managed in a facilitative or participative manner but are happy with being consulted on their opinion before the authority makes the decision. Only an open, growing person in the Achievement-Orange level will appreciate the participative approach of an Agile team. Even worse (we may lament), someone centered in the Amber level who has stopped growing, and is basically just living life day-to-day, will prefer to be managed in a paternalistic way! A similar person centered in the Orange level will prefer a consultative management approach. This helps us make sense of the reports from many Agile coaches that some of their team members just want to be told what to do, so how can they self-organize? It begs the question for us as transformational leaders of how we can respect people who are centered in altitudes other than our own, appreciating the views and qualities they offer, and allowing them their own destiny.

Spiral Dynamics: Continuing Graves's Work

Don Beck and Chris Cowan, former students of Clare Graves, took his research further into more modern times. They called their model and book *Spiral Dynamics* (1996) and updated Graves's conceptions with work from psychology, biology, complexity and systems science, and other fields. A key concept they introduced sheds light on the evolution of both people and cultures, as originally discovered by Graves—namely, *memes*.

In biology, genes are a prime mechanism of evolution. In the psychosocial world, evolution can be said to be carried by memes. **Memes** are ideas, behaviors, or styles that spread from person to person through imitation. Fashions are a good (if somewhat trivial) example of memes. Internet memes are the latest subset of this idea. Strong memes replicate, whereas weak ones tend to die out (thus the connection to evolution and survival of the fittest). The Agile paradigm can be seen as a set of related memes, which will have great relevance for us in finding fertile ground for planting Agile meme "seeds."

The term *meme* was first introduced by Richard Dawkins in 1976, then used by Mihaly Csikszentmihalyi to identify the origins of human behavior, in contrast with a gene's relationship to our physical characteristics (Beck & Cowan, 1996, p. 30). John Perry Barlow further articulated how this social evolution progressed, saying that memes are self-replicating and reproduce across human ecosystems, mentally and socially, similarly to how genes reproduce and mutate.

Beck and Cowan (1996) expanded this theory, proposing the existence of a kind of "meta-meme," which they called a systems or *values meme* (vMEME). These vMEMEs act like attractors for thinking styles within people and cultures, coalescing into what Integral calls altitudes. With the concept of vMEMEs, Beck and Cowan articulate the mechanism by which Graves's findings apply to individual development (the I quadrant structure of our mindsets) as well as how Graves's conceptions act like a cultural attractor (the WE quadrant), bringing together beliefs, value systems, and worldviews into coherent wholes that form organizational cultures.

According to Beck and Cowan, certain vMEMEs that are in harmony resonate like notes in a musical chord, while vMEMEs in conflict lead to troubled individuals, companies, and civilizations. In other words, certain vMEME stacks (or layered collections) work in harmony, whereas others conflict with each other. Further, vMEMEs can be expressed in both healthy and unhealthy ways. Beck and the late Cowan maintained separate websites and various training and applications using these concepts.

Now that we've presented the basic idea of altitudes within the context of organizations—the context most familiar to us—we want to broaden this concept and talk about evolution within each quadrant, a concept we will return to in Chapter 9 in more detail.

Evolution Across Quadrants

As Wilber (2008, p. 77) states:

> The emergence of the complex neocortex in the Upper-Right quadrant [IT] corresponded with the arising of higher intelligence in the Upper-Left quadrant [I]. All four dimensions evolved simultaneously (and continue to do so!) into higher waves of consciousness and complexity.

Tracing the history of evolution in all four quadrants, Wilber goes on to say:

> This deepening from simpler to more complex, less conscious to more conscious, can be traced across the billions of years of Kosmic evolution. Each new level transcended and included all that went before, always growing into ever-greater degrees of novelty and awareness. For instance, in the I quadrant, the self evolved from *instinctual* to *magical* to *egocentric* to *achiever* to *sensitive* to *holistic*; correspondingly in IT, from the *reptilian* to *mammalian* to the *complex neocortex* brains (and into *SF1*, *SF2*, and *SF3*); in WE, from *archaic* to *magical* to *early mythic* to *late mythic* to *scientific-rational* to *pluralistic* to *holistic*; and finally in the ITS quadrant from *survival clans* to *ethnic tribes* to *feudal empires* to *early nations* to *corporate states* to *value communities* to *holistic commons*.

Figure 3.1 provides a representation of this evolution within each of the four quadrants, with corresponding names for the appropriate developmental scheme that is applicable within each quadrant. Note the correspondence across quadrants at a similar level, whereas altitudes across quadrants address very different things (e.g., the mind of an individual in the I quadrant versus a social structure or socioeconomic system in the ITS quadrant).

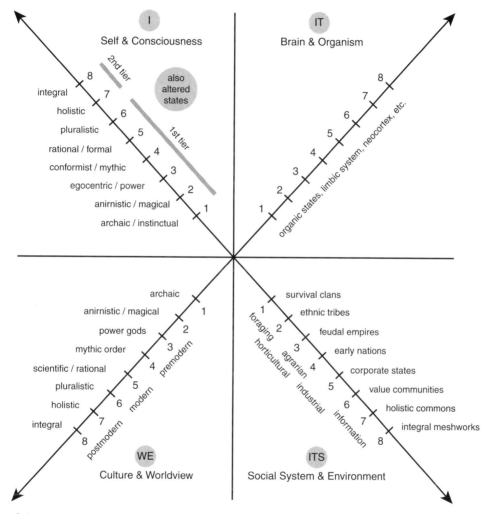

Figure 3.1

Example names for developmental stages within each quadrant, from Wilber

Generic Altitude Names

Figure 3.1 shows a different evolutionary schema for each quadrant. While this approach is the most accurate for representing evolutionary progress within each quadrant, it is a bit cumbersome to have four different labels, each of which corresponds to the relevant level of complexity within its corresponding quadrant. When Wilber devised the Integral Model, he wanted a unifying concept for altitude that had meaningful application across quadrants. He tends to use various generic names depending on context but always anchors them with a specific set of colors. These colors were originally taken from Spiral Dynamics, but Wilber later adapted them to be more neutral in terms of methodology and to correspond to the order in the colors of the rainbow. The colors are otherwise arbitrary, having no inherent meaning.

Laloux addresses altitudes that concern organizations, as well as the individuals within those organizations (rather than the whole world, as Wilber does). We could say they focus primarily on the WE quadrant and to some extent on the I quadrant. In working with Agile Transformations, we are concerned with business processes, Agile and other practices, organizational policies, structures, systems, culture, mindsets, and other phenomena. It will simplify things if we can reference a generic, neutral concept of altitude, regardless of which quadrant it addresses. This cross-quadrant altitude gives us a single point of access to the evolution of any given phenomenon, regardless of which quadrant perspective we are taking at the moment. This is the power of the Integral Model, as it provides a comprehensive meta-map of all phenomena. In doing so, it offers a type of Cartesian addressing system for any given thing, by specifying its quadrant and its altitude; Integral calls this a *kosmic address*.

Since our use of Integral is concerned with organizational life, we have decided to restrict ourselves to four or five Integral colors—namely, (in order of complexity) Red, Amber, Orange, Green, and Teal. In Table 3.2, we list the color and an identifying name for each altitude, after Laloux, who largely adapted the Integral and Spiral Dynamics traditions. These name and color combinations are Impulsive-Red, Traditional-Amber, Achievement-Orange, Pluralistic-Green, and Evolutionary-Teal. In *Integral Psychology* (2000b), Wilber maps many different developmental schemes to others taken from psychology, sociology, brain science, anthropology, and various Eastern and Western wisdom traditions. Table 3.2, in turn, maps various researchers focusing on different quadrants to our generic altitude to give readers a mapping for other schemas they may encounter.

Taking one example and following a row across in Table 3.2, the generic Integral name of Traditional-Amber corresponds to what Graves called *D-Q* (with respect to the I quadrant development of individuals, and later called *blue* in Spiral Dynamics), and also to what Kegan calls the *socialized mind* in his mental complexity (*orders of mind*) scheme, to *expert* leadership in Bill Joiner's leadership Agility system, to Conformist-Amber in Laloux's organizational name, and to *mythic* in Gebser's schema regarding the evolution of social structures (corresponding to the Agrarian Age and early states in sociocultural terms). Each of these could also be described in the term relevant to their quadrant or by a generic Integral label, such as Traditional-Amber.

Table 3.2   Adapted in part from Wilber (2000b), plus reviews of Graves, Beck, Kegan, Laloux, Joiner, and others

Generic Altitude Name	Values/ Personality: Graves (Beck)	Sense of Self: Kegan	Leadership: Torbert (Joiner)	Organizations: Laloux	Worldviews (Sociocultural): Gebser (Wilber)
Mature Integral: Turquoise	B′-O′ Wholeview (Turquoise)	Self-Transforming Mind	Ironist	[Hinted at, but not named]	(Global) Integral (Informational)
Emergent Integral: Teal	A′-N′ Flex Flow (Yellow)	Self-Transforming Mind	Existentialist (Catalyst)	Evolutionary-Teal	(Nation)
Postmodern: Green	F-S Human Bond (Green)	Self-Authoring Mind	Existentialist (Catalyst)	Pluralistic-Green	(Industrial) (Empire) Mental (Adv-agrarian)
Modernist: Orange	E-R Strive Drive (Orange)	Self-Authoring Mind	Achiever	Achievement-Orange	(Industrial) (Empire) Mental (Adv-agrarian)
Traditional: Amber	D-Q Truth Force (Blue)	Socialized Mind	Technician (Expert) Diplomat	Conformist-Amber	(Early State) (Agrarian) Mythic
Warrior: Red	C-P Power Gods (Red)	Imperial Self		Organizations at this altitude are generally engaged in illegal activities or corruption	(Village) (Horticultural)
Tribal: Magenta	B-O Kin Spirits (Purple)	Impulsive Self		Insufficient complexity to form an "organization" as such	Magic (Tribes) (Foraging)
Archaic: Infrared	A-N Survival Sense (Beige)	Impulsive Self			Archaic

Integral Altitude and Agile Transformations

Let's return to the topic of evolution across the four quadrants and how that evolution impacts organizational transformation. Here's Wilber (1996) again:

> All 4 quadrants show evolutionary levels. The left-hand quadrants measure development in terms of interior depth, or awareness (consciousness). The right-hand quadrants measure development in terms of exterior complexity. However, because all 4 quadrants tetra-arise, an increase in interior consciousness corresponds, at least generally, with an increase in exterior complexity.

It is this comment—that evolution happens "at least generally" in a consistent way across quadrants—that concerns us in organizational transformations. In saying this, Wilber is referring to a scale measured in decades (or even longer). Evolution within the four quadrants proceeds largely in parallel, but not in lockstep, especially not within a short time scale like years. The exterior complexity of the environment around our organizations has increased dramatically, particularly in the last 10–15 years (just think about the Internet, social media, changing international political landscapes, and COVID-19). Meanwhile, the related consciousness development of people and organizations (the I and WE quadrants) has not kept pace. We are out of whack! In specific terms, the internal awareness or complexity that drives our leadership—and the values and ways of thinking that create our organizational cultures—has lagged behind the development of sophisticated processes and frameworks for developing products like software. As Robert Kegan (1994) says, we are "in over our heads" because we are not up to the challenge in some fundamental way. When leadership recognizes this deficit, it becomes a wake-up call, and an opportunity to pursue further personal development.

A colleague of ours, Al Shalloway, made this point quite succinctly. Al has worked with a large range of clients implementing Lean and Agile methods for many years. Here's how he captured the dilemma:

> We have been quite clear for a number of years about how to produce the best results in software through Lean and Agile processes, quantifying cost of delay, etc. [pointing to IT and ITS]. What is much less clear is how to do the leadership and cultural pieces to match." (Personal communication)

In our experience working with leaders and organizational culture, we see this dynamic play out repeatedly.

Michael's Take

From the very first Agile Transformation effort I worked back in 2001, there has always been a gap between the level of the Agile practices we were implementing (Pluralistic-Green and sometimes Evolutionary-Teal) and the level of leadership mindset and organizational culture that was prevalent. With only a few exceptions, the organizational cultures were centered in Achievement-Orange with some Traditional-Amber subcultures; if there were pockets of Pluralistic-Green culture, it was largely within the internal Agile community or the occasional small organization with a more visionary leader. Generally speaking, the leaders were a mix of Achievement-Orange moving to some extent into Pluralistic-Green. This caused a mismatch between the practices I was teaching and coaching and the mindset of the leaders and their culture. A notable exception was a Green-Teal leader in charge of a business unit of 200-plus people who took upon himself to learn Lean thinking and practices in detail, so that he could lead classes for his people. He was totally committed to this way of thinking and to empowering his people. The coaching team thrived under his leadership. Another exception was the leader of the engineering department of a medium-size business, who was probably centered in Orange but moving strongly into Green. He gave his full commitment to the Agile implementation and saw the need to change the culture; he was in part successful but had strong headwinds within the overall Orange nature of his organization's culture.

As we mentioned earlier in this chapter, we in the Agile community know how to work with the IT and ITS quadrants (e.g., visualizing workflows, quantifying the cost of delay, envisioning and measuring value streams, implementing process frameworks), but we have not been able to successfully alter the underlying forms in any of the quadrants, thereby limiting the use of these new innovations. This is rooted in the lack of corresponding evolution in the I and WE quadrants. It would be easier for executives and other leaders to successfully implement these new IT and ITS forms if their own inner complexity were a match—this topic will be our primary focus in Part II. This deficit accounts for many of the failures of clearly superior, more complex ideas that hold great promise— Lean Startup, product development flow, Lean thinking, empirical processes, Scrum and Kanban, and more. When these methods do succeed, their greater complexity can lead to a maturing within the I and WE quadrants, since all four quadrants arise together in any given situation. But our experience is—and the research bears this out—that the left-hand quadrants provide a constraint on how far right-hand evolution can go. To make a practice really work, we need intention (I) to match behavior (IT).

Michele's Take

Years ago, I worked with a large insurance organization that was undergoing its first Agile Transformation. The business was sponsoring and leading this change. One of a number of successful outcomes with that client was specifically focused on Leaning out a number of its processes, which were hindering the company's ability to practice Agile effectively at the team level. Doing this required me to challenge some of the mental models that had created the processes many years prior but were now causing severe bottlenecks. It required me to work directly with the mindset of "because we've always done it this way." As the managers began to see the benefits of working differently, they were willing to radically change some of their processes. Intention had to match behavior to bring about a healthy Agile practice. The constraint, which had existed for quite some time, was in the left-hand evolution.

Taking a simple IT quadrant example, a procedural process with many detailed steps and no latitude for judgment is less complex than an emergent process guided by a few rules or patterns. It is not that one is inherently better than the other—that will depend on the circumstances. In our complex world, however, the emergent process is frequently called for (recall the distinction between complicated versus complex). If we look from the corresponding WE perspective, the procedural process will appeal to traditional (Conformist-Amber) cultures, while the emergent process will fit more with postmodern cultures, such as Pluralistic-Green or Evolutionary-Teal. The currently dominant Achievement-Orange thinking will embrace such processes to the extent that they produce what Orange values: success, in the form of results. But if the organizational culture is not a very healthy form of Orange (or still has aspects of Amber thinking), it will likely reject, or inappropriately modify, the emergent process in response to its own cultural antibodies (and we could argue, the unfulfilled ego needs of its leadership). Of course, this risks not meeting the IT and ITS complexity needs in its environment, but it is the best this culture and mindset can do.

Earlier in this chapter we shared the concept of *transcend and include* as the way to evolve through the altitudes (personal or organizational evolution). This is a good place to bring the concept back to your awareness, given the challenge just described regarding an unhealthy form of the Orange paradigm and aspects of the Amber orientation when a complex circumstance requires an emergent process. Likely, a first step is to work on getting to a healthy Orange level before trying to move into the Green or Teal altitude, so that you are actually able to *transcend* and *include* the healthy and valuable and leave what is limiting you as you move into the next level.

One example of how this shows up when organizations are shifting to Agile practices is in the metrics and measurements that get created. If organizations are already operating from an Orange center of gravity and using metrics, measurements, and rewards that produce unhealthy behaviors, that situation will not naturally change just because the company adopts Agile behaviors. As an Agile leader or coach, the way to begin evolving as an organization is to meet people where they are (in Orange) and help them establish metrics that matter; within the Orange value system, this might include things like productivity, efficiency, innovation, and goal attainment.

Pluralistic-Green and Evolutionary-Teal ways of thinking and valuing are generally a better match for today's complexity. Evolutionary-Teal, for instance, has more degrees of behavioral freedom because it is less rigid and able to solve problems more effectively, with the ability to bring multiple points of view to the task. Unfortunately, far less than 10% of the population has evolved to this stage. Most leaders understand their organization's need for agility and are drawn to the promise of the Agile framework for this reason. But in the end, it is the altitude of the mindset within which change is approached that fails to deliver the intended results. Agility is ultimately about being really great at going through change. Indeed, how you go through the process of change determines your results. For this reason, the level of development of their thinking underlies how people work with both the human and organizational processes of change.

Many Agilists focus on the IT and ITS quadrants because they are elegant and straightforward, and—when changes there are applied appropriately—lead to dramatically better results. The problem is the lack of general understanding of the corresponding levels of mature leadership and evolved culture. We need to give more conscious attention to that gap to achieve better results, since it severely limits our effectiveness. It is the focus of an outsized portion of the remainder of this book, though we will surely not ignore the right-hand quadrants.

Summary

Altitudes represent the level of complexity within each quadrant. We explored four primary altitudes, applicable to the kind of organizations in which most people work: Amber, Orange, Green, and Teal. We use these generic names across quadrants, since they represent similar or parallel (but not the same) ways of being and doing relevant to the given quadrant. Understanding the altitude in the context of your organization is critical because people centered in a given altitude will not be very responsive to ideas and approaches from a different altitude. Thus, this is an important implementation factor that will help you work more effectively with people where they are.

From Insight to Action

To put this chapter on altitudes and evolution into action in your world, try doing a simple assessment to determine where your organization currently operates:

- What do you believe your own altitude is, as far as your "center of gravity"? Which values most strongly resonate for you? Reread the descriptions of each altitude to make this determination. Be aware of the difference between the set of values you espouse (preach to others, aspire to) and the set of values you actually live by when reading the descriptions.

- What do you believe is the altitude of your team? This might be the change or transformation team, a group of Agile coaches you work with, or a leadership team. You are looking for a center of gravity, not just one answer.

- What is the primary altitude of the overall organizational target of your Agile Transformation?

Chapter Notes

1. Deming first attempted to teach people in the United States but was rejected. He found a home in the more Pluralistic-Green–oriented culture of Japan. Then, when the Achievement-Orange U.S. automakers saw his success, they wanted to get it for themselves. Again, however, their Orange mindset caused them to focus on tactical things they could understand, related to success and cutting costs, rather than the underlying—and Green—philosophical notions, such as leaders as teachers and truly valuing people, that made the whole thing work. See, for example, Jeffrey Liker's *The Toyota Way* (2004).

2. To be precise, those thinking from a value perspective that is prior to Amber, such as Impulsive-Red.

3. This is also known as outcome-creating (or creative) leadership in the *Leadership Circle* universal model of leadership (Anderson, 2016). It is covered in detail in Part II of the book.

4. Some students in Graves's classes were undergraduates, others were graduate students in education or industrial management, and still others were from a program for mature students. Many members of the latter two groups had full-time jobs, so they were more mature than the usual undergrad students might be expected to be (Graves, 2005, p. 44).

5. The researchers found that 60% were easily classified into one of the five conceptions, while the remaining 40% were mixtures of the five types, almost all of which were either centered in two adjacent conceptions or had a preponderance of at least 50% in one conception (p. 56). Note that this is significantly different than if the 40% had been classified as random collections of multiple types.

6. The judges put conceptions into categories independently, then worked together to come up with common categories. An individual conception was placed in a category only if there was unanimous consent among all of the judges. As each year progressed with new judges, they were given both the new (unclassified) conceptions from that year and the old ones. A remarkable degree of consistency was seen: In most cases, all judges agreed with each other and with the previous years' classifications (p. 93). Altogether, Graves studied more than 1000 people, which is a very large sample in this type of research (see Steve McDonald, www.eman8.net/blog/?p=489).

7. We were not able to obtain permission to quote from the summary of Graves's findings, *A Never Ending Quest*, so all references are in our own words, doing our best to faithfully interpret the text. The interested reader is strongly encouraged to read Graves's work in the original, which is available directly from the publisher. It is an amazing story!

8. Graves, not wanting to prejudice his data, and frankly having no real theory to fit them into as they emerged, had very neutrally labeled the first set of what he called "life circumstances" as "A" and the corresponding developmental stage as "N." Subsequent circumstance–stage pairings continued as B-O, C-P, and so on. Two students of Graves, Don Beck and Chris Cowan, added the color names when they wrote their book, *Spiral Dynamics*.

4

Lines of Development

The developmental lines lens is the capability lens. It is used to assess specific capability lines within each quadrant that pertain to that given quadrant's perspective, rather than merely looking at the entire quadrant. Therefore, **lines of development** are a way of measuring altitude within a specific domain that falls within a quadrant. Using this lens helps to understand which new capabilities are needed to enable the desired result. Because your organization is likely more evolved in one domain than in another, by assessing each line, you become able to focus development in the relevant areas needed for the change to be successful.

Developmental Lines

Wilber's research defined more than 24 different lines of development for people, although there may be more or less depending on how you define each line. Many theorists have devoted their life's work to researching a single line of development, such as the cognitive (Piaget), emotional (Erikson), spiritual (Fowler), and moral (Gilligan, Kohlberg) lines.

As human beings, we all have innate abilities—that is, different natural talents, capacities, or competencies that we are born with (e.g., musical, artistic, mathematical). Then there are the learned abilities we have cultivated by devoting energy and time to developing areas that we were interested in or that may have been imposed on us by our parents or society. In our adult years, as we begin to intentionally develop ourselves so that we are able to work with the complexity of our own environments, we will discover areas where we need to build more capabilities to be able to work with the complexity. We may also undertake such development for personal growth, as we face our personal challenges and need a more skillful means with which to work with them. (We will address these efforts in more depth in Part II.) For example, if I have a tendency to be overly complying with others, that can limit my ability to take a stand for what's important to me. This might mean (as one example) that I need to work on my emotional line of development, so that I become more skilled in dealing with difficult emotions. This effort is like going to a gym and working on a specific muscle that needs to be strengthened. These capabilities or "muscles" are what enable us to achieve our desired state.

Integral practitioners use developmental lines as an assessment tool to diagnose current capabilities and then to effectively address the gaps in needed areas. Figure 4.1 provides an overview of the kinds of lines that can be included in an Integral assessment. In this table, each line within a quadrant has correlates in the other quadrants. For example, as the cognitive line develops in the UL (I) quadrant, there are corresponding behavioral developments in the UR (IT) quadrant, intersubjective capabilities in the LL (WE) quadrant, and grammatical systems in the LR (ITS) quadrant. Again, many variations of developmental lines are used, depending on the context within which Integral is being applied.

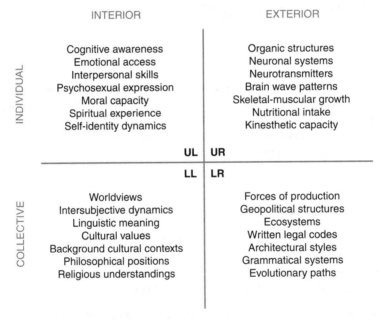

Figure 4.1
Examples of Integral developmental lines (Source: Integralacademy.eu/about/about-integral-theory)

Just as we develop these capabilities as individuals, so organizations must develop the needed capabilities for the complexity of their context. And just as people don't typically attempt to develop to a high altitude in all lines, so organizations don't necessarily pursue high altitudes in all possible areas.

We have identified a number of developmental lines for each quadrant (covered in Part III), based on our thinking about what could potentially be required for each quadrant to evolve to a more Agile way of being as an organization. Again, you might choose more or fewer lines depending on what you are trying to do. Think of this development as a way to take a broad dimension and break it down into subcategories (or subdimensions) that allow you to more easily assess that dimension as a whole. It is also a way for you to see more clearly what your landscape is and to prioritize your focus, leveraging areas that will catalyze your change efforts.

Because the quadrants co-arise in any given situation, and because all are equally important to attend to, a given altitude in a developmental line within a quadrant will likely impact and be impacted by a developmental line in the other quadrants and the altitude in which that line is expressed. For example, in the I quadrant, the altitude expressed for the emotional intelligence developmental line will impact the altitude of the shared worldviews developmental line. This is why we often say that the transformation of one quadrant requires the transformation of another. We do not mean that all developmental lines in all quadrants need to be equal or operating at a high level, but rather that the organization and the people must be able to achieve their desired results, based on which developmental lines are important to build capacity in.

Developmental Lines and Agile Transformations

As previously mentioned, each organization has its own unique capabilities, along with areas that need further development to enable the desired changes. Thus, one developmental line in a quadrant may be expressed from an Orange altitude, while another line in the same quadrant may already be at the Green altitude. Not only is this the case within quadrants, but also this pattern holds across quadrants and within different areas of your organization, as well as at different holon levels! Whew, that's quite the constellation.

Approaching change from a conscious stance, we attend not only to the quadrants and altitudes, but also to the specific domain areas in an Agile context. From each quadrant's perspective, we see the following:

- **I Quadrant:** Lines of development focus on the overall level of leadership maturity, working with individual beliefs about the change, the new way of working, leadership beliefs and vision, and leadership effectiveness and alignment to a Lean and Agile mindset. *Example:* Emotional intelligence.

- **IT Quadrant:** Lines focus on the practices and behaviors needed to enable an Agile way of working at the enterprise level and on bringing an organization's products to market. *Example:* Technical practices.

- **ITS Quadrant:** Lines focus on the organization's structure and systems, its adaptability to changing conditions, and the flow of value to achieve the level of agility desired. *Example:* Flow of communication.

- **WE Quadrant:** Lines focus on the health of the culture and of relationships needed to enable collaboration, innovation, and collective effectiveness, moving into a transformative "we" space and away from an "us versus them" mentality. *Example:* Shared worldviews.

In Part III, we will more fully cover the specific lines of development we are using in our transformation work and their mapping to the quadrants as well as altitude levels.

From Insight to Action

To put this chapter on developmental lines into action, take the developmental line examples just given for each quadrant, and assess what altitude you believe each of those lines is being expressed at in your organization and what indicators lead you to that conclusion:

- **I Quadrant:** Emotional intelligence

    - Altitude expressed:

    - Indicators:

- **IT Quadrant:** Technical practices

    - Altitude expressed:

    - Indicators:

- **ITS Quadrant:** Flow of communication

    - Altitude expressed:

    - Indicators:

- **WE Quadrant:** Shared worldviews

    - Altitude expressed:

    - Indicators:

Summary of Part I

So far, we have explored the following:

- **Holons:** The fundamental whole/part building blocks of organizational life, from people to teams to departments to organizations, and agency/communion and integration/transcendence.

- **Quadrants:** The four fundamental (horizontal) perspectives we use to look "at" or to look "as" any given organizational situation and any given holon.

- **Altitudes:** The levels of evolutionary complexity represented by any given instance of a holon, in a quadrant, and for a specific developmental line.

- **Developmental lines:** The capability lenses we use to assess development in particular lines within each quadrant that are needed to develop the capability needed to achieve a particular goal.

That's the basic Integral Operating System that the IATF is built on and the foundation for how we will further explore the use of this system for your work in Agile Transformations, transitions, or change efforts for achieving enterprise agility. Before we move to Part II on transformational leadership, take a moment to integrate what you have learned so far in Part I by performing a few simple exercises of applying Integral thinking to your current Agile change effort.

Applying Integral Thinking to Your Agile Transformation

To integrate your learning from Part I, try this simple exercise. Recall the earlier scenario of using the Integral Model to assess the situation of the fish dying in the lake (presented in Chapter 2); now the scenario to consider is your Agile Transformation effort. To scale this exercise, you might think of a particularly large obstacle with the Agile Transformation rather than the entire effort (Figure 4.2).

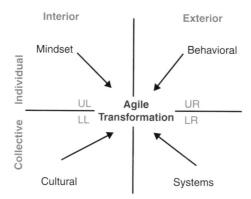

Figure 4.2
Integral assessment: looking at your Agile Transformation

From the lens of each quadrant, reflect on and answer the following questions:

- **I Quadrant:** What specific mindsets, beliefs, and values held by key individuals (whether leaders, team members, or others) affect the transformation effort? What altitude(s) do these mindsets express? What holon level do they arise from?

- **IT Quadrant:** What actions and behaviors are being exhibited that affect the transformation effort, both in a supportive manner and in an opposing way? What altitude(s) do these behaviors seem to express?

- **ITS Quadrant:** What structures, systems, and policies affect the transformation effort? What altitude(s) do these structures, systems, and policies arise from? What holon level(s) do they involve?

- **WE Quadrant:** What attributes of your current culture impact the transformation effort? What altitudes are being expressed, and are two cultural altitudes in conflict (e.g., Orange versus Green)? Does this play out differently at different holon levels (e.g., the culture of Agile teams versus overall organizational culture)?

As we move to Part II: Transformational Leadership, you will begin to understand more deeply how your own way of being as a change leader or coach impacts the results you are getting, and how you can more consciously go about your life's work.

PART II

TRANSFORMATIONAL LEADERSHIP: UPGRADING THE LEADER'S OPERATING SYSTEM

Part I of this book describes an approach to Agile Transformations based on Integral thinking, while Part III articulates a meta-framework for a new organizational operating system for Agile Transformations. In between the two, Part II focuses on upgrading your existing *leader's operating system* (LOS) to the level required to lead a transformation.

For at the center of real transformation is leadership. It is **leadership** at every level, at every turn—from the wake-up call, to the vision, to the strategy, to the implementation, learning, course-correcting, and sustaining; it is the opposite of delegation. Without leadership, the best we can hope for is a managed movement from one state to a more or less similar state, not transformation. Because of this centrality, Part II emphasizes the type of leadership we need to drive a transformation: what it looks like, what it allows for, and how we can grow into that set of capabilities. It is important to understand that the term "transformational leadership" and the specific role of "the transformational leader" are not necessarily synonymous. Throughout this part of the book, we will be talking about transformational leadership, and a transformational leader, as anyone who is part of leading an organizational transformation, and in our context, an Agile Transformation. This includes executive and senior leadership, middle management leaders, the person who may have the formal title of "transformational leader," the change sponsor, enterprise Agile coaches, consultants—in short, anyone who leads any part of an organization that is involved in transformational change.

The various roles mentioned here will have different responsibilities and different levels of engagement, but all are considered "instruments of change." Moreover, all must accept leadership—of self and others—as the foundation of the transformation process. Transformational leaders understand that the most important tool they have for transformation is their own selves. The effort to grow and develop themselves is therefore the central task of a transformation. This is what we mean by "upgrading the leadership operating system."

A Note on Our Thinking about Integral Leadership

You may be surprised that we have chosen to write about transformational leadership rather than "Integral leadership." We made this decision given our conviction that the bar for being centered in the Integral level of leadership (as opposed to outcome-creating/self-authoring mind) is unrealistically high; estimates are that fewer than 5% of leaders are at this level. And yet, our world screams out for a radically new kind of leadership. We've been wrestling with questions underlying Integral leadership—what it really looks like in practice, how many leaders are actually at an Integral stage of development, what it takes to get there, and how will you know when you are there—for quite some time.

With the gravity of the decision regarding what to focus on in this part weighing on us, we wanted to go to a source of wisdom for some kind of confirmation, as well as for a deeper dialogue and exploration. The universe was more than generous, giving us two of the most credible and profoundly wise sources on the topic: Bob Anderson, creator and founder of The Leadership Circle, and Ken Wilber, world philosopher and creator of the Integral Model. Wow, when they both said "yes" to our invitations, we were overjoyed and humbled.

Our conversation with Bob served to reinforce where we were heading. While Integral leadership is indeed rare, there is also an accelerating quantity of research around it (by Bob and Jennifer Garvey Berger, for instance), due to the world's need and a growing level of consciousness in the leadership field (Anderson interview, June 4, 2019). Bob himself is a clear exemplar of Integral leadership in our view, offering himself fully to our dialogue. (You might check out his Coaches' Rising seminar on Integral leadership with Jennifer Garvey Berger at https://vimeo.com/334146708/e50fd54d0f.)

Our discussion with Ken led us to a similar conclusion, grounded in his two admonitions about what it takes to lead a successful transformation: (1) We must get better at the ability to take the perspective of others, and (2) we must learn to see our own seer (Wilber interview, July 26, 2019). We will have a lot more to say about these insights throughout Part II, but for now we acknowledge the contributions of these two men, who helped us reach a working conclusion, and to rethink transformational leadership and how we can develop and grow Integral leadership. Developing new capabilities is like developing muscles that are weak because they aren't used often. If you begin to exercise those muscles consistently and intentionally, eventually you have new, well-developed muscle. Using that analogy, we believe that by consistently using Integral thinking (specifically the IATF) with the disciplines in each quadrant, we can begin to develop more Integral leadership.

Our discussions with Bob and Ken gave us encouragement to articulate the following definition: A **transformational leader** is an outcome-creating leader who uses the Integral Disciplines, both in their mindset (consciousness; left-hand quadrants) and in their actions with the organization (behaviorally; right-hand quadrants) to catalyze personal and organizational transformation. By using the Integral Disciplines—which represent a defined focus of evolution within each quadrant's perspective—transformational leaders move themselves, and their organizations, in the direction of the Integral stage. Indeed, if used properly, the Integral Disciplines enable us to see our own seer, as well as more reliably take the perspective of others.

Let's briefly define what we mean by the Integral Disciplines here for our purposes in developing the LOS, then come back to a fuller articulation in Part III.

The **Integral Disciplines** are the handful of key organizational disciplines—a branch of organizational knowledge consisting of sets of Integral practices, perspectives, and goal matrices—that together lead an organization toward overall organizational agility. The five Integral Disciplines capture the essence of evolution in that quadrant and are supported by several developmental lines in the quadrant, all aligned with the overall Integral Discipline. In addition to providing focus for the organization's change plan, we can use these disciplines as a tool in our own leadership development.

The five Integral Disciplines are

- **Conscious change:** We must take a proactive (conscious), disciplined, and sustainable approach to organizational change, holding the system as the client and working at all holon levels, from all four quadrants, using an intentional, structured, disciplined approach.

- **Evolving consciousness:** To move from the status quo to change, we have to work with evolving the consciousness of individuals in the organization. As transformational leaders, we can go about this in a conscious, strategic, disciplined way, by utilizing vertical leadership development.

- **Evolving product innovation:** If the goal is not just doing Agile but achieving organizational agility, then an organization must go beyond a customer-centric focus to an organization-centric approach in creating its products, hearing all voices of the system.

- **Evolving systemic complexity:** Designing, shifting, and shaping the organization's collective set of beliefs, mores, and mental models in the direction of—and to create a hospitable environment for—organizational agility requires growing systemic complexity, evolving from Achievement-Orange to Pluralistic-Green thinking and acting.

- **Evolving adaptive architectures:** Designing and implementing organizational structures, governance, and policies that optimize flow, value creation, and human well-being is the focus of this discipline.

Even if we as transformational leaders cannot yet fully shift our meaning-making stage to the Integral level, the cognitive line of development is sufficiently advanced in most of us that we can at least understand and use the distinctions of Integral stage thinking. Employing the Integral Disciplines becomes a kind of structural aid to help us act from that understanding, even before it is an integrated part of who we experience ourselves as being (within our meaning-making function); it is a bit like "fake it until you make it." Another angle is that using the Integral Disciplines gives us a "state" experience of Integral leadership; with practice and persistence over a period of time, this state experience can turn into a more reliable "stage" of development. In turn, our center of gravity changes to the higher level with repeated practice. In short, we can act ourselves into a new way of being.

As you read Part II, we hope to ignite in you a conviction about the centrality of transformational leadership, foster a deeper understanding of the characteristics of a transformational leader, and inspire you on your journey toward this new way of being.

5

Transformational Leadership

A quick LinkedIn search on the phrase "transformational leader" tonight yielded 762,137 connection results and 14,656 jobs! More disheartening is that one job description after another cites criteria such as implementing Scrum, implementing scaling frameworks such as SAFe, development of Agile training material, conducting Agile maturity assessments, program management, and … well, you get the picture. An hour into this search and there was still no mention of personal transformation, personal responsibility, or words that represent the true definition of "transformation."

Organizations mostly react to the Agile industry, creating titles and job roles based on what consultants and the industry in general come up with. Mostly, there hasn't been conscious thought about the term *transformational leadership* and what it actually means.

A **transformational leader** is someone willing to be the vessel of change, willing to hold a vision outside existing norms, and willing to personally be transformed in service to that vision. Transformational leaders recognize that they are the most important instrument in the change. They realize that they cannot take their organization further than their own level of development. This is why we know that for leaders to lead transformational change, they must go through their own transformation process. Transformation is often a perilous path, so it requires courage. Transformation is a long path, so it requires an open heart. Transformation is a fraught path, so it requires a steady will. Finally, transformation is a challenging path, requiring an open and growing mind.

In this chapter, we fully explore the concept of transformational leadership, key aspects of its characteristics, and the business case for developing to this level—in short, a full description of the end state covered in Part II of the book.

The Context for Transformational Leadership

Why is transformational leadership so important in our Agile Transformation efforts? We will make the case here that transformational leadership, as we define it—the work of an outcome-creating leader who uses the Integral Disciplines—is the thing that your transformation to organizational agility needs to be successful. Making your own leadership development a priority, helping you grow to the outcome-creating level, is the first step in upgrading your leader's operating system (LOS).

The Leader's Operating System

Men do not attract that which they want, but that which they are.

Men are anxious to improve their circumstances, but are unwilling to improve themselves.
—James Allen, *As a Man Thinketh*, 1905

The process of becoming a great leader is the same as that of becoming a great person.
—Warren Bennis, who first coined the distinction between
"management" and "leadership," 1989

The idea that, as leaders, we have an operating system is a powerful metaphor. Earlier in this book, we used a parallel metaphor regarding the Integral Agile Transformation Framework (IATF), calling it a meta-framework for organizational transformation, which uses the Integral Model as the operating system. The LOS points to the reality that our leadership effectiveness is determined not just by *what* we do, but by *how* we do it—by our *meaning-making* system, our order of consciousness, brought to bear in how we carry out tasks and in our leadership presence.

When we look from this point of view—and at the data from researchers like Bob Kegan, Bill Torbert, Bill Joiner, Susanne Cook-Greuter, and our friends Bob Anderson and Bill Adams at The Leadership Circle—we see that there is a structure to our meaning making. And, as Anderson and Adams (2016) point out, the primary determinant of the performance of a system is its **design**. The nature and structure of our thoughts, beliefs and assumptions—conscious and unconscious—create our reality; thus, *consciousness is the operating system of performance*. Our performance is always consistent with our level of consciousness. So, if we want to break through to higher levels of performance, **we** must be restructured (Anderson & Adams, 2016, pp. 35–37). In short, if we want greater business success—especially in an organizational transformation—the highest-leverage path is to go inside to allow ourselves to be restructured. This is what we mean when we talk about upgrading your LOS.

Just as Agile implementations focus almost exclusively on the IT quadrant of behavior and practices, so most leadership development efforts focus on the *outer game* of competencies, skills, and knowledge. Certainly, those are important, but in general they are not differentiating of great leadership: The *inner game* runs the outer game, so the leverage occurs when we upgrade our inner game, the LOS. The following two chapters are about how to do that; this chapter sets out the context and builds the business case for doing so.

Developmental researchers define the inner game as being composed of our meaning-making system—our decision making, our values and spiritual beliefs, our level of self-awareness and emotional intelligence, the mental models we use to understand reality and act, and the internal beliefs and assumptions that make up our personal identity (Anderson & Adams, 2016, p. 31).

> Great leadership is connected with the deepest parts of ourselves. It has more to do with *character*, *courage*, and *conviction* than it does with specific skills or competencies. Leadership requires *wisdom*, *self-knowledge*, and *character development* at psychological and spiritual levels. (Anderson & Adams, 2016, p. 29)

In corroborating evidence from both spiritual thinking and biological science, we see that the beliefs and the heart have more bearing than we might typically realize. From a spiritual context, *chakras* are the circular vortexes of energy (*subtle energy*) that are centered at seven different points on the spinal column, and all seven chakras are connected to the various organs and glands within the body. The lower chakras (first, second, and third) are the seat of emotion, whereas the upper ones (fifth, sixth, and seventh) are the seat of thinking; they are joined together in the fourth chakra, the heart center, which integrates emotion and thought into feeling (and belief), which in turn guides what we do. In parallel, biologically speaking, the electrical field of the heart is 100 times stronger than that of the brain, while the heart's magnetic field is up to 5000 times stronger than that of the brain (Braden, 2019). The claim that leadership requires wisdom, character development, and bringing the heart online has a basis in long-standing science and spiritual tradition.

Perhaps most importantly, the LOS can be seen as the primary determinant of leaders' practical effectiveness, which can be quantified using a tool like a 360-degree assessment, as their leadership quotient.

Leadership Quotient

Leadership quotient (LQ) can be defined as leadership effectiveness divided by leadership ineffectiveness. When we use the Leadership Circle Profile (LCP) in our work, a shorthand calculation is dividing an individual's score for the outcome-creating competencies on the LCP by their score for problem-reacting tendencies. A score of 1.0 indicates a leader who has an equal effectiveness to ineffectiveness; in short, that leader has a neutral effect on the organization.

The LQ score for an organization, then, measures the degree to which its leadership provides a competitive advantage or disadvantage. If the organization has an LQ of less than 1.0, its leadership is a costly competitive disadvantage; we have all seen organizations where this was true but rarely acknowledged or measured as such. In contrast, organizations with LQ scores greater than 1.0 are moving into the range where their leadership is a distinct competitive advantage. In top-performing businesses studied by Anderson and Adams, the LQ was 4.0; for bottom performers, the LQ was 0.4. This is a 10-fold difference (Anderson & Adams, 2016, p. 17). (Note: This study is described in more detail later in this chapter.)

For leaders to find out their own LQ is an act of both courage and shrewdness. Only by getting data on our own leadership effectiveness—through a 360-degree tool, deep conversation, and/or by asking for feedback—can we hope to evolve our own complexity to meet the challenges we face in an ever-complexifying world. So, what difference does our LQ score really make in terms of business results?

Leadership Effectiveness and Business Performance

Most, if not all, leadership researchers would agree that the collective consciousness of most senior leadership teams is not complex enough to lead in the world we find ourselves in. For example, 75% of adults are classified as having a Reactive mind or being in the transition from Reactive to Creative (Anderson & Adams, 2016, p. 72). This "center of gravity" creates corresponding organizational structures, policies, and culture where true empowerment is simply not possible, despite all the Agile and management training to the contrary. When we are "run" by our Reactive side, we do not feel comfortable being in deep relationships at work, letting "subordinates" fully participate in decision making, or finding the strengths (as opposed to the weaknesses) in others, all of which reinforces their need for us.

This fact was confirmed by the Full Circle Group (the consulting side of The Leadership Circle) in its consulting history. Consultants would routinely design meetings and change events for clients from the Creative level of mind and happily find that people would rise to the occasion. The problem was that they would then be unable to maintain this level of functioning after they left the structured event. This outcome was perplexing until the consultants fully understood that the client's leaders were not continuing to lead from that Creative level (Anderson & Adams, 2016, p. 74). In fact, most change efforts are an attempt to create a Creative-level culture, but they fall short because that can be sustained only with leadership functioning at the Creative level or above—resulting in lots of activity (IT quadrant) geared toward creating a high-performance organization but ultimately ending in failure (p. 73).

Bob Kegan, in his book *In Over Our Heads* (1994), makes a parallel point about many of our institutions, such as education, marriage and childrearing, and work practices, where the societal norm is a bar set for someone with a self-authoring mind—someone who acts on their own principles, has an internal locus of control, and so on. This level is simply not a reality for most people, and so there is constant disappointment.

You may be thinking that this is our collective experience in Agile Transformations: The practices and culture of Agile were designed from a Pluralistic-Green (with elements of Teal) state of mind but cannot be authentically or fully implemented in the Achievement-Orange (or Traditional-Amber) cultures of most organizations. When we did a mapping between Agile leadership characteristics (e.g., servant leadership, trusting teams, regular release of valuable products, collaboration orientation), we found that there was essentially a perfect correlation between those Agile leadership concepts and the outcome-creating competencies of The Leadership Circle. Correspondingly, we found no correlation between the Agile concepts and the problem-reacting tendencies (https://leadershipcircle.com/en/agile-leadership/, "Agile Leadership and Outcome Creating Competencies," Leadership Circle Blog, February 14, 2019). Our conclusion, reinforced in repeated experiments with workshop participants engaging in the same mapping exercise: It is impossible to be an Agile leader without being able to work at the Creative level (or above).

Moving the average level of leadership up is an inner game play; all the Agile training in the world will not get us there. It's not about well-crafted arguments, better process frameworks, or implementing CI/CD or dev-ops on an enterprise-wide scale! Until the leadership of an organization can hold the necessary transformational container together, Agile "installations" are doomed to underperform. We must restructure both the inner game and the LOS.

Let's turn now to business performance and leadership. The Leadership Circle did an extensive research project on 500 organizations (later extended to 2000) on the relationship between business performance and leadership (Anderson, 2006). Researchers created a *Business Performance Index* (BPI) consisting of measurements for revenue, market share, sales, profitability, quality of products, and overall business performance. They then asked a cohort of managers from the same industries as the various organizations to rate the performance of the organization that a given leader leads compared to industry standards. The 50 highest-ranking businesses were identified through this process, and the LCP profiles of each organization's leaders were combined into a single aggregate profile; a parallel process was performed for the 50 lowest-ranked businesses. The resulting profiles are shown in Figure 5.1. The bottom line to help you read the charts: Green on the top half is good (Creative), but green on the bottom half is not so good (Reactive).

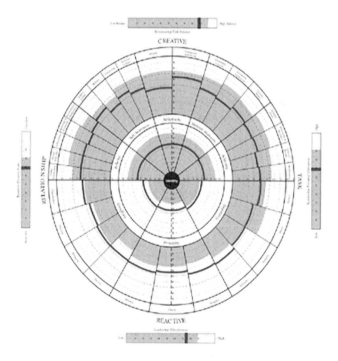

Figure 5.1 (Continues, next page)

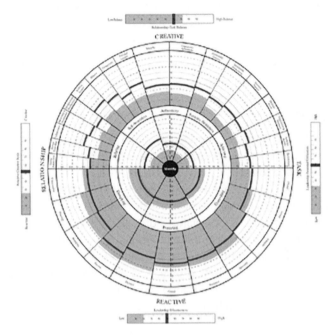

Figure 5.1

Aggregate profiles of the leaders of top- and bottom-performing businesses [Anderson, Robert J., & Adams, William A. (2016). Mastering leadership: An integrated framework for breakthrough performance and extraordinary business results. Hoboken, NJ: John Wiley & Sons.]

Notice the large disparity between the two composite profiles: The top organizations had leaders (left profile) who were highly outcome creating but relatively low problem reacting; the bottom-performing organizations (on the right) showed the reverse pattern. Further, the top leaders underestimated their strengths and overestimated their weaknesses (humility? higher self-standard?); the bottom leaders did just the opposite.

Researchers specifically compared the leadership effectiveness scores of the top 10% to the bottom 10%. The top performers had an average leadership effectiveness score at the 80th percentile, while bottom performers were down at the 30th percentile (Anderson, 2006, p. 15). The correlation was 0.61—a strong positive correlation. This level of correlation means there is a 38% probability that if you improve leadership effectiveness, you will improve business performance (p. 14).

These results also track with Zenger and Folkman's research on the competitive advantage of great leaders, which found that leaders at or above the 80th percentile on a robust 360-degree assessment produce twice the results of those in the middle 60th percentile range. In other words, two (out of ten) top-performing leaders have *double* the performance of six (out of ten) medium performers; put differently, one great leader at this level outperforms *by a factor of six* each middle performer. That's a serious competitive advantage that organizations can maximize with their leadership development efforts (Zenger & Folkman, 2009).

A related question is, Does leadership effectiveness increase at each progressive stage of development? Anderson and Adam's results are shown in Table 5.1.

Table 5.1   Leadership effectiveness by level of development (Anderson & Adams, 2016)

Altitude	Leadership Effectiveness	LQ
Reactive (socialized mind)	40%	0.67
Creative (self-authoring mind)	65%	1.9
Integral (self-transforming mind)	90%	9.0

Collectively, these studies suggest that the performance of an organization strongly depends on the level of consciousness of its leadership. Our conclusion is that if your Agile Transformation does not have a serious leadership development effort going on in parallel with the implementation of Agile practices—given both the effect that upgrading the LOS has on business performance and the strong correlation between outcome-creating level of leadership and Agile principles—you will be leaving money on the table, putting the Agile change initiative at serious risk, and unlikely to fulfill the promise of Agile.

Michael's Take

Two leaders I have worked with illustrate this point. The first—I'll call him Mike—was a vice president of engineering, a brilliant strategist, and a knowledgeable Agile advocate with a strong technical background. And he was a bully: He had a sharp, incisive mind that he used to drill into people's assumptions and inadvertent mistakes. People did learn things in meetings where he interrogated their work, but they dreaded going to those meetings in the first place. As a result, the culture of his organization reinforced behaviors for their brilliance but not for connection, collaboration, or honesty when people didn't know the answer or made mistakes. The culture of his department was brittle and did not grow.

By contrast Doug, another business vice president and Mike's peer, was an outcome-creating leader (or higher). He was easily able to tolerate disagreement, not needing to be the smartest guy in the room, and had a keen interest in hearing others' ideas and catalyzing their creative spark. Doug had a highly innovative organization that ran cutting-edge experiments that excited everyone in the greater organization. His Friday afternoon discovery sessions were eagerly attended by a sizable crowd within the company, all excited to see the latest developments. People did not fear Doug as they did Mike; they went to him to get help thinking through their challenges, and they felt supported by him. When people went to see Mike, they could not show vulnerability, which stifled their natural creativity. Doug's organization was a hub of innovation and commitment.

One final note: The Leadership Circle has a database of approximately 200,000 leaders, who were assessed by more than 2 million raters. This offers a treasure trove of data to examine differences between various demographic groups. For the most part, there are very minor differences between cultures across countries around the world; likely the biggest difference is due to gender. The bottom line: The way women lead in the early twenty-first century is decidedly more effective, on average, than the way men currently lead (Anderson, 2016, p. 104), with strengths in relating to others, collaboration, being team players, and getting results (Table 5.2). Interestingly, this seems to map a recent meme in Agile thinking, that Agile tends to be "feminist."

Table 5.2   Women's average leadership scores compared to men's (Anderson & Adams, 2016)

Altitude	Women	Men
Relating (relationship side of wheel)	56%	39%
Achieving (task side of wheel)	53%	41%
Leadership effectiveness	53%	41%

The Business Case for Transformational Leadership

Adding it all up, the case is clear:

- Agile leadership is essentially impossible without moving to a self-authoring (outcome-creating) stance.

- Business performance suffers greatly at lower levels of leadership development.

- The actual structure of the LOS at socialized mind levels is not designed to create change but rather to maintain the status quo.

- The culture of the organization—long known to constrain or thwart Agile success—is reinforced and co-created by leaders.

- Therefore, the higher the level of collective development, the more likely that the organization will achieve Agile Transformation success and greater business performance.

Collective Leadership Effectiveness

> *Effective, collective leadership is your one competitive and strategic advantage that no one can copy.*
> —Dave Schrader, PhD

Peter Senge (1990) notes that the collective intelligence and performance of most groups is well below the average intelligence and performance of the members. In short, we often "dumb down" when we come together. If instead we are able to raise our collective leadership intelligence—in essence, upgrade our collective LOS—we can create a competitive differentiator that will decidedly improve our business performance, not to mention making our organization a better, more humane environment for employees to work in, a more collaborative space where we can engage our clients, and with a leadership perspective that is more sustainable for the internal and external ecosystems.

How does this play out in the research? If we look at leadership culture in the highest- and lowest-performing businesses from the business performance study mentioned earlier, the top businesses had an 80% Creative score as an overall culture, and a 30% Reactive score. The leadership culture of the bottom performers was skewed to 30% Creative and 70% Reactive. The LQ of the highest-performing businesses was 2.7, while that of the lowest-performing companies was 0.4.

To reshape the leadership culture in organizations—and the collective leadership effectiveness—we must find a way to expand our systemic consciousness and culture complexity. Based on extensive work with hundreds of top leadership teams, Anderson and Adams (2016) say: "The quality of the leadership conversations determines collective effectiveness, which determines collective intelligence, which determines business performance. As senior leaders, the quality of our conversation and our relationships correlates directly with the results we create" (p. 25). The most consistent feedback they receive after working with a senior team for a year is that

> [T]he difference that made the difference is that we can now tell the truth to one another and have courageous conversations that get results. We can now take on complex and politically charged issues, central to moving the business forward, and we quickly cut through the complexity and personal sensitivities to arrive at high-quality decisions. (Anderson & Adams, 2016, p. 25)

Our experience is fundamentally the same. When we work with leaders in an Agile Transformation using good 360-degree data for each leadership team member, the precise feedback about their leadership—as well as the debriefing of it in the company of each other—creates a mutual vulnerability and human bond that dramatically changes the tenor of the conversation that members are able to have with each other. The revelations are deep, honest, and often moving. When a leadership team can have truly genuine, human dialogue with each other, the game forever changes. A different way of working—for them and for their teams—is truly possible.

Two client stories will illustrate the point.

Example

We worked with two senior leadership teams from different organizations with dramatically different results, based on the nature of their collective leadership and openness to feedback.

- The first was the leadership team for a key business unit within a large health care company, whose senior leader was Margaret. We took Margaret's team through a multiple-day leadership development workshop. We made good progress on day one, but then on day two—as we confronted problems we had both observed and heard in interviews with team members—it became clear that the team was unwilling to confront Margaret's rather controlling, and somewhat toxic, leadership style. The issue was clearly present in the room for all to see, but no one was willing to take on the elephant in the room (except us). On several occasions, the team could see the elephant but made the (unconscious) decision to go in a safer direction of staying with the status quo. The result was that the team shifted from the possibility of having an open and honest, if difficult, conversation to focusing on tactical work as an avoidance mechanism. They were "safe," but they did not have a breakthrough.

- The second client was the senior team of a large technology distribution company, whose leader was Mark. By contrast to the first team, this leadership team really rose to the occasion. Led by Mark's courageous and vulnerable acknowledgment of his own feedback report—which pointed out numerous weaknesses in his leadership—the team had demonstrably different conversations than they had ever had before, reaching new levels of candor, authenticity, and vulnerability. The energy was electric; you could feel their excitement and relief. For us as coaches, it was a very moving couple of days. The conversations were not easy or all rosy, but they were genuine and respectful. A follow-up several months later confirmed that the gains were not short-lived. Mark reported that the team's conversations were never the same.

Leader-First Transformation

This leads us to our bottom line: If we are to succeed in attaining organizational agility through an Agile Transformation, the place to start is by developing the senior leaders. We need to help them individually and collectively look in the proverbial mirror, to honestly assess and find out how they are likely the most important limitation—though perhaps also the greatest asset—in helping the organization transform. As Agile Transformation professionals, when going into an organization that wishes to transform itself, we should regularly be making the recommendation that the coaching start with leadership, not with teams. We don't focus on running standup meetings per se but rather on catalyzing the work of helping leaders grow their LOS. If we collectively took this approach, it would radically shift the game. The challenge: Are we courageous enough to take this stand, and how many senior leaders are ready to start with themselves?

Having made the case for transformational leadership from a business perspective, we now want to draw a sketch of what it looks like on the ground and to explore where the idea came from historically.

The Essence of Transformational Leadership

There is a calling, a global world calling, for humanity to wake up to the change that is happening, wake up to how we are "being" with and changing our world (this drive has become all the more poignant during the COVID-19 crisis). If you are truly a transformational leader—not just in title only, but someone who is called to catalyze transformational, breakthrough kind of change—then you are called to this global consciousness work. We must not ignore this calling; to do so would be to go back to sleep. Organizations are being called to do more than create products; they and their leaders are being called to bring the consciousness of humanity into the workplace, into society, for the changes the world needs.

How does this calling play out in your day-to-day world? Imagine this is you. As the transformational leader, you have discovered that there is an "us versus them" mentality between the business and technology areas in your organization. The business sees the Agile Transformation as a technology-driven implementation and expects to "get it right" with minimal involvement from its executives. Further, as the transformational leader, you have good relationships with both the business and technology people. It turns out folks from both sides are coming to you, complaining about people from the "other side," putting you in the middle of their conflict. They expect you to be the middle-man, to solve the problem, to rescue them. This puts you in an awkward position. It also confronts you head on with your motivations and intentions in this leadership position. How you react will either be from a transactional leadership stance—fixing the problem—or be from a transformational leadership stance—helping the people and the system to change. The transactional response is the autopilot response and typically the first one that most people make, unless they are awake and consciously making a choice from an outcome-creating stance rather than instinctively reacting in their normal manner.

Becoming a transformational leader challenges us to make room for our own deep passion for change, coming up against the personal limitations in us that prevent this change from occurring through us. When we face these issues, we draw on the deepest resources within us—emotional, psychological, ancestral, spiritual. We find ways to tap into the internal voices of inspiration and vision that come through us rather than the ego voices that only go to the limits of our own mind. In addition, we draw on external resources of trusted colleagues, friends, and family who can help us see where we are exaggerating our own importance or, conversely, selling ourselves short.

Our experience working with many transformations is that there is often a fundamental disconnect between how Agile Transformations are perceived and how the reality of achieving organizational agility plays out—the true goal. As we've discussed, organizations need organizational agility and believe that installing an Agile process framework will get them there. Generally speaking, there's a somewhat naive misunderstanding that the real intention of an Agile Transformation is not "installing the Agile," but actually transforming the organization, and not just transforming it externally, in terms of its practices and structures, but also internally, through its mindset and culture. In short, Agile Transformation seeks to reshape the *way of being as an organization*. If that is our goal, only transformational leadership—not transactional leadership—will get us there.

Moving from Transactional to Transformational

Transformational leadership is not a new term. It was initially introduced by James V. Downton as "**transforming** leadership" and then further developed by leadership expert James MacGregor Burns (1978). Bernard Bass built on MacGregor's work to include the psychology behind the *transforming* and *transactional* leadership approaches and then tweaked the term to be "**transformational** leadership." We continue to evolve our thinking of what it truly means to be a transformational leader.

We compare transactional leadership and transformational leadership in Table 5.3.

Table 5.3   Transactional versus transformational leadership

Transactional Leadership	Transformational Leadership
Reacts to issues from patterns of habit; maintains the status quo.	Creates outcomes that matter guided by passion; a catalyst for change.
Rewards individual success; guided by leadership's goals and expectations.	Inspires teamwork and cross-organizational collaboration for the higher organizational purpose.
Operates within existing culture and norms; conservative.	Consciously cultivates the desired culture by modeling new behaviors and ways of thinking.
Operates within existing structures and system; using workarounds to get things done.	Evolves more adaptive organizations by seeing the limitations of existing systems and structures and co-creating solutions that allow for more agility.

The Role of Consciousness

Let's go back to our scenario, digging a bit deeper to understand how we can make choices from conscious awareness. We do not often think about consciousness, though we experience it all the time, typically without being aware of it. When we do, it can become self-consciousness: We are aware of ourselves being aware; it can be an awkward internal moment. At the same time, our awareness is precisely what makes it possible for us to change, to create, to recognize a new idea, to see that a process needs changing, or to come back to ourselves.

If we look closely—perhaps by meditating or praying—we see that awareness is always on. Consciousness does not turn off, only our mind does; consciousness persists, though we sometimes go to sleep. When we "wake up," if we look back, we realize awareness did not suddenly appear; rather, we just became aware that it was there. We become aware of our awareness, or you might say, we "see our seer." Seeing our seer, making the subject-to-object switch, is an essential element for any transformation to be possible. The only way to do this is to become more consciously aware of our way of being in the moment.

If we have lost conscious awareness within the preceding scenario—if we just become absorbed into the problem—we may instinctively (like a reflex) try to defend our friends when they are criticized, believing we are being a good friend. We may take the bait about being a hero, tasked to fix the problem. There is plenty of reinforcement, both within ourselves and in our environment, for taking the actions of a hero. We won't take the time to think, Whose problem is this? Or, at what level can the problem be solved? When we pause to reflect and challenge our thinking, however, conscious awareness is starting to come online.

If we become internally still enough to pause and reflect, we may start to consider how we can actually be effective in this situation, moving toward our goal of organizational agility. The transformational leader uses conscious awareness to examine a thorny issue: If the "us versus them" split persists, can we ever get to a good outcome, a place where creativity and innovation are happening, where everyone enjoys working?

The transformational leader then digs even deeper, into the underlying beliefs that drive us to want to be seen as the hero. When we see deeply into those beliefs, we begin to understand what makes us feel safe, or heard, or needed, or smart, or worthy. Aligned with that deep place of conscious awareness, we realize these beliefs we have constructed for ourselves are mostly untrue. Freed from such false beliefs—ones that no longer serve us—we are able to look objectively at the situation from a place of non-ego, for the sake of the outcome that will benefit the whole. From this place, we become able to make a real choice in the moment rather than reacting without even being aware of our motivation or the impact on the whole system. We have woken up. This is the transformational leader in action. Such a leader stands in contrast to the many leaders with "good intentions," but not necessarily "conscious intentions," as they go about their change efforts.

Becoming more conscious is not something we can achieve from an intellectual place. Instead, it is an experiential journey, one that requires us to move from talking-the-talk to authentically walking-the-walk. We must actually aspire to be a conscious leader; without this intention, it will not happen. The move from transactional to transformational leadership is undeniably a transformational journey as a human being first. Simply put, you cannot be a conscious leader without being a conscious human being. And you cannot become a transformational leader without first becoming consciously aware of your current way of being as a leader.

Taking the Perspective of Others

The second essential element for transformation to happen is being able to take the role or perspective of others. When we truly take the role of another, it means we attempt to look "as" them. We are looking through their lens to see the world as they see it. This is different from just hearing another's perspectives before making decisions. The fundamental shift is developing the ability to deeply understand the needs and perspectives of others, based on understanding how things look through their worldview (like their altitude, quadrant, developmental lines, and other lenses). The two ways of seeing our clients are to look "at" them—that is, to observe them through these different lenses—and then to look "as" them—that is, to see what it must be like for them, how they come to their conclusions, what their underlying beliefs are, how they go about their day to day, and what they value. In this stance of mutual deep understanding, we are able to co-create and find solutions that meet all needs. We shift from taking a position on key challenges to identifying them. We begin to see that we are only a part of the system, which is only part of the truth, and not the truth of the whole. In this way of seeing, we are able to develop a win–win–win capability (me, you, and the situation as a whole); rather than a win–win, we are serving a higher purpose together. We are able to reframe our perspectives when we deeply listen and truly understand the perspective of the other. This move has to take place not only in individuals but also in the organization as a whole. For such win–win–win thinking to be possible, it must be designed into the culture and into the incentives and reward systems.

Looking "as" another person is possible only from a place of consciousness, presence, and curiosity, which allows us to respond in a more empathetic and compassionate way. When our situation calls for more candor, it is important that we first pause, reflect, and then respond from a place of compassion and curiosity. When we come from that place, our candor is more readily taken in by the other person. The inability to "look as" another person from curiosity and compassion, and to genuinely see their perspective, is what blocks us from co-creating. It is what keeps us locked in the us-versus-them or me-versus-you reactive mindset, making one right and the other wrong; it becomes the barrier to transformational change.

Michele's Take

One of my coaching clients was working on his ability to be more curious with others rather than advocating for his position or idea. We created his metaphor as the "fiery advocate." What he was advocating for, of course, was positive change, but his current way of interacting with others was shutting down his ability to see their perspective, simply because he was so attached to an outcome he perceived was the right one.

Several months into our coaching, he shared with me that he had an opportunity to meet with the CEO for the first time. As he began to "advocate" to her his ideas and approaches, he had a moment of self-awareness—seeing himself in the way of the fiery advocate and seeing her completely checked out and seeming very overwhelmed. In that moment, he took a breath, challenged his thinking and made a very different next move. He simply said, "I've been here telling you things I think you need to do. Instead, I want to know how I can help you." He went into inquiry mode and became truly curious. The interaction took on an entirely different quality. He began to see "as" her, a new CEO, overwhelmed and hearing from so many people what she "should" be doing, and now here's the Agile transformational leader doing the same thing. By standing beside her, looking as her, he was then able to be in relationship with her. It required him to detach from his desired outcomes to be fully with her and to take her perspective.

In Anderson and Adams's second book, *Scaling Leadership* (2019), the beginning of the shift to Integral is first described as moving from being self-authored to just being authored—neither authored by others nor exclusively by our own sense of personal purpose. In this new way of being, we let go of our self-authoring to being authored by something larger than ourselves, something that urges us to serve a higher calling, a calling to create what the future needs. As Anderson shared with us, it is "moving from self-authored to authored by one's own 'higher-power'" (Anderson interview, 2019). In the transition from outcome-creating to Integral leadership, we are transitioning toward a self-transforming mindset. It is at this level of leadership that we become more capable of dealing with challenges without blaming, taking sides, or becoming attached to our own ideals. In the scenario, we don't feel the need to take sides or to fix the problem; instead, we look for the systemic causes of the conflict, attempt to see the world from both sides' points of view, and neutrally hold the transformational container between the groups that can allow for change.

Transitioning to an Integral way of being as a leader allows us to see ourselves, our organization, and our world from a systemic point of view—full of irresolvable polarities, good intentions, conflicting positions, and at times discordant worldviews—that all contribute to creating our results.

It allows us to not take ourselves so seriously, to see that we are continually a work in progress. As we become more comfortable with our own shadow/disowned parts, we see that the systems we are trying to change, as messed up as they are, are not that different from us (Anderson interview, 2019).

We believe that to become a transformational leader, capable of leading organizations through massive transformation and successfully thriving in the midst of today's complexity in unique and innovative ways, it is imperative to shift toward Integral leadership. Our work is helping people and organizations use the Integral Disciplines to develop this capability.

Summary

Transformational leadership is a uniquely developed form of leadership, essential to catalyzing an Agile Transformation and to leading in an Agile environment. It is our growth as a human being that leads to more effective leadership.

In Chapter 6, we describe what each of the three developmental levels of leadership look like so that you get a sense of where you're starting. Then, in Chapter 7, we explore ways to develop from one level to another.

From Insight to Action

This chapter is about what it really means to be a transformational leader. It is worth doing some reflecting on the premise of the chapter for yourself. Specifically, reflect on your journey to the place of leadership where you are now, and take some time to journal about the following questions:

- What is one gift, talent, or characteristic that has helped you get to where you are now? What is a current limitation that stands in your way of being a leader and change agent?

- How is that limitation impacting your results?

Another powerful action we suggest is undertaking a leadership 360-degree assessment for yourself. Make sure it gets at your underlying level of development and your personal psychology. In addition, sit down with 5–10 colleagues and ask them for detailed feedback on your leadership.

6

The Developmental Landscape

We live in a globally connected world, amidst more complexity than ever seen before, which leads us to the need for global human development. *Vertical development* increases the ability to think in more complex, strategic, systemic, and interdependent ways. *Horizontal development* increases knowledge, skills, and competencies and is focused on making the person better within their current way of being. In vertical development, you are transforming the person. Ironically, in spite of the high demand for transformational leaders in organizations, the investment in people is typically focused on horizontal—not vertical—development. The daily challenges that leaders face, causing so much distraction and constant change, produce highly reactive leadership in an autopilot "doing" mode, when what is really needed to break through the status quo results is leadership in a "being/thinking" mode of conscious intention. Moving to a consciously aware and intentional leadership stance does not happen accidentally, nor does it happen by attending a training course or learning a new skill. Instead, it happens when leaders become aware of their way of being as a leader, see their limiting patterns and beliefs, and then consciously embark on a journey to develop a new way of being.

The Core of Development: "Our Story"

In the last chapter, we used the metaphor of an operating system for our meaning-making system, revealing our *order of consciousness* brought to bear in how we carry out tasks and in our leadership presence. We also learned that to be more effective, we have to "upgrade" our operating system. If our inner game runs our outer game, and our inner game consists of our meaning-making system, and our internal beliefs and assumptions make up our identity, how then do we "develop" ourselves? This is where our "story" comes in.

Our interpretation of our reality, the way we make meaning, is really just a "story"—one that started before we were even born. It started with the culture we were born into, and it continued from our birth into our early childhood, telling us how we should organize ourselves and our lives: what's good, what's bad, what's right and wrong, what our spiritual or non-spiritual beliefs should be, what money means, what success means, what education means, what makes us special, what should make us happy or sad, and so on. This "story" is constructed by our culture and interpreted to us by our parents to inform us of what it means to be human. And, of course, why would a baby or a child question what adults know best? To be fair, children have a need for a story, some kind of story that helps them find their place in the world.

But then the time comes when that original "story" no longer serves us. This is the beginning of the end of the socialized mind level of consciousness. (See Kegan, 1994, where the concept of "orders of consciousness" is explained.)

When we see from the socialized mind, the world fits more neatly into categories, into societally defined ways of conforming, into forms that make social interactions easier and less conflictual, but nevertheless forms that do violence to the urgings of our soul, putting them into a straitjacket. It is here that we are creating and writing our ego's story, based on the stories we create to belong, to fit in the world, to feel worthy to belong to something, to someone. At this stage, we aren't really questioning this story much, except to ask if it fits in with the stories of everyone around us. There are three characteristic ways of creating this story, based on what is our most adaptive skill set within the human communities we inhabit: skills of the *heart*, skills of the *head*, or skills of the *will*.

The transition to being an adult takes us beyond the strong binds of our "story," beyond the narrative we have believed in, into a journey of exploring our true selves and constructing our story from new premises. There is no age limit on this quest, and the journey is different for everyone. The longer the original "story" is reinforced, or if healthy support for this transition to adulthood is lacking, then the more entrenched this "story" becomes, the more it becomes reality, and the more it becomes tied to our personal identity. When this transition doesn't happen, people find themselves working in organizations in job roles that they aren't equipped for. The socialized mind, while enforced by our organizational cultures, doesn't support the work that individuals, teams, and organizations are being called to do. The socialized mind, trapped in the story, finds it difficult to truly take another person's perspective, because doing so would threaten the story or the person's **ego**—the thing that needs this particular story to survive. Trapped in the story, we aren't aware of our blind spots, or how our way of being is even showing up in the moment. We are just doing what we always do, without even thinking or seeing how our limiting beliefs are hindering us in that moment; we're on autopilot. Therefore, when we are unconscious and unaware of our way of being and unable to take another's perspective (by looking *as* them), we block the ability to make forward progress as a whole system, creating what needs to be created.

The more we free ourselves from the "story" of who we believe we are and what makes us worthy in this world, the more we connect to our genuine selves in the present moment. When we connect to being fully human, we no longer compartmentalize ourselves but rather begin to feel the connection between our mind and body and a longing to be in harmony with ourselves.

The self-control that we have "mastered" so that we don't look stupid or make mistakes that might cost us something, separates us from the harmony of our true self. Think about a time when you were sitting in a meeting and had an instinct, a knowing of something—of an idea or a break-through that needs to happen in the room—but you did nothing. You did nothing because you were trapped by your story. Reflect on the feeling in that moment. Did you feel in harmony with yourself? Were your mind and your body in harmony? Or were you trying to "think" your way out of it? You most likely felt tension in your body, so your mind either worked to get rid of the tension or just ignored it.

Here's the thing: Harmony cannot be controlled. It is not done alone; it is the opposite of control. Just think of how harmony works in music. Harmony is a living, moving state, where we are in tune with the whole and focused on co-creating rather than focused on ourselves. Being in harmony with our humanness is being with our wholeness—they are inseparable. We feel harmony when we are operating in our wholeness, and when we are operating in our wholeness, we feel harmony. In this state of harmony and wholeness, we find our true calling and our sense of purpose. This is the level of consciousness we refer to as the **self-authoring mind** (Kegan, 1994), where we become the authors of our own lives.

As we grow into this self-authoring mind, we feel ourselves grow. We can no longer rely on the values of others, their approval, or their condemnation to correct our behavior; instead, we must rely on ourselves. We are the ones accountable—not someone else's value system or someone else's judgment. Our internal complexity has increased, as we use our gifts to sense what's needed in the world. But we still have a story that makes our ego feel secure, a story of who we are, an identity that we insist on defending. Defending that identity—whatever it is in the moment—takes us away from seeing the truth of the moment. The way the game is played is that we don't *see* the facts that don't fit our story and that don't protect the identity we are defending. Instead, we see things—in fact, we subconsciously check for them—that conveniently "prove the case" of how we want to see ourselves: whether generous, in the right, discerning, open-minded, or good or bad (since being wrong or weak or defective is often an unhappy part of our story). Seeing the "story" in its truth requires self-honesty, the ability to tell ourselves the truth. This self-authoring story is still "our story," one that we have written and that we hold on to, sometimes for life, unless we have one more wake-up call.

Our culture continuously reinforces the belief that you can find the secret to success, career fulfillment, relationships, financial security, and your life's purpose by following an approach or by making the right decisions and actions. This mantra also reinforces our "story" that we can self-manage or control our lives. In turn, we humans continue to manage our way into finding this sought-after end through self-help books and programs, diet and exercise routines, religion, and all the various "things" that we hope will bring us our heart's desire for living in purpose and harmony. Unfortunately, this obsession with self-improvement, without awareness, pulls us away from the present and from the presence of our whole self that already exists. If you have ever truly danced, played a musical instrument, painted a beautiful painting, or engaged in a form of creative expression, you have experienced the connection of your mind and body, of your wholeness, of being fully present and in harmony with yourself. Self-consciousness doesn't exist in these moments; self-control is released. The experience is just a pure expression of you, all of you—not compartmentalized, not separating mind and body. This is the experience of letting go of our "story." We aren't *something*; we just *are*. That is, we just are our whole human being, in full experience of our human self.

This chapter is about understanding our current reality as individuals, as human beings who are shaped by our "story," and realizing that we can take a journey to discover the beliefs and assumptions that make up this story. When we more fully understand the narrative of our story, along with all its controlling and limiting beliefs, we can begin deconstructing that story and transcend to the place where we feel connected to our true being. In this move to a self-authoring mind, as we become connected to our inner truths, we recognize that we are no longer defined by the story and thus better able to speak our truth.

There is one final landscape to examine beyond self-authoring. Our society, as it moves into post-modernism, is beginning to explore the idea that we are all connected by something larger than ourselves. Rather than looking at our differences, we are beginning to look at our similarities and seeing that we are all tied to the whole of our planet. Climate change, for example, is one issue binding the world together as a whole. If we don't all join together and let go of our differences so that we can focus on our joined reality, our planet will likely suffer catastrophic extinction in the not too distant future.

As we develop a **self-transforming mind**, we become more willing to see the fictions of our own ego. As we question our own philosophy, our own story of any kind, we see the paradoxes inherent in our being. Rather than choose one or the other, we come to hold both as part of the **container** that we are—the container of consciousness that never goes away, that never rejects us; the consciousness whose nature is compassionate, accepting, and loving. As we sink into the ground of our being, we can take amusement in our story, rather than making the proving of it a deadly serious game. In this new story, the ego is seen for what it is, just a story, so there is less to protect; the ego's desire to prove something fades away and our connection to others becomes even more authentic, more immediate and in the moment. It is this self-transforming mind that brings about real, lasting, transformational change in our lives and in the world; this is the level of Integral leadership.

While the majority of individuals haven't shifted to this self-transforming level of consciousness, our society is pushing us to develop this way of thinking and being so that we can solve our world-scale problems. As we evolve from self-authoring to self-transforming, we will experience "states" (moments, occasions) of the self-transforming mind. The more intentional we are about our development, the more often we will find ourselves in these state experiences, until eventually we are operating mostly from that place.

The way of being of our organizations across the globe is even further behind in developing this level of consciousness. The world's imperative to develop a self-transforming mind is inarguable: This mindset is needed to survive and thrive not only in our future of work but also in our world, period. This is the landscape for which reluctant development is no longer an option.

Deconstructing the Levels

Now we want to break down each of the three primary levels in some detail, using a combination of descriptions from Robert Kegan's extensive research on what he calls *orders of mind or consciousness* (i.e., socialized mind, self-authoring mind, and self-transforming mind) as well as the nitty-gritty of how that shows up in leadership practices in organizations, through the lens of The Leadership Circle (i.e., Reactive, Creative, and Integral) developed by Anderson and Adams (2016, 2019). We also mention the work of Bill Torbert (Rooke & Torbert, 2005) and of Bill Joiner and Stephen Josephs (2007) in this regard. Our purpose is to give you a realistic description of the logic of meaning making in each stage, both from research findings and from our personal experiences in working with ourselves as well as with other leaders.

Kegan's Orders of Mind

Robert Kegan (1982, 1994, 2009) is a psychologist, now retired from Harvard Graduate School of Education, who is perhaps the most well-known and respected researcher in the area of adult development. His findings are pioneering but also reflect the overall findings of many developmental researchers, including Spiral Dynamics and altitude.

The heart of Kegan's research is a developmental line he discovered that he refers to as *orders of consciousness*, a series of developmental stages (or platforms) from which we make meaning of the world. Each subsequent stage is more complex than the one before and represents a new way of making meaning for the self in the world. In short, Kegan's model describes the evolution of the self. The less complex self believes that it is the only thing that exists; a more complex self sees its social context (social conformity); an even more complex self sees its relativity within the whole field of human experience. Thus, we develop by uncovering greater awareness, and developing makes us even more aware. The transition from one stage to the next is signified by the subject–object movement, as we mentioned earlier and describe in detail in Chapter 7.

Kegan's model includes a total of five levels, including two stages that show up in childhood and early adolescence. The three stages we will review represent the level at which most adults operate. The third stage is the *socialized mind*, the fourth is the *self-authoring* mind, and the fifth is the *self-transforming* mind.

Let's examine Kegan's orders of mind and the subject–object relationship. The things we see as aspects of our experience, we hold as objects that we can look *at* and therefore more easily decide how to work with them. In contrast, what we are *subject* to—the lens through which we look—is invisible to us; we aren't aware of it. For example, a very young child is aware of her perceptions, such as how hot the sun is or how silky smooth a nice piece of fabric feels. But such a child has a different relationship to her emotions: When she is angry, she is clearly angry from our viewpoint, but she herself is not able to identify (or manage) that emotion. When she is sad, everyone can tell. We say that the child is *subject* to her emotions. That is, they are not an *object* in the sense that she *has* emotions; rather, she *is* her emotion. Therefore, the child cannot control or decide what to do with her emotions; they have her.

As children grow older, they are able to realize that they have an emotion, like anger, and decide whether and how to express that emotion. The emotion, to the older child (or adult), is an *object*, subject to some level of decision and control. That doesn't mean the person might not act impulsively at times, get angry, and later regret it; the difference is that she now has the complexity of mind to see that she has emotions and to realize that she has some control over them. The young child does not.

A very clear summary of Kegan's basic thinking is given by Peter W. Pruyn in his Developmental Observer Blog, entitled *An Overview of Constructive Developmental Theory* (2010), parts of which are paraphrased here. According to Pruyn (2020):

> We can … think of the subject/object relationship as describing what we *have* in our perceptions, versus what *has us*. What can be seen as *object* represents the *content* of one's knowing. Meanwhile, what one is *subject to* provides a clue about the underlying *structure* of one's knowing. Each order of mind is subject to its underlying structure.

Development from one stage—or order of mind—to the next proceeds when what has been the subject (or the lens through which one was seeing) now becomes the object. The subject of the lower stage becomes an object in the next (higher) stage. We could say *vertical development* is learning to look *at* what we previously (and unconsciously) were looking *through*. Vertical development is about cultivating a greater level of awareness of our world and how we respond to it.

Let's look at each of the three major levels for adults with this lens.

- **Socialized mind.** The socialized mind takes as its object one's needs, interests, and desires. It takes as its subject (looks through) the social environment in which one has been socialized. This socialization is critical in developing into an adult and typically happens sometime during adolescence. Prior to this order of consciousness, the child is entirely self-centered and unable to enter into meaningful, adult social relationships or agreements, such as having a driver's license, getting married, voting, or signing contracts. Because relationships (and approval) by others is critical, one tends to be guided, or even controlled, by what others think, how one is expected to fit in with peers, the team, the profession, the organization, family, and so on. The social milieu has become internalized, so a major fear of the socialized mind is losing favor with the tribe.

- **Self-authoring mind.** The self-authoring mind takes the very social milieu in which one lives and is now able to see it as an object: to consider it, reflect on it, and critique it. Individuals with a self-authoring mind can consider the opinions and expectations of others, then decide what to do for themselves, thereby establishing an *internal locus of control*. They have their own internal compass and are self-directed, independent thinkers. They are not subject to a reactive mind but can choose how to lead or respond, based on circumstances, not based on whether people will like them or whether they can stay in control. For example, as we become more self-authoring, we begin to question the religion we adopted as a result of family tradition, and we think about what we really believe inside and what's true for us. People at this order of mind are subject to their own personal philosophy or ideology: They cannot see it as object but rather see through it (like the proverbial fish in water).

- **Self-transforming mind.** The self-transforming mind is able to take a step back from authoring one's own thinking and question one's own and others' ideologies—considering them,
critiquing them, questioning them. What am I missing? What am I assuming that may not be
true? and other self-challenging questions are asked when we develop to this level. A very
small percentage of the population is stably functioning at this self-transforming level (something like 5%). In the example of the person who questions their religion at the self-authoring
stage, that individual would now begin to question whether their upbringing and their biases
are influencing what they believe and begin to think that other beliefs are also true and possible.

Imagine each order of mind depicted as a diagram: We can visualize the socialized mind with the
self inside the social milieu (which it is subject to); the self-authoring mind is outside the social
milieu, looking at (and critiquing) it; and the self-transforming mind self-examines multiple self-
systems and their many identities.

Having summarized Kegan's orders of mind, let's turn now to the more pragmatic descriptions of
The Leadership Circle, whose levels map closely to those in Kegan's model. Specifically, the socialized mind is essentially the same as problem-reacting (Reactive), the self-authoring mind maps to
outcome-creating (Creative), and the self-transforming mind is what Anderson and Adams call the
Integral level.

Problem-Reacting Leadership

Let's start with a schematic of the Reactive/socialized mind structure, then provide an example.
The Reactive level has three primary types or ways of manifesting: Complying, Controlling, and
Protecting. The identity structure of the Reactive person is based in "lack": Our worth and security
are defined by our being X, where X is a strength related to either

- Relationship—the Complying style, or

- Getting results—the Controlling style, or

- Our intellect—the Protecting style.

The underlying, and usually unconscious, belief that drives this structure is the following:

- "I am worthwhile and safe if I am X, and if others see me as X," or

- "To be is to be X." Run backward: "Not to be X is not to be" (Anderson & Adams, 2016).

So, for a Complying-style person, to exist is to be liked, to be valued by others, and to belong. If that
person is not those things, the individual will feel a true existential threat—as if they are in danger
of not existing. Likewise, a Controlling-style person feels the need to get results at any cost, while a
Protecting-style person needs to be right or seen as smart at any cost. This process goes on largely
unconsciously, meaning the underlying belief is processed by the brain as a given, not as something
that could be constructed differently.

Example: A Complying Leader in Action

Sue has excellent listening skills; this is one of her core strengths. People give her feedback on what a great listener she is and state that she has a heart of gold, but they don't know what she really stands for or what she values. Her feedback says that she doesn't take a firm stand on anything and is wishy-washy. This is because Sue has a strength for listening to people, but she lacks the courage to advocate for what she believes and for what she wants. This lack of courage is costing her in integrity and authenticity and in being decisive and achieving results. However, her strength of listening is what makes her feel safe and safeguards the relationships she cares so much about. Her belief is that if she advocates for what she wants, rocks the boat, and brings her own needs to light, she will be rejected and no longer be loved by others. This belief is her story, and so long as she stays trapped in her story, she will not be able to experience a change or transformation in her leadership effectiveness. Sue's strength of listening has become outmatched, and the more she doubles down on her strength of relationship through listening and caring connection, the less she is building a capability (another strength) that she needs in her new role. The complexity of her role has increased, which requires complementary competencies that are typically in tension with each other.

So, here's what is happening: Sue tightly embraces her strength of listening and connection. When she is thrown in over her head by the situation (a more complex leadership role, for instance), instead of developing the new skills needed (e.g., a focus on results or on navigating conflict), she relies on her old strength of relating to others to get her out of her dilemma. Unfortunately, that doesn't help. Sue, like everyone functioning from a Reactive level of mind, is stuck in a negative feedback loop structure that causes them to react to most situations using X (the strength with which they identify), instead of some other strength that might be more effective in the situation (such as from a perspective like *situational leadership*; Hershey, 1969). The negative feedback loop structure also means we cannot create change using this leader's operating system (LOS), since it is designed, by definition, to maintain the status quo. When the world was far more stable than it is today, this type of leadership sufficed. Today, it typically falls far short.

When we operate from a Reactive mindset, our motivating driver is personal success as judged by others rather than by our own self. Highly Reactive leaders operate more from a group-centric place, which is why we experience a high degree of silo thinking in our organizations. Leaders who are stuck in the "us versus them" mindset are operating from a highly Reactive place, motivated and driven by their need to be secure by being the best, the smartest, or the most liked. In this mindset, the leaders are still trapped in their "story," where their self is constructed from a socialized mind. Reactive leadership is leadership authored by others, driven by a need to stay safe.

The transition to outcome-creating leadership (the Creative level) is marked by two changes: giving up some of the old assumptions that have been running us (e.g., I am valuable only if I have results/intelligence/heart) and presenting a more authentic version of ourselves. We start to grapple with questions like these: Who am I? What do I care most about? What do I stand for? How can my leadership be an expression of what matters most? To make this transition, we have to listen to the call of our inner voice and realize we may disappoint others, contradict the norms we grew up with, and risk failure. Anderson says it is an inside-out process, and that is our experience as well. That's why stillness helps, because we are not trying to look to the outside, but rather to the inside, to decide what really matters.

Outcome-Creating Leadership

The identity structure in the Creative level is based in sufficiency rather than lack: Fundamentally, I am enough as I am; I don't need to do or be anything in particular to have the right to exist. Because of this radical new belief, I choose to express my authentic self in my leadership, not trying to gain the approval of others, adopt their ideas, or apply their standards. I have found my own voice. In finding my own voice, I have spent time understanding what I stand for, what I care about, and what my heart really wants and believes. I step outside the circle of everyone and see that I am a separate self with a separate identity. This is a very empowering place to stand, because it is a place where I begin to make my own meaning of life and decide what I want to *create* in it, instead of what is expected by others. When I find my own voice, I am now no longer instinctively motivated by fear of not meeting the expectations of others, afraid that I might fall short and lose my value as a human being in my organization.

Many leaders find it difficult to express their vision, purpose, or values in ways that are authentic and deeply felt. Achieving this goal starts by answering the questions that we are grappling with in the transition from Reactive to Creative: Who am I? What's important to me? What do I most care about? What do I want to create? What vision do I hold deeply? What is the outcome I want to create that is larger than just me and that I want to serve?

The move to outcome-creating leadership is the move from being stuck in the stance of "playing it safe" to being able to balance the tension between safety and purpose. If I have understood my purpose, and I've answered the questions about who I am, then I next have to be willing to move into a new place of playing on purpose for what I most desire. What is required for us to do anything great is courage. It is making moves that sometimes seem extreme. It is taking bold actions in service of a vision. Our organization's complex challenges demand bold and, yes, risky movements from leaders. Without this, we will never experience transformation; we will be stuck in the status quo.

Example: An Outcome-Creating Leader

Dianne is a leader who believes in an organization where people feel accountable for their contributions and openly seek input from others so as to produce better ideas. She cares about the business results of the organization and the specific contributions of her group. She fosters this environment through her ability to create strong connections with others and to develop an environment of team versus individual success. She expresses her vision from a heart-centered place, with a strong, direct, and honest style, while remaining open to listening and hearing the perspectives of her colleagues. When she advocates for her vision or position, she then inquires and genuinely listens to the perspectives of others. Under her leadership, people feel heard and respected, and they openly share their ideas and even failures. This leads to greater contributions and accountability to new ideas that contribute to their business results.

When we move to outcome-creating leadership, we shift to being authored by self, driven by our purpose to make a contribution to something larger than just our own self-ambition. Rather than allowing others to evaluate whether she is living her own truth, Dianne evaluates her contributions by her own internal standards. It is not that she doesn't listen to others but rather that she does not use them as the yardstick of evaluation.

Integral Leadership

The Integral level of leadership is harder to describe, as it is less clearly understood than the Reactive and Creative levels. Only 5% of the population is at this stage, so it has been studied less than the other stages (Anderson & Garvey-Berger, 2019). Research is starting to ramp up, however, as the Integral level of leadership becomes ever more important to help solve the complex problems in our world. Today, it can be described with some effort and some openness on the part of the reader, who may need to stretch into the logic of this new level.

At the Integral level, the visionary leader at the Creative level expands the perspective to include systemic welfare and becomes the architect of the whole system and its future. Whereas Reactive leaders think on a week-to-month time frame regarding actions (focusing on problems and projects), and Creative leaders think in terms of years (visions and strategies), Integral leaders consider the very long-term impact of what they do, focusing on systemic design from the ecosystem level; this requires considering a time frame of decades. (Some Native American traditions have the idea of considering the impact of what we do down to the seventh generation after us—a very wise perspective.) When looking from a decades-long perspective, integration and optimization of all the stakeholders become critical. That is, we look at systems design from an ecosystem point of view; we become servants and architects of the entire system to benefit not only our business but also the whole ecosystem. In the Reactive level, we play not to lose; in the Creative level, we play to win; at the Integral level, we play for all.

At the Integral level, servant leadership is actually possible in a genuine way, since the ego does not run the show. We are not striving to "look" like a servant leader (Reactive) or even to express that as one of our values. Instead, we can't help but be a servant in our leadership. Our internal complexity, our ability to simultaneously hold perspectives that are polar opposites, and our fundamental transcendence of the ego identity all put us in a position to take in the needs of the whole system. As we really rest in the fundamental nature of the universe, we realize that its nature is compassion, that there is a unity underlying all of existence. Identifying with this foundational level, we naturally become a servant of the whole. This transition simply expresses our true nature, which has now become clear to us.

As we see in the example, the Integral mind is able to hold opposite ideas (my approach is best, her approach is best) and to put off resolving complex problems too early. Such leaders can hold the tensions inherent in a situation and let themselves become the container for an alchemical transformation to take place, where the opposites somehow come into alignment in some previously unforeseen way. When we live at the Integral level, we move from believing we are a complete self, expressing its purpose in a clear vision, to being an ecology of selves, some in conflict or dynamic tension with others, including ones we previously did not want to own. As we embrace our shadow

Example: An Integral Leader

William is a leader of a small start-up. He is motivated to see major change within his industry, since he knows if they do not change, the world will be a lesser place. He focuses not only on his own company and its results but also on improving the industry as a whole. He sits on several committees that work across the industry to do this, even though some might say it's not a particularly good use of his time as the CEO. When he visits working groups within his company, even though he is CEO, William shows up less with directives or even goals and more with questions from his own curiosity. Team members find him provocative, intriguing, an eager listener, and more like a philosopher than a boss. He genuinely seems to care about people, is highly curious about their experiences and ideas, and has a knack for captivating people with his visions, when he expresses them. He always asks groups how he can help them and really seems to mean it.

William can at times act in almost contradictory ways. On the one hand, he might say he sees the need for greater integration between the functions. On the other hand, he sometimes encourages people to explore their own paths. He doesn't appear bothered by this apparent contradiction, even when others are at times perplexed. William will sometimes take the opposite position to what he was recently saying on an issue; when someone points this out, he sometimes says, "Yes, you're quite right. I was beginning to believe my own thinking, so I'm looking for help in exploring the opposite point of view. What do you think?"

sides, the energy formerly used to repress those parts becomes liberated. We feel even more our true selves: a complex, multidimensional, flawed, beautiful, tender, strong, outrageous, at times pathetic being that is, in a human sense, perfect.

This deeper engagement of the shadow side of the self taps into underdeveloped strengths, which might otherwise appear to be weaknesses or dark elements. We realize that the conflicted function and dysfunction in the larger system are also in us. As Anderson and Adams (2019) say, "We are, individually and collectively, a microcosm of the system we are trying to lead and change" (p. 82). Our woundedness, as transformational leaders, is precisely how we can be helpful to, and lead, others as they go through a transformation themselves. If I can be compassionate toward my own flaws, absurdities, and darkest parts, then I can also hold the system I'm helping to transform in the same skillful way.

As a corroboration of the power of the Integral mind in the organizational change context, Bill Torbert ran a longitudinal research project on the developmental level required of CEOs to create sustainable organizational transformation (Rooke & Torbert, 1998). Only the CEOs who were measured at the Integral level of mind were able to create sustained, measurable change. Hence, we recommend that outcome-creating leaders use the Integral Disciplines to help move themselves toward the Integral level to be in a position to lead a successful transformation.

In addition to the more or less individual level we have been discussing, we can grow leadership at a systemic level, both within ourselves and within a group. We now turn to this topic.

Collective Leadership Development

We mention collective leadership effectiveness here in this chapter on the development landscape because we recognize that it is not individual leadership effectiveness alone but rather a journey of lifting the collective effectiveness of leaders that is the only way organizational transformation is possible. Individual leadership development is necessary but insufficient to change the DNA of your organization; to shift mindset and culture requires scaling your leadership effectiveness. Collective leadership effectiveness (or ineffectiveness) heavily influences our results and generally how things go in organizations; collective effectiveness is a primary determinant of organization culture. It takes focused intentional work on ourselves to individually develop, and it is an even more conscious, focused effort to do this collectively.

Individual, collective, and systemic development is a critical business imperative. Just as individuals have an internal operating system that must be upgraded, so does an organization. Raising the consciousness of the leaders of an organization is the lever for a complete shift in the organization's results. But it is not an easy journey. It requires the most senior leaders of an organization to recognize that it is their collective leadership effectiveness that will be their strategic competitive advantage. Can you imagine if senior leaders had that wake-up call and made that their number one initiative for the year!

Michael's Take

A few years ago, I had an experience that exemplifies when this priority was lacking. Tim headed a business unit within a well-known global technology company. He committed his entire leadership team (25 people) to a two-day workshop, with myself and colleagues, to debrief their 360-degree reports. If you haven't been through such a process, it is striking how intensive and powerful it can be for a leadership team to receive this sensitive data together as a group. The vulnerability in the act of honestly looking at themselves—both individually and collectively—can lead to significant insights and changed behavior (as we saw in the example in Chapter 5).

Despite our clear recommendation to Tim (and his team) that he be in attendance for the entire workshop, he left for long periods on several occasions (meetings with his boss and others). Tim's absences were not clearly explained or designed around, and the impact was palpable in the room: Tim was not really "in" the process. Even though everyone else was there the entire time, the leader did not set the model. This sent a clear message. The adverse impact was not just Tim's issue, since his management chain clearly did not prioritize this work. The overall leadership culture of the organization did not value developing their leaders—likely, they felt their other work was just too important—so they did not prioritize the session. The sad part for me was how much the rest of the group received the data in such an earnest way, really wanting to improve themselves. From a brief follow-up, I learned there was an impact for some on an individual level but not on the collective.

It is the collective consciousness of the organization's senior leaders that is the primary culture carrier. Indeed, an organization cannot perform at a higher level than the consciousness of the senior leadership. This collective consciousness, and the systemic consciousness described in Part III, together create the results the organization achieves. The leaders' level of consciousness is designed to create exactly what they are creating. Achieving breakthrough results—results never before achieved—can happen only when they decide to work on their collective effectiveness as one of their highest priorities.

Summary

We have outlined what the LOS looks like at three levels of development: the socialized mind (Reactive), the self-authoring mind (Creative), and the self-transforming mind (Integral). This is the landscape of development. To be a transformational leader requires developing beyond the problem-reacting level to at least the outcome-creating level (plus using Integral perspectives). The next chapter addresses how development moves from one level to another.

From Insight to Action

A few reflection questions to integrate the material in this chapter:

- Which of the three levels did you most identify with: socialized mind, self-authoring mind, or self-transforming mind? One sign that you are "identifying with" a given level is that you read about it but did not think that it was any big deal; it just seemed "normal" to you.
  - What did you consider to come to that conclusion?
- Which of the three levels was most difficult to understand or to imagine yourself as acting from that order of mind?
  - What was difficult about it?
- What do you believe is the implication of this material for your Agile Transformation effort?

7

The Developmental Path

When we are on autopilot, the world may seem easier, but it does not give us the results that we want. So, how do we develop our consciousness to become a transformational leader? How do we develop our inner capability, allowing us to meet the external complexity in our world with our own inner complexity?

Awareness is the beginning of the pathway to inner development. As we've said, developing is not about fixing ourselves. It's more about accepting ourselves, who we are at the core. It's about tuning into the authentic version of ourselves—not limited to our bodies or minds but the inner reality of our soul and existence. Our inner being—and its ability to deal with the outer complexities we face every day—is oftentimes starving. When speaking of this inner lack, we sometimes say that we need "food for the soul." When we feed this inner need, we develop our inner complexity. Without a focus on our inner complexity development, we feel a greater and greater distance between our ability to work effectively and the incredibly complex situations we face as leaders. That distance can be resolved only through inner work. As we do this work of raising our level of consciousness, our ability to see ourselves as "enough" starts to dissolve our need to "prove we are enough"—to react, to defend, to criticize, to pretend, to judge, to please, to control, to envy—all the reactive tendencies that are limiting us from realizing our true potential. While it is seemingly so simple, this soul journey—to just realize that we are enough—is surprisingly a long one, fraught with the battle of our minds and wills to protect our image of this person we created, our story. The beauty and paradox of it, the realization that we are enough, *is* the beginning of becoming our authentic self. In that process, our way of being, of going and seeing in the world, changes, and we embody the person we were meant to be all along.

How Development Actually Happens

You may be saying to yourself, "This sounds good. I'd like to develop myself, but how exactly do I do that?" There are various beliefs about how human development and change occur and are sustained. Beliefs about this change process vary from focusing on practices or new "actions" to focusing on inner beliefs, to having coaching conversations to spark new insights, and so forth. From an Integral perspective, development and change take place by using an approach that incorporates all four quadrants. Just as organizations have to focus on all four quadrants for transformational change to be successful (the subject of the Integral Disciplines in Part III), so do we as individuals need to take the same approach. We can break that process down by quadrant:

- **I quadrant:** Change occurs when people connect to their deeper beliefs, values, and truths, previously unseen by them. That is, what was unconscious comes into their conscious awareness. Change comes with a new inner awareness and an inner wisdom or knowledge of self. People begin to see what they are aware of and see it with a new lens, through introspection and reflection.

- **IT quadrant:** Change comes about by taking specific action, using new deliberate behaviors that are in line with the desired way of being. We hold ourselves accountable to these new actions and behaviors and we build strength and confidence when we accomplish things we were previously unable to do.

- **ITS quadrant:** Change comes about in this quadrant by understanding, from a systems view, how we fit into the system, and by looking at roles, expectations, operating structures, and current capabilities in those areas that allow us to contribute to the whole. This quadrant focuses on our fit in the system, so the work here is to help people better understand and build the knowledge and capabilities needed to create this fit or to figure out what a better fit might mean for us.

- **WE quadrant:** Change comes about through meaningful interactions with others, having shared meaning-making experiences, and perceiving in a more systemic way. Through conversation and hearing other perspectives and schools of thought, we see new possibilities and ideas that we would not have had alone. By tuning into systemic consciousness, we see the impact our system has on our mindset, our beliefs, and our shared values. From this lens, interactions with others challenge or disrupt our own meaning-making system.

Our Integral approach to development not only considers all four quadrants but also the approach used to integrate them, rather than seeing them as separate quadrants to focus on individually. All of the quadrants are interconnected and arise together in our way of being in the moment within a specific context. This is like the use of our Integral approach, in an organizational context, when we look through the lens in one quadrant at what is happening; the context from another quadrant's lens is also at play in this situation, and then the context from another quadrant. So, just as in organizational change, in individual change we use an approach that encompasses and integrates all quadrants.

You might be wondering, How do the problem-reacting and outcome-creating approaches fit into this view of quadrants? Let's take our previous example of Sue, who was a high Complying

Reactive leader. She has great listening skills and forms strong caring connections with people. When we look at Sue's primary (also referred to as "orienting" or "native") quadrant focus, we find that she relies on the WE quadrant lens. Sue's "autopilot" reaction at work is to approach a situation first from a WE perspective. She rarely thinks about approaching a situation from an upper right or IT quadrant perspective, because this feels unimportant to her if relationships aren't valued first. If she is involved in an interaction with a high Controlling Reactive type—let's call him Joe—with an IT quadrant orientation, she will typically become passive; that is, she will do what is expected of her so she can maintain the relationship with Joe and his team.

When we look at this interaction, we see the cost to the organization: Sue's valuable ideas and thoughts are not voiced or taken into consideration, and she is likely feeling exhausted and uninspired by these interactions and therefore not producing her best work or achieving strong results. Joe's high Controlling Reactive type is costing him energy, making him feel overwhelmed and compromising his caring connections with others. He feels alone and as if the world is resting on his shoulders if he doesn't get results. This also costs the organization: It leads to lower diversity in ideas and innovation, as well as morale and motivation. Either Sue or Joe could choose to move into an outcome-creating stance and the interaction would likely shift.

Here's an example of an outcome-creating move (many are possible):

Example

In the moment of the reactive-to-reactive interaction, Sue could simply disclose to Joe that she is feeling "passive" and state why that is the case. Let's assume that Joe has a habit of cutting Sue off when she speaks, so that she can't finish her thought. Sue might disclose something like this: "Joe, I'm finding it hard to contribute to this conversation, because I am unable to finish my thoughts when you interrupt me. I would really like to share what's important to me and what I feel is a valuable contribution. Will you agree to letting me finish my thought before responding?"

In addition to focusing on the quadrants for sustainable change, we are working with our lines of development. Just as our orienting quadrant limits our perspective, so we have some developmental lines that are not sufficiently mature to ensure we have the capability needed to achieve our developmental goals. We can think of these as muscles that need development. If we are weak in the I quadrant, for instance, where we struggle to give voice to our own meaning or to know what we really want, we might need to develop certain capacities where we lack strength to make this possible.

Ken Wilber has identified more than 24 different lines of development, though there may be more or less depending on how people define them. Some of these common developmental lines include cognitive, emotional, spiritual, moral, and interpersonal areas, among others. Knowing which lines are most crucial for anyone to make progress toward their developmental objectives, and then understanding what their current level of capability is in those lines, is how we work with developmental lines.

Our high focus on self-development—personally as human beings, and professionally as leaders—can sometimes seem overwhelming. It is a focus on the future (what's not here yet) and on the gap (the significant distance between where we are now and where we want to be rather than living in the present with who we already are). This is one of those tensions that we must pay attention to. How do we balance this polarity? On the one hand, we speak of stillness, presence, and being with the present moment; on the other hand, we speak of a developmental need to focus on the future, the gap. To balance this polarity, we use a *transcend and include* approach. This means asking, "What is the current me that is healthy and honoring and contributing to my goal that I want to keep, and what do I need to let go of that is no longer serving me?" This is just like the organizational transcend and include approach used in the move from Amber to Orange, from Orange to Green, or from Green to Teal. In healthy development, we aren't deconstructing or getting rid of everything from the past, but rather we are taking the healthy aspects with us and letting go of what is no longer serving the organization we want to have. Development of individuals and teams and organizations essentially uses the same approach!

We've established that change starts with a wake-up call: becoming aware of the impact on others, on an organization, or in the world. It is good that we get feedback, and perhaps even we do complete a 360-degree assessment such as the Leadership Circle Profile. Even so, those steps alone will not change us. Gaining awareness is a great start, but sometimes after we receive this information, we can feel helpless about how to actually change. It's not quite as simple as making a decision to show up differently. If it were, we would have many more outcome-creating or Integral leaders in our world!

So, let's explore further what the developmental path entails.

The Subject–Object Switch in Action

As we mentioned previously, the subject–object switch is a fundamental principle in all human development. In this section, we provide more explicit examples to understand this switch in the context of our own development.

Let's look at how this works in an organization. The things we see as aspects of our experience, we hold as *objects* that we can look *at* and therefore more easily decide how to work with them. For instance, I may see my work environment as a kind of object—the players, the political interests, the hierarchical structure. In contrast, certain things about the environment may be more hidden assumptions: We may all hold the same belief that failure is bad, and if we allow it to happen, that means we are not worthwhile. This belief is not an object; instead, we are *subject* to it. It is the lens that we look through and therefore invisible to us. We could say it runs us. Recall that developmental progress can be characterized at a high level as what was once subject in the previous stage becoming the object of awareness of the next. Let's look at this idea in a broad context.

When I adopt a certain way of being in the world for a long period, I become so accustomed to this "me" that I'm not aware of how this "me" operates. I actually am not even thinking about it; I am blind to it. It just *is* me, it's *who I am*, and who I've always been. It has become my *identity* (my story). In this way, I am "subject" to my current way as a human being—it is the lens through which I look at the world. It is also referred to as my proximate self, and as such I do not see it as an object.

Development as a human being happens when this unconscious way of operating my life (subject) suddenly is seen by me, giving me a conscious choice to do something with it (since it is now an object). Sometimes this understanding comes to our awareness through feedback from someone, and sometimes it is recognized because we experience a tragedy or extremely difficult challenge (a "wake-up call"). When we see ourselves from an objective point of view, as if outside of ourselves looking back at ourselves, then we can begin to disidentify with our story. It is only after we become aware of our current way of being that we can begin to develop a different capacity for a new way of being. We can then work on those capabilities that will allow us to meet our developmental goals.

Example

Jill is a giver. She's been a giver most of her life. It started early in life, as the middle child in her family. She mostly focuses on others' needs and gets her own needs met through being needed and giving to others. Her driving energy is pride in being needed and even indispensable. She avoids giving her opinion in meetings when she feels there is tension and conflict in the room, because she does not want her ideas to be rejected. Jill goes out of her way to do things for others, even anticipating what they might want, but at the expense of her own needs—which she doesn't really think about, because she's always been this way.

Jill has a wake-up call during a particularly stressful period at work, with new management responsibilities and critical business deadlines. In a key meeting with her boss and his peers, she agrees to take on a big new assignment. Her colleague looks at her in disbelief; she whispers on the side to Jill, "I can't believe you just took that new project beyond what you are already doing. You're so stressed right now; you need to take care of yourself."

Her colleague's observation annoys Jill at first, but over the course of the day and into that night, she realizes the truth of it. She knows she does take on too much. But in that moment, she didn't want to let her boss and the executive team down—she believed they were desperate. At that point, her "giver" took over and she couldn't say "no." In this moment of reflection, Jill clearly sees her own pattern; it has now become an object of her awareness. From here, Jill can begin to see the pattern in lots of places, at work and even at home. If she maintains her awareness, she can examine the underlying belief that drives the pattern ("I won't be worthwhile if I sometimes let people down"), then see the pattern in operation in real time, and finally decide to choose differently in the future.

Michele's Take

In Chapter 3 on altitudes, I began to share a little about the Integral Coaching Canada™ method in terms of *transcending and including*: transcending the limitation of your current way, and including aspects of your current way that will still serve you, all in the context of your developmental goal. This is a very different feeling from "changing yourself to be something else" or "fixing yourself"—something that many people will feel when they get feedback from a 360-degree assessment. The way we go about this evolution of transcending and including is to create a way for people to make the subject–object switch.

One way that I have found to be grounded, practical, and effective is through the use of metaphors. Integral Coaching uses metaphors for your current way of being, which depict the honoring and valuable aspects of you and at the same time show the limitations clearly—so you see them in the moment of an action or a reactive response. The new way of being is an entirely different metaphor that doesn't negate the honoring part of your current way; instead, it helps you build the capacities and capabilities needed for your developmental goal, with the guiding metaphor integrated into your daily life and practice.

Here's an example from one of my clients, Torsten, showing how we used metaphors and developmental objectives to help him make the subject–object switch from his current way of being in his topic to the way of being that he desired:

Development topic: I want to be more able to speak and articulate my truth, in the moment, without concern for what I believe others might think.

Why he felt this was an important developmental goal for him:

- So that he could have a stronger stance in what he believed was important
- So that people didn't experience him as distant or passive but as fully present
- So that, as a coach, ultimately he could be of more service to others and to their growth
- So that his current way of being, as a "giver to others," would have a bigger impact

His metaphors:

- *Current way:* The way of the Silent Thinker
- *New way:* The way of the Gentle Speaker

What is honoring about Torsten's current way is his thoughtful way, his ability to remain calm, to not react or overreact, to be patient with people and appreciate their views. As a Silent Thinker, he is also a great listener. He is humble and kind. Collectively, all of these characteristics are very honoring and helpful to him. What the way of the Silent Thinker closes down is the ability to be able to speak his own truth, to more fully step into the space and share his views, to have an impact. When he is silent, people experience him as distant or passive—and they can't really get to know him or what he stands for.

The new way as Gentle Speaker is still Torsten. He has not lost his gentle, kind way. By not making his current way "bad," and by including the aspects of it that are healthy into the new way, he is able to observe himself without judgment. The metaphors help him see himself in the moment—to see who is talking and to notice the patterns around when the Silent Thinker chooses to remain quiet and when the Gentle Speaker chooses to speak.

This is the beauty of transcending and including in development, whether it involves an organization or a person. When we try to negate everything that was or is about someone or something, that effort will be met with resistance. When Torsten is able to gain more access to his body and emotions and see his way of being in the moment, either as Silent Thinker or Gentle Speaker, he is now consciously aware of who is speaking and acting, and this awareness gives him the ability to choose his next move. This is the outcome-creating versus problem-reacting stance. Torsten has been doing practices to build capability or "muscle" in specific areas to be able to articulate his meaning, to be expressive, to work with his body to notice what he is feeling, to name it and use it to inform his next action. The work he has been doing has helped him get more in touch with his personal values and boundaries, so he can express them to others. This is the developmental shift.

Fundamentally, in part through the use of the metaphor about our current way of being, we are beginning to see ourselves in action, to take our self as an object, or as Ken Wilber says, to "see our seer."

Seeing Our Seer

Seeing our seer, or becoming aware of what we are aware of, is one of the key elements for transformation to be possible. It is making the subject–object switch as we discussed earlier. The more we see ourselves and our way of being in the moment, the more we then become able to make different choices in those moments. In turn, the more the desired new way of being becomes the new norm for us. A number of practices can help us see our own seer and implement this fundamental strategy for facilitating the subject–object switch as a way to grow our leadership vertically. Let's take a look at self-awareness and foundational development practices, meditation, prayer, journaling, and a client example of seeing oneself from the outside.

Self-Observation Exercises

If you work with an Integral coach, self-observation exercises are key to developing from your current way of self to the desired way you wish to be. These exercises are the first step in developing toward your goals, and their sole intention is to help you become really familiar with your way of being in a specific context or area in which you want to develop. Through consistent, daily practice exercises in which you hone in on aspects of your actions and behaviors, emotions, thoughts and beliefs, and how you see things, you begin to see your patterns and triggers and to understand more deeply what is driving your behavior.

These practices are created with questions and observations that provoke you to inquire more deeply into your underlying assumptions and beliefs. When you do this over a period of time, without judgment of yourself, but with compassion and curiosity, you create the capacity to develop muscles in areas where you need to grow to meet your developmental objectives.

Foundational Developmental Practices

Along with self-observation exercises, you also want to develop specific capabilities that are needed to reach your developmental goals. For example, you might be weak in one quadrant or developmental line (emotional, interpersonal, moral, or spiritual, to name a few) or in other areas that are limiting your growth. The goal of developmental practices is to develop muscle in those areas, much like going to a gym to work underdeveloped muscles.

For example, a developmental practice for someone who needs to move away from being the "expert" to being more open to other perspectives might be to have this person ask at least two or three questions, from a genuine place of curiosity, in a meeting that invites other people to share their views. This works well especially for reactive tendencies that might be perceived as distant, critical, arrogant, and autocratic. As the person begins to become more curious by asking more questions consistently, they begin to show up differently to others and to see how their distant or critical reactive tendencies weren't serving them well. This then closes the gap between the distant or critical tendency and creates a new relationship with others.

The Practice of Meditation

Meditation is the fundamental practice for seeing our own seer. By focusing on a mantra, the breath, or some other relatively neutral object, we start to see the way that thoughts arise, dwell for a time, and then dissolve. We begin to see that "we" are not the same thing as our thoughts; we begin to identify more with witness consciousness, or pure awareness, rather than with our story. This is what Wilber calls "waking up" to the fact that the fundamental ground of being is non-dual awareness, and that at that level, there is no separation, all is one. The more we identify with witness consciousness, the less attached we are to ego. Bill Joiner, in a study of leaders at different developmental levels (Joiner & Josephs, 2007), reports that of the leaders at Catalyst stage and above (roughly equivalent to beginning the shift to a self-transforming mind), all of them engaged in meditation practices.

The Practice of Prayer

Many people believe that prayer and meditation are at odds with each other. In the traditional, more ritualistic view of prayer, this may be true for some. However, when prayer begins to shift from a ritualistic, religious activity to a spiritual experience with deeper meaning, you are able to access a healing energy for yourself and to send it to others. This healing energy can be scientifically verified, which is why so many people believe in the power of prayer. When you use meditation combined with prayer, it can be quite a transformational experience.

When you meditate, you relax into your being, you begin to let go of your story, your identification with your thoughts, and you feel the groundedness of your being, the internal stillness. When you begin to pray from this state of consciousness, you are more open and available to healing energy and communion with the Divine or your soul. This prayer and communion change you; they unleash transformation from within. This combination also helps you see yourself in a truly compassionate way, embracing grace and allowance for being fully human.

The Practice of Journaling

Many years ago, journaling was more likely to be the subject of a self-help class or an article than to be presented as a leadership development technique. We now recognize that the regular recording of one's thoughts, reflections, feelings, and struggles is a great way to see our own seer, to take ourselves as object; journaling has become a leadership practice. The more regularly we keep such a journal, the more it becomes an ingrained reflection practice, and the more deeply it becomes embedded into our psyche. Rereading my journal over time creates visibility into my own developmental journey, helps me see my own patterns of thought and the typical dilemmas I get into repeatedly, and develops compassion for myself as I empathize with the me I was three months ago, a year ago, or many years past. Like meditation and prayer, journaling reveals our inner self.

Michele's Take

My coaching client's (let's call her Sue) topic was "to be more self-confident and be able to articulate my thoughts and ideas more succinctly to senior leadership so I can gain their respect and be a trusted partner." Sue is very competent and passionate about her work. She tends to go all in and do whatever it takes to make things happen. She is a fast thinker and a faster talker, and she gets things done. It was important to her for others to see and validate her work. Since people could count on Sue to get things done, they would frequently ask her to take on additional duties.

Sue had taken on the Agile Transformation leader role, but she was not being seen or treated as a trusted partner to other leaders. She could see how other Agile leaders could command their attention and respect, and she felt dismissed or undervalued. One of Sue's challenges was to let go of outcomes she expected from others, even in meetings. Her emphasis on sticking to the agenda, and walking away from the meeting with her intended outcomes accomplished, did not allow for others to be heard or for them to feel a connection with her. Her development work was to listen more, to detach from expected outcomes, and to communicate with others so that they felt heard and a part in contributing to the idea or plan.

I offered Sue the metaphor of "Amelia the Competent Pilot," which depicted her current way of being in this situation. Using this metaphor, Sue was able to get a distinct image/visual of herself and her behavior in the moment of being the competent pilot. While her competence was a very honoring thing, it wasn't getting her where she wanted to go. So I offered her a new way of being metaphor, the "Connected Ballroom Dance Partner." This dance partner had to learn to connect with others in a deeper way. The dance partner had to move out of the head space and more into the feeling, emotions, and heart space. She had to become more curious and listen more.

Through specific self-observation and developmental practices over a span of six months, Sue developed the capabilities needed to reach her goals. She was elevated to a new position in her organization, with a greater sphere of influence, and given opportunities she had not thought possible. This six-month journey was one of seeing herself, of looking at herself from the outside objectively and with compassion, so she could more deeply understand her way of being as the competent pilot and slowly begin to make different choices in the moment. Through this development, she was able to stop in the moment to see herself, challenge her thinking, and choose a different way to act.

Taking the Perspective of Other

Besides the ability to see our own seer, the other key to transformation is taking the perspective of another—a colleague, boss, friend, partner, enemy, or even disowned parts of ourselves.

Looking "As"

> There is no feeling in a human heart which exists in that heart alone—which is not, in some form or degree, in every heart.
> —George McDonald

The ability to take the perspective of other, or look *as* the other, requires us to develop a whole different level of capacity than just being able to look *at* someone to assess them. We more often adopt the latter perspective, as depicted in Figure 7.1.

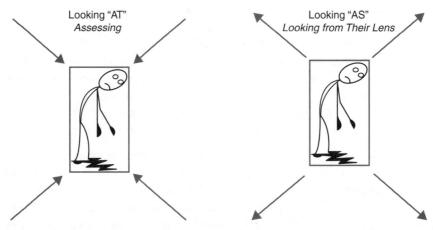

Figure 7.1
Looking "at" versus looking "as"

To step into another's shoes, or to see through their eyes, requires us to be fully present, curious, open, and receptive to the other person's heart, body, mind, and spirit. In addition, it requires us to have the same level of awareness about our own way of operating, about our biases and reactive tendencies, and about our strengths. To find compassion for others is to see how we are connected to the other, even the people we resist. When we feel compassionate toward another person, we have an inner experience of our shared humanity. With compassion and empathy, we are able to accept them as they are, and to see how we are not so different. This does not mean that we merge with the other person or move into an intimate and emotional connection, as we must be rooted in our own sense of identity and an unobstructed view of their separateness. This is especially true for a client or someone we are coaching. Having compassion does not mean we lose our ability to be direct or to have courageous conversations in which we fully speak our truth. When we come to the encounter from a place of heart and compassion, it facilitates a space of safety and trust, enabling truthful, authentic dialogue. Creating a practice of looking *as* the other, especially your direct reports or most important colleagues, will move you to greater development.

Shadow Work Development

The inner journey takes us on a path into our shadow. The **shadow** of our self is the part of our psyche we're not aware of, sometimes because it's hidden or mysterious, but other times simply because we deny it. Our shadow holds our unfelt emotions, our repressed impulses, our unacceptable behaviors, and our unlived aspirations or dreams. The hiding of our inner self happened throughout our childhood as a result of our parents, peers, and society sending us signals to repress our emotions, our inner desires, and our dreams. Many people believe the shadow contains only the repressed "bad" parts of us, but it can also hold our authentic voice, our creativity, our genius, and even beauty (sometimes called the "golden shadow"). What our shadow contains depends on what we deny most vigorously, so everyone's shadow is different. When we project our "good" shadow, such as idolizing someone's talent or brilliance, we often project our best talents or brilliance onto them. In that way, we give them our power. When others live out the "bad" part of us that we repress, we will likely be triggered to attach to them in the form of resentment, contempt, or even hatred. The shadow holds tremendous power over us, because without awareness, we go through enormous pains to keep it from our consciousness and deny our wholeness.

The difficulty of the journey lies in the need to face this shadow, to move from an unconscious place of not seeing what is painful to see to a conscious place of clearly seeing it, and to be present in this raw, exposed place long enough to work with it. People, organizations, and society, with their ideals and notions of civilization, have collectively repressed emotions—basic instincts we all have—and created a world of unconscious beings wearing beautifully colored, ever-so-deceiving, social and professional masks. To take this mask off is to expose ourselves and our shadows—that which we believe is likely not acceptable either to the other or to ourselves.

On a psychological level, the idea of the shadow encompasses those parts of ourselves that we disown because they somehow threaten our identity or make us feel bad (guilty or shameful) about ourselves; in short, they threaten our ego story. The irony is that we recognize our shadow frequently, albeit not in ourselves, but in someone else when they "trigger" us: that person in another department who carries themselves a certain way, who talks a certain way in meetings, and who makes you want to scream or even do them bodily harm in your mind's eye. In this other, we see a reflection of those unwanted parts of ourselves. Maybe the person is arrogant, controlling, or just totally oblivious to how they come across. Whatever it is, we "hate" it because we don't like it in ourselves, but we can often only see it in them. That's what gives the shadow the charge that it has for us: We are busy trying to defend our identity against that attribute, so we work hard to see it in others and to *not see* it in ourselves. This takes a lot of energy, so working with and releasing shadow defenses can give us access to more energy.

One simple shadow practice from the Integral world is called the **3-2-1 shadow process**. It involves taking a third-person perspective on some shadow material or person, then a second-person perspective, then a first-person one. Here's an example. Suppose I find myself triggered by someone in a meeting who questions the argument I am making for a certain course of action. The man, who works in product marketing, implies that I might not have my facts straight, and the way he does that feels condescending, not respectful. I get very angry and want to put him in his place or else storm off. I don't do either, but I am clearly triggered, thinking about the scene over and over again in my mind, with lots of emotional charge. Do I just shrug it off, or do I retaliate? The most effective method to develop myself is to take it into shadow work.

The 3-2-1 shadow process has three parts:

1. *Take a third-person perspective on the situation.* I describe—in writing, verbally, or in my mind's eye—the "facts" of the situation, describing the person, the situation, the "offensive" action, and so on. I don't attempt to sugarcoat things or "be fair"; I just tell it straight as I experienced it in third-person terms: "The group was talking about X. Jack from product marketing acted like I didn't know what I was talking about; he acted like a jerk in front of everyone, very disrespectful."

2. *Take a second-person perspective on the situation.* I "dialogue" with the person, Jack in this case (although a situation can also act as the trigger). In my mind's eye, I "talk" to Jack—not to argue with him, but to ask him what his message is for me. What does he have to teach me or help me learn? Why did he show up, right now? Here, we are treating the figure not as a literal person but more as an internal image that has attracted our attention, which can lend us its wisdom through dialogue.

3. *Take a first-person perspective on the situation.* I actually become Jack and see the world from his perspective; I describe myself *as he sees me*. This part can be a bit painful or awkward, because it is giving credence to the shadow element's (Jack's) perspective on me. And that is the power of the 3-2-1 shadow process—taking his perspective fully. He may see me as the jerk, or perhaps he sees me as a threat or superior to him. Be open to whatever insight comes up.

Especially in the last step, we are acting in a truly Integral way: We are seeing a multiplicity of perspectives, all of which have their partial truths, even those that feel threatening to our ego's story. When we authentically do this, we are going into our shadow; we are moving away from the autopilot place of looking *at* the other person to a conscious place of looking *as* the other person. In taking the first-person perspective, we are reintegrating the shadow element rather than pushing it away; we are seeing how that perspective really is *our* perspective, just (previously) unthinkable.

This is shadow work! We have gotten out of our own way by taking a perspective on ourselves; we have found our shadow. It requires courageous authenticity to be present in this experience; this is the experience that will move us from our reactive stance to creating the outcome we genuinely desire. An unexamined shadow keeps us on autopilot, which maintains the status quo. In contrast, working with shadow is cleaning up, making us a vessel for the change that wants to happen.

The Shift from Reactive to Creative

The shift from a Reactive to a Creative level is a journey of becoming frustrated with the lack of purpose in your life, of failing to gain real satisfaction from fulfilling other people's wants, needs, and expectations. The informal name says it all: *authored by others*. When we allow others to set the course of our life and decide what it means for us to be successful, and when we evaluate what we did in a meeting by their standards rather than our own, we eventually become fatigued. We perceive ourselves as lacking integrity and hear a nagging inner voice that often seems to speak in quiet tones, which gets overridden by the voice of our reactive story.

This is the place where people start to become "tired of the rat race," where the transactional style of leadership and Achievement-Orange cultural standards take their toll on the human soul. We long to get back to a human connection with our work and our life. In a moment of stillness, we are aghast that we may be wasting our short life on unimportant measures of status and external success.

The outcome-creating stance serves as a beacon that encourages us to stand in our own authority, to make our own choices, and to assess ourselves by our own standards. We recognize a transition is under way when we start to experience ourselves as marching to the beat of our own drummer. We may become interested in new hobbies or self-development practices, or we may change our associations or our church, as we become more authentic to an inner listening. Part of any development, as we have said, is the subject–object switch. Somehow during this transition—through meditation, prayer, some kind of self-awareness practice like journaling or self-reflection, or a painful experience leading to a wake-up call—we start to see how often we are influenced by what other people think. We begin to see where we sacrifice our own authentic voice because of a fear of being rejected in some way, and we recognize that this rejection is tied to our self-worth. In the heat of those moments, we are not typically aware of these relationships, because we are not in a state of self-awareness. Instead, our ego is running us. That means we aren't choosing our action but rather are acting from habit. As we become more keenly aware of our patterns, we begin to see this objectively in the moment, which then gives us a choice.

In Buddhism, there is a set of slogans for developing the mind to greater awareness, called Lojong Training. One slogan particularly relevant in this context is the following: **Of the two witnesses, hold the principal one.** Judy Lief (https://tricycle.org/trikedaily/train-your-mind-of-the-two-witnesses-hold-the-principal-one/) offers some insightful commentary about this slogan:

> This slogan is about aloneness and confidence. It gets to a core issue on the path . . . which is the fact that each of us must travel it alone and by ourselves. Of course we may be in a community . . . but within a [community] of one hundred members, there are a hundred different paths. . . . We come

in alone, we go out alone, and in between no matter how many friends and acquaintances we may have, we are still alone at a fundamental level.

It is hard to accept this kind of existential aloneness in ourselves or in others. We want people to really know us. . . . But no matter how much we bare our hearts, we can never convey the fullness of our experiential reality.

According to this slogan, if we want feedback as to how we are doing, we must rely on our own judgment. But it is unsettling to realize that no one else really knows what is going on with us. . . . Instead of looking directly at our own experience, we try to find it in what is reflected back to us from outside. But that reflection is not all that trustworthy. People are easily fooled by appearances and judge what is going on according to their own biases and preconceptions.

It is easy to become so used to looking for the approval of others that we lose confidence in our own self-knowledge. Only we really know when we are being phony or genuine, aware or unaware, compassionate or uncompassionate. No matter what may be going on at the surface, and how confused we may feel, deep down we know exactly what is going on and what we are up to. That is the witness we must hold.

This is not to say that we won't benefit from hearing feedback from others, since we can use such information about our impact to wake up our own inner seeing and knowing. The danger is if we take their perspective as the *standard* by which we judge ourselves. As Leif so poignantly states, only we truly know when we are being authentic or when we are lying to ourselves. Some deep part of our consciousness never goes to sleep, though the internal habit of mind of telling ourselves our story can obscure that awareness—that voice is so loud.

When we step into this place of self-authority, we become driven by our purpose, our vision. We may experience our purpose almost as if it were alive and looking for us, wanting us to realize its vision. When we lock onto that purpose, we stop being driven by fear; instead, we are pulled forward by our passion to make the world different in some way. When we are not driven by fear, our reactive parts tend to calm down. We see our own arrogance, and we choose not to express it in a critical moment. We understand that it comes from the desire to make us feel safe, but we do not let it run us, for that will compromise our purpose and our ability to fulfill our vision. Instead, we stop, check, choose, and act.

Michele's Take

One of my coaching clients, Tamara, started her development journey to be a better leader and coach by getting feedback using the Leadership Circle Profile. As she came to a greater understanding of her underlying beliefs and the mental constructs that had created her story, she created a metaphor that helped her see when her reactive tendency of being complying was showing up (objectively), as well as a metaphor that helped her see herself when she showed up in the way she most desired—fully expressing her authentic voice. When she began working on her own effectiveness and shifting from the Reactive to the Creative level, the results with her clients also began to shift.

As she reflected on her journey, she said to me, "I used to come into organizations with the pressure of my own mind to perform and deliver. I really wanted to prove myself, and my ego got in the way. Entering a system mindfully, with an open mind, without judgment, and honoring what is already there, helps me to see and hear what the system really needs."

The Shift from Creative to Integral

The movement from the Creative level to the Integral level is more subtle than the movement from the Reactive to the Creative level. The Creative level is about finding yourself, finding your inner voice, and firmly authoring your life with your own values, principles, and vision. The shift to the Integral stage is more about the self beginning to dissolve. Rather than being subsumed by other people's preferences, the self is put more in service to a larger whole; thus, the level involves a stance beyond the self. Development is always about transcending and including: We are starting to transcend our ego, our story.

In the transition out of the Reactive stage, the object of focus in the subject–object switch was the values of others that we had unconsciously internalized as our own. In essence, we see how much we are a slave to what other people think of us, which then becomes an object of our awareness. By contrast, in this new shift, we start to see our principles and values—our own self-authoring—from an objective point of view. We naturally turn a critical eye to what we value, to our purposes, and to what we create. Were we overly influenced by our familial upbringing? Has my cultural heritage as a European American, White male made me insensitive to certain key aspects of life? Is my circle of friends too narrow? Or my spiritual beliefs?

In the transition to the Integral level, the shadow parts of me—my arrogance, my intellectualizing tendencies, my lack of body awareness, and even "golden shadow" aspects like my tenderheartedness—start to become less threatening. I become curious about them rather than trying to hide them. I explore them, express them in a light way, laugh at them. I find that I am not one self that authors my life but rather many selves, some contradictory or antagonistic, each unique. I am a complex *ecosystem*—more like a rain forest than like a sophisticated machine that can be programmed. I realize my "personality" is only a loosely constructed story that appears to hold things together. When I look really closely, I see that my "self" is put together in a much more tenuous way than that. When I relax into that reality, I feel more peace: There is really nothing to prove. I feel more compassion, for there is less basis for judging others; instead, I see others as like me, in our tender humanness, with compassion.

There is a shift to an even deeper purpose, beyond the values of my singular self. There is an awakening to the wonder of the world, of the way the future is calling each of us to evolve it in a new way. The world becomes filled with signs, clues of what we should do to serve the highest good. In the Reactive level, we were centered in our group—whether professional, organizational, or otherwise. In the Creative level, we became centered in ourselves and our vision for organizational benefit. At the Integral stage, we look for the highest good for the world, for all of life. We long to be of service not as an ambition or to conform by being a good "servant leader," but because we cannot truly find fulfillment without being of service. Our deepest joy is in humbly serving the greater good. This is the deepest expression of our soul and what it wants. This perspective was always there, lurking in the background, so coming into this realization is like coming home to ourselves. Previously, our story was so strong, so loud, so all consuming, but now it recedes.

At this level, we become capable of holding polarities. I might believe that I must speak up, advocate for my position, and not allow myself to be stepped on—now I'm ready to act. At (almost) the same time, I am uncertain if this is the right time for action, if I am overreacting, or if I am not seeing the other person's side of things. I seek clarity—clear seeing. Then, I start to judge myself for not being decisive, for holding back. I may recognize this as my inner pattern and feel self-compassion.

Then suddenly, the situation resolves itself, without me "doing" anything. In fact, what I have come to understand is that this is the way that I hold polarities internally within me, allowing them to be worked out. Hesitation to act is not indecisiveness, though I might judge it that way in some moments. Instead, the stillness of holding the polarities creates a kind of alchemy where the "lead" of the conflicting polar positions is turned into the "gold" of reconciliation and, perhaps, resolution.

A further example: When two (or more) people are in conflict, and each presents their "side" of things to me, more and more I find myself agreeing quite vigorously with both of them. There are no true or complete perspectives, only partially true ones, all of which form the whole. From this place, it is clear that I want to hear all the voices in a system, that I would naturally embrace taking an Integral perspective on things, and that I don't have fixed positions on myself or on others. In fact, I often disagree with myself, or rather two parts of my inner ecology of selves disagree with each other. The more I move into witness—holding the transformational container for myself—the less conflict I feel, and the easier it is to find a win–win–win solution.

Integral leadership is well equipped to lead complex organizational transformations. At this stage of leadership, the leader is focused on the welfare of the entire system, including the design of the whole system. There is a shift to a larger systemic vision, going even beyond the organization to a society-centric vision. This Integral stage, which Bob Kegan terms "self-transforming," is what enables a leader to also be systems-transforming. Leaders operating with an Integral mind no longer see themselves as separate from the system, trying to change the system. By seeing themselves as part of the change that needs to happen, they are able to lead from an authentic, servant leadership stance. This takes us back to the case that being a transformational leader, who is able to transform an entire organizational system, requires the leader to develop this self-transforming capacity.

Using the Integral Disciplines to Foster Development

As we've suggested, the *Integral Disciplines* have two very powerful functions: (1) to help outcome-creating leaders move themselves into a more Integral stage, by working in an Integral way on a day-to-day basis, and (2) by focusing on the five disciplines, to leverage the IATF, as an organizational operating system, to achieve the goal of organizational agility. We will talk more about how the Integral Disciplines are used as part of your organizational transformation in Part III. Here, we explain briefly how each Discipline helps us develop ourselves more fully into transformational leaders.

The main point of making the Integral (four-quadrant) distinctions is to develop capability (muscle) in each of the quadrants and their underlying disciplines. We all have a native (primary) and secondary quadrant orientation. Likewise, we all have more skill in one quadrant than another (orientation doesn't necessarily equate to skill in that quadrant). Due to this orientation and skill preference, we need to develop the capability to consciously pay attention to all quadrants and all relevant developmental lines. By doing this over a period of time, we are developing and evolving our own Integral leadership.

An abbreviated description of the five Integral Disciplines and their relationship to our leadership development follows (full definitions appear in Chapter 8):

- **Conscious Change.** Organizations seeking to become Agile need to get really good at change and how they go through the process of change. Doing so requires leaders to take a proactive (conscious), disciplined, and sustainable approach to organizational change. Taking a holistic and leader-driven approach to change pushes us to grow in multiple ways. The Conscious Change Discipline moves us away from an autopilot prescriptive change process and toward a process that uses conscious thinking and planning that incorporates factors from all four quadrants using an intentional, structured, disciplined approach. This grows our Integral leadership. Working on these abilities in ourselves moves us toward the Integral level.

- **Evolving Consciousness.** We do not generally question our inner game, our assumptions and beliefs, how we got here, what's contributed to it, or how we change as human adults. But whether or not we ever question them, they guide our everyday actions and limit us, keeping us stuck at the status quo. For example, an arrogant, critical inner state is much more likely to trigger resistance or defensiveness in others. It will not serve to change the situation at all and, in fact, may even make it worse. By working on our own development first, we grow a critical capacity that can make us truly transformational leaders. This Discipline is the direct focus of Part II of this book.

- **Evolving Product Innovation.** When an organization moves to using Agile practices, the shift requires its members to move from goal-centric practices (such as waterfall programming) to customer-centric ones; this shift is more or less built naturally into Agile thinking and practices. If the goal is not just "doing Agile" but achieving organizational agility, then the organization must go beyond a customer-centric focus to an organization-centric approach in creating its products (as a way of transcending and including). One of the key barriers to using this approach arises when we fall into an us-versus-them mentality, in which we are not able to effectively take the perspective of others in different departments or different geographic locations. Using this orientation stretches us as leaders, pushing us to work across organizational boundaries, to *see as* those different groups, if we are to become effective in creating synergies with the natural diversity of an organizational system. The boundary-spanning practices are a way we can effectively work with others across boundaries.

- **Evolving Systemic Complexity.** Designing, shifting, and shaping the organization's collective set of beliefs, mores, and mental models in the direction of—and to create a hospitable environment for—organizational agility requires growing systemic complexity. For instance, it requires evolving from Achievement-Orange to Pluralistic-Green thinking and acting. As we examine our own mental models and the effectiveness of our relationship systems, we are pushed into more Integral ways of relating: taking the perspective of others, seeing our own meaning-making process, confronting our group shadow, and seeing the systemic effects of the group conscience. As we help evolve the culture, we naturally come up against the inside of our group's meaning making. In turn, we are forced to confront our common assumptions and cherished beliefs and our jointly held mental models about the world and what our system needs to do culturally to exist. We have the opportunity to create a deliberately developmental culture and deliberately developmental relationships, where evolving consciousness—on both an individual level and a collective level—is valued in the organization alongside achieving business results.

- **Evolving Adaptive Architectures.** Designing and implementing organizational structures, governance, and policies that optimize flow, value creation, and human well-being is the focus of this discipline. As far as our own development, this Discipline stretches our design thinking skills, our understanding and recognition of systemic effects in bottlenecks and governance logjams, and our flexibility in allowing for changing structures that can create uncertainty or discomfort in us if we are easily ego-triggered. The stable hierarchical structures of the Traditional-Amber altitude are in part designed to mollify the relatively fragile identity structure appropriate to that level. If we can grow ourselves and others beyond the Reactive level, we will enable greater adaptability in our policies and structures.

By working with each of these Disciplines, not only does the organization benefit, but also we ourselves are forced to grow, especially as we stretch into our non-orienting quadrants.

Increasing Collective Effectiveness

Developing as a leadership **collective** is another dimension of development. As we've mentioned, an organization's collective effectiveness as an extended leadership team or collective is a competitive advantage that cannot be duplicated and that is fully under the control of the organization's leaders. Using such mechanisms as leadership coaching cohorts, facilitated by a leadership coach or even peer-led, can create a supportive yet challenging environment in which growth can occur. Banding together and making vertical development a norm within the leadership ranks take away any stigma or vulnerability people may feel in exposing their weaknesses.

According to The Leadership Circle research, the two most highly correlated dimensions of a leader's effectiveness are purposeful vision and teamwork. Put simply, to build high-performing leadership teams, leaders must be extremely clear and highly focused on their vision, strategy, and performance. Achieving this requires a conscious, intentional long-term focus on their individual and collective development and identification of developmental goals, individually and collectively. Leaders must also create an environment where concrete, helpful feedback is welcomed and consistent, and where leaders hold each other accountable to their developmental goals, in deliberately developmental relationships. Without rich feedback from others, we may be blind to how we are showing up and perceived by others. Your organizational system, and the leaders around you, experience you. They see how you behave, they see what makes you effective or ineffective, and they see and perceive this same thing in a collective leadership team. Here, we aren't referring to just the people skills of a leader. A highly effective leader has a healthy balance between relationships and tasks and attends to the full spectrum of both.

Receive this feedback as a gift, and don't try to resist, deny, argue, disbelieve, or discount it. Open your heart and your mind, and explore the feedback from an objective stance. What might be a pattern? What do you know is essentially true about your leadership team and how you are leading others? How do you close yourself off? How do you limit the growth of your employees? How do you send mixed messages about what is truly important? How does your collective reaction limit your organization's further growth? Moving into a place of deep discovery as a team is the beginning of increasing your collective effectiveness.

Summary

In this chapter, we have outlined the development path for transformational leaders, looking at practices for development (meditation, journaling, prayer, shadow work) and examples of the subject–object switch within each level of development. Overall, Part II has provided a detailed overview of what it means to become a transformational leader, one capable of leading an Agile Transformation.

From Insight to Action

In Part I, in your Insight to Action exercise you used Integral thinking to look *at* your Agile Transformation and assess it from the lens of each quadrant. In Part II, we've focused on *you*, the transformational leader, and how you are the most important "tool" in your work. Indeed, it is your impact and effectiveness in the use of any framework or tool that determine your results. In this exercise, rather than looking *at* your organization from each quadrant and altitude, take a few moments to look *from* your own reality. In Figure 7.2, notice that you, as the Agile leader, are now in the center. As you tour the quadrants, from your own perspective and your own way of going about the transformation, what do you now see?

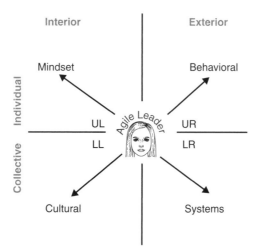

Figure 7.2
Looking as yourself in each of the quadrant dimensions

- **I Quadrant:** As you think about the Agile Transformation or change effort you are leading or guiding, in this moment, what emotions or feelings do you have about the current situation and what beliefs are you holding about what is possible? What is most important to you? What do you believe is the altitude expressed in what you value most? Why do you believe this is the altitude you come from?

- **IT Quadrant:** As you work on the transformation effort, what do you notice about your own actions and responses to that work? What kind of action response is called forth in you (e.g., tactical, strategic, forceful, passive)? As you observe your own behavior in your response to the work, what altitude do you see mostly expressed? What is your reasoning?

- **ITS Quadrant:** As you do your work on the change effort, what do you notice about your way of working within the constraints of the system? How are you supported by the current structure and environment? How are your efforts thwarted by that structure? At what altitude do you believe you mostly operate when working within the constraints of the current organizational structure? How do you come to this conclusion?

- **WE Quadrant:** What are you experiencing in how the organization's culture impacts you in the change effort? As you look inward, what do you notice about how the culture and quality of relationships affect your way of working with individuals, teams, leaders, and all levels of the organization? How do they affect your ability to engage in collaborative conversations that generate new insights in others as well as in yourself? What altitude do you believe you operate in as you work with others and with conflict or cultural barriers to change? What is your reasoning for choosing this altitude?

- Lastly, as you look at all quadrants, what do you notice about your primary way of working with challenges in regard to your quadrant orientation and altitude? How might you give more attention and intention to other quadrants? How might you be more curious about your way of seeing and listening to the organizational system?

Other actions you might take for developing your transformational leadership:

- Get 360-degree feedback, either through interviewing direct reports, colleagues, and your boss or by using a formal 360-degree assessment instrument.

- Taking in your feedback and your own self-assessment, decide on your developmental goal. Choose one of the developmental practices outlined in this chapter, and commit yourself to doing it for at least one month, ideally multiple times per week (if not daily).

- Start a peer group, or find a partner, to start a coaching/development group. Such a cohort is a very powerful mechanism to develop yourself over time by getting feedback and providing mutual accountability. A peer cohort also helps develop your collective effectiveness.

PART III

ORGANIZATIONAL TRANSFORMATION: PUTTING THE INTEGRAL COMPASS TO WORK

The first part of this book described the Integral approach to transformation, while the second part focused on upgrading your existing leader's operating system to the level required to lead such a transformation. This third and concluding part focuses on the articulation of the full Integral Agile Transformation Framework (IATF), which can most properly be termed a "meta-framework." We customized the IATF, based on our experience with Agile Transformations and in studying and applying Integral thinking, to be a comprehensive guide for organizational transformations. The chapters in Part III first provide an overview of the IATF and then concentrate on the Integral Disciplines—the five key focal vectors for designing, implementing, and measuring an Agile Transformation. The last chapter guides you, as a transformational leader, in beginning your transformation effort.

8

The Integral Agile Transformation Framework: An Overview

Development comes about when we are able to take more perspectives; the Integral Agile Transformation Framework (IATF) is a vehicle to shift our development because it creates a discipline or a platform for us to take these perspectives systematically. It helps build different muscles or capacities both for ourselves as transformational leaders—to help us show up differently to lead our organization through change—and for our organizations in their practices, structures, mindset, and culture. We can easily take a familiar perspective out of habit. The beauty of the IATF, by contrast, is that it gives you a new set of lenses with which to see things that you may have never seen before. It takes you out of autopilot mode and into presence with what is happening in the moment, which then gives you more options in how to respond. Our goal in writing this chapter is to help make that power real for you by applying Integral thinking directly to the tasks of organizational transformation. The IATF can be seen as an organizational operating system for transformation, which, after upgrading your leader's operating system (LOS), puts you in a good position to fully embrace this approach.

The IATF is an Integral model uniting each of the four quadrant views, the developmental lines within each quadrant, and each of the altitudes expressed for those lines, which can be applied to any level of holon (individual, team, program, organization, and even society). It is a highly robust model, pointing to more areas than we can easily pay attention to in a single sitting but is useful beyond measure in reminding us of what there is to see, practice with, and take into consideration. Recall that we compared the Integral model to a compass and a map: The IATF is both compass and map, helping us see more clearly and act more effectively. The IATF is an infinitely expandable map that accommodates all the approaches we could take to achieve enterprise transformation. In that sense, it is a *meta-model* and, therefore, not in "competition" with other organizational, process, scaling, or change models. Rather, each of those models or approaches will have a *place* (one or more "kosmic addresses") within the IATF and, in turn, a clear *relationship* with any of the other models or approaches you want to consider, either now or in the future. This allows for comparing and contrasting approaches—that is, where each is strong, where it is missing elements, where it is likely to be compatible with other approaches, and where it is unable to offer an integral, comprehensive approach. You will be able to map your client situation into the IATF to determine the appropriate tools, models, frameworks, and approaches for the situation in which you find yourself.

For you as a transformational leader, the IATF provides a powerful method for working with your organization as a complex adaptive system. But it is equally important to remember that the IATF is only a tool: While it is a way for you to more clearly see your complex system, you should not become attached to your assessment of what you believe you see in terms of quadrant orientations or altitudes. Instead, you should remain curious and in inquiry mode rather than being fixed on your views and attached to your map. When you keep "self as instrument" in the forefront of your awareness, you recognize when your own quadrant orientations, level of thinking, biases, and meaning making are limiting your ability to more effectively work with the organization and with leaders. Furthermore, you are better able to allow for emergence and accommodate what is arising in the moment.

How Do We Use the Map?

Taking an Integral approach to enterprise transformation means that we consider multiple perspectives on the situation or the holon of interest. For instance, what is the primary *altitude* of the individual person, team, program, or organizational system we are working with? We could say that that is looking *at* the client or situation. We also want to look *from* their perspective, through their eyes (looking *as*) to see what they see. A person who views the world through an Achievement-Orange lens will see the world in a much different way than one who sees the world primarily from a Pluralistic-Green perspective. Of course, since we see the world primarily through a given lens, we also need to be aware of our own biases and limitations. For instance, if we see the world through an Achievement-Orange lens, we may tend to see a project as an accomplishment to be achieved and perceive that we will be "installing" the IATF, or some other framework, that we then hope to implement to make the transformation happen. Conversely, if we see the transformation from a Pluralistic-Green value system, we will more likely be motivated to inspire a new way of being and valuing in the organization rather than just focusing on the "doing" aspect.

In our work, we use our Integral lenses to see more clearly how the client makes meaning of the world (I), how they go about getting things done (IT), what types of structures they build (ITS), and how they are in relationship with others (WE). Asking ourselves these types of questions is what it means to use the Integral Operating System (IOS). (Recall that another name for the IOS is the "all quadrants, all levels, all lines" [AQAL] view.)

To summarize, a given "something of interest"—whether a team, an executive leader, a product development process, an organization's culture, or its performance management policies—can be distinguished or mapped in relationship to its counterparts, or to any other thing, by assessing four dimensions:

1. What is the **primary holon** (individual, team, organization) of interest, or what holons are interacting?

2. What is the **primary quadrant** (I, WE, IT, or ITS) emphasized or privileged (since there is almost always a bias)?

3. What is the **primary altitude** (or level) of functioning (e.g., Amber, Orange, Green, Teal) being exhibited or acted out of? Alternatively, which altitude values are in conflict (e.g., the Orange goal fulfillment conflicts with the Green need for consensual decision making)?

4. What **developmental lines** (lines within each quadrant, relative to the evolution of that quadrant) are applicable to the situation, and how do they help us see where growth could be applied?

Given that this is a framework for Agile enterprise transformations, to be effective for our purposes we also need to narrow the generic quadrants I, WE, IT, and ITS down to more relevant (and specific) designations. We will outline these in the next section at the organization level; later in the chapter, we will look at the team- and program-level designations for the quadrants. We will continue using the altitude designations of Amber, Orange, Green, and Teal, as these have by far the most relevance for organizations adopting Agile. In Chapter 9, we will layer in the concept of developmental lines (how complexity evolves within each quadrant) and our own concept of *Integral Disciplines*—the primary vectors to focus on in an Agile Transformation.

In essence, we are moving from using a high-level map of the world (the IOS) to a detailed map of our neighborhood, complete with our favorite bakery, natural foods market, night club, and gym (the IATF). Let's look at the enterprise transformation quadrants first.

The IATF Quadrants

The creation of the IATF came from an awareness, a "seeing," of how marrying Integral and Agile together can make transformation possible. Integral is used in many different fields of study—from medicine to art to psychology to business and leadership—so the model needs to draw your attention to what is most important in an organizational change context. Figure 8.1 shows the four quadrant names with this Agile Transformation focus. In this section, we make the quadrant perspectives real by detailing both the subject matter and the relevant methods for each quadrant at the organizational, program, and team levels. We also provide examples of typical methods used in Agile implementations and explore how they map to the quadrant perspectives. In Chapter 9, we will look at how things develop within each quadrant—that is, the movement from less complex to more complex altitudes.

INTEGRAL AGILE TRANSFORMATION FRAMEWORK™

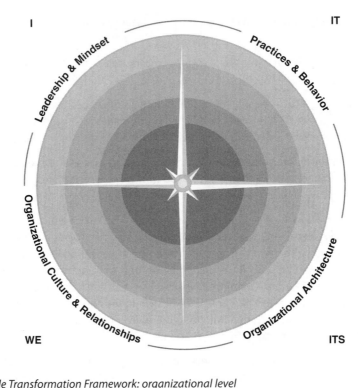

Figure 8.1
The Integral Agile Transformation Framework: organizational level

Leadership and Mindset (I Quadrant)

As we've discussed at length, for organizational transformation success, nothing is more important than leadership. Leaders cannot delegate this level of change; they must actually lead it. Recall that the I quadrant is about our intentions, values, beliefs, feelings, emotions, and, more generally, mindset and overall internal experiences as a person.

When we are assessing our organization from the point of view of the *Leadership and Mindset* quadrant, we might ask questions like these: What is the belief of the Agile sponsors about why they are doing an Agile Transformation? What was the wake-up call for them that spurred the change? How open are leaders to new information and perspectives that will impact the transformation? What emotions are present in individuals when speaking of the change?

In our Agile initiatives, we often pay most attention to competencies, skills, training, and similar aspects. All of these are IT quadrant perspectives and part of what we call the "Outer Game." The I quadrant is about the "Inner Game": how people make meaning of their world, their self-identity, how they feel about the Agile Transformation effort, and so on.

Common approaches to Agile that highlight the I quadrant include the distinction between *being* Agile and *doing* Agile. The being side emphasizes our inspiration, our motivation, and our inner experience of—and integrity with—the Agile principles and values. We see that this "being" distinction comes from an I quadrant perspective. The being side can be known by each person only as an inner experience. Yes, it can be talked about and shared, but ultimately it can be experienced and known only from within our individual experience—something not directly accessible to others. We cannot expect people to "take on an Agile mindset," because change cannot be imposed on someone. Transformational change is an inside-out practice. Another I example—being a servant leader—is largely an issue of our inner motivation for leading (consider how different it is to be motivated by achieving status or power versus serving people and the greater good) and our sense of self-sufficiency (our ability to feel as if we are enough rather than as if we are deficient, and our ability to develop ourselves in an internal way that allows us to access such motivations and capabilities). Other I-oriented approaches include the following:

- Bill Joiner's Leadership Agility

- Bob Anderson's Leadership Circle

- Professional coaching (Coaching is not limited to the I quadrant, but most practitioners' use of such skills tends to overemphasize this perspective.)

Insight to Action: Leadership and Mindset Success Factors

Several factors from this quadrant perspective affect the success of an Agile enterprise transformation and should be considered for assessment and intervention. Here are some examples of "Leadership and Mindset" questions that you might reflect upon:

- Assess the maturity and adaptability of leadership at all levels. The maturity or complexity of a given person's leadership includes their internal capacity around emotional intelligence (EQ), their LOS's meaning-making capacity (Reactive to Creative to Integral), and (especially at a team level) the depth of commitment felt by individual contributors to craftsman's pride. Unless outcome-creating leadership is activated, the Agile values will simply not be achievable.

- Evaluate the extent to which leadership is engaged, committed, and actually leading the transformation rather than delegating the effort. (This is the focus of forming a change team and designing the change initiative, topics addressed in Chapter 10.)

- Assess the level and quality of employee engagement. This is a mindset issue for the individual, which then becomes a cultural issue. Unengaged employees may be the single largest source of unfulfilled potential in organizations in our time. This factor may already be assessed by human resources personnel on an ongoing basis, but it could also be addressed in your transformation effort.

- Evaluate the alignment (experienced internally) between people's values and the Agile values, and how this plays out as they participate on teams and in organizational activities.

- Assess the extent to which people are able to speak their truth. Embracing Agile means embracing transparency, visibility, accountability, feedback, and courageous authenticity. If the culture of an organization stifles the voices in the organizational system, and if it contributes to people feeling the need to put on a "corporate professional mask," you will only achieve the status quo—you will not see transformational change.

- Notice the emotions present in people who are part of the change, as well as in the individuals who are being impacted by the change. Leadership, mindset, and engagement point us to the most easily overlooked areas in a transformation and urge us to focus on these needs. If we think of Agile as just a set of software development practices to be competent in and trained on, then we will have missed the point (this is perhaps Achievement-Orange thinking). Instead, from an evolutionary development point of view, in addition to learning new knowledge and skills, we must develop our internal capacity to enact and embody the Agile values and principles (i.e., develop the Inner Game). This is true whether at the team level or the leadership level.

Practices and Behavior (IT Quadrant)

In the last 25 years, owing to enormous technological advances, products have become much more intelligent. Today, there are more types of users, more types of organizations, and different perspectives on "value." With these changes occurring at an accelerating pace and with increasing complexity, product design now has to include more than just economic and user values for the given organization; that is, it has to account for an increasingly wide range of social and economic values for the industry and even for society as a whole. This complexity of product innovation requires us to adopt even more perspectives outside of the Agile delivery team, to the organization, and even outside the organization. The practices we use to develop products are obviously central to Agile. Agile practices are brought into organizations for the very purpose of changing the way people work together and how they create the desired business results and innovative value. Recognizing the importance of this factor, we made *Practices and Behavior* the primary focus of the IATF's IT quadrant. Ultimately, organizational agility will come about only through the use of progressive practices that optimize collaboration and cross-boundary synergy. Likewise, successful practices will come about from a combination of the right behavior (IT) with the right intention (I). If we merely go through the motions (behavior without intention), we will be unlikely to achieve the results we expect.

A common Agile approach that emphasizes the IT quadrant occurs when we focus primarily on specific Agile behaviors and practices, breaking down the details of the practices, observing whether they are going well, and teaching and mentoring people how to engage in them. This is the strategy adopted in many Agile implementations and is often a strength of Agile practitioners; however, when it becomes the singular focus, it reduces transformational change to merely "installing" Agile practices rather than producing the desired organizational agility. Behaviors and practices have the virtue of being observable from the outside, objectively, including any artifacts created by the practices (e.g., a software build history, the number of bugs, observing or recording the stand-up meeting, the documented results of a retrospective). This is useful when we wish to measure and make objective assessments of where we are at—hence, its appeal in a business results and scientific measurement context. However, this approach does not capture the intentions of the people engaged in the practices (the I quadrant perspective), so we're in danger of missing important information if we do not also look there. Practice = behavior + intention; without the underlying intention (belief or value) of the practice, the value is lost. In general, Agile process frameworks are often IT-oriented descriptions, often being described as empirical process frameworks.

Insight to Action: Practices and Behavior Success Factors

Several key factors from this quadrant should be assessed and considered for intervention in your Agile enterprise implementation. Here are a few reflection questions for you to consider as you look at your current Agile practices and behaviors:

- Evaluate the actual practices used to create products, involve customers and other voices, and measure success to determine the level of product innovation occurring at present in relationship to the organizational agility goal.

- Evaluate the alignment between how the practices are carried out (behavior) and the intention they were created from, to identify instances of just "going through the motions." This gap—for instance, a Green customer-centric practice that is enacted with an Orange intention of selling more to a captive customer audience—creates tensions between delivery teams and product owners or management.

- Assess the maturity of collaborative and relationship competencies, within teams, and also across organizational boundaries (e.g., across horizontal and vertical levels, between departments or functions, between geographic regions, including external stakeholder groups). The gaps identified are a potential target for interventions to increase boundary-spanning competency, enabling a more cross-organizational collaborative culture capable of operating with the agility needed to respond to the complexity and pace of change, and to disrupt the market with innovative products.

- Assess the consistency of your *practice* of software craftsmanship and modern Agile engineering practices (your actual *behavior*, not just what you say that you value) to evaluate the maturity level of technical practices. The state of these practices will greatly determine the agility of your products and the ability to make future changes, impacting the total cost of ownership.

- Look at the extent to which the organization considers its impact on society and the planet. This level of vision may be beyond what most organizations can currently do in a serious way, but it will become increasingly important (the COVID-19 pandemic has made this abundantly clear). Overall, when assessing our organization from the point of view of the "Practices and Behavior" quadrant, we want to ask questions like these: How aligned are the organization's current practices to Agile practices? How is the customer involved in product development? What metrics are captured at the team level and how are they meaningful to business leaders? How can we meet the organization where it is and help it evolve its practices and behaviors to a more organization-centric level, including all voices in the system, aligned around a shared unified vision and the organization's brand and purpose?

Many Agile efforts, while focusing on this quadrant perspective, lose sight of the need to focus on practices at a multiple-holon level—not just within teams but also across the organization. Moreover, when Agile practices are "installed" within the organization, the deep intention designed into the practices is often lost, along with the benefits. The result is what people often refer to as *doing* Agile but not *being* Agile; both are required. In other words, rather than introducing a practice with an appropriately corresponding intention (as is possible with Evolutionary-Teal development), we are re-creating the existing practices and their way of thinking (Achievement-Orange).

Organizational Architecture (ITS Quadrant)

The structures and environments we create may either enable or limit our culture and mindset. They may enable or limit how adaptive the organization can be in making significant changes or achieving significant organizational agility. Likewise, they either enable or limit innovation. Transformational leaders need the ability to see the "whole" system and the environment to realize the organization's vision around transformation. Indeed, "seeing systems" is a critical competency for a transformational leader.

For agility to be possible, organizations must architect their structures and systems so that value creation and flow of value are optimized. An inflexible structure will limit the likelihood of achieving this outcome and make responding to changing market conditions almost impossible. Since this ability is paramount to organizational agility, we have chosen to name the ITS quadrant dealing with these concerns *Organizational Architecture*.

The "Organizational Architecture" quadrant reminds us to look at the overall social system and environment of the company and its work and to "see" things like organizational policies, organizational charts, systems, workflows, and emergent effects (hence, the criticality of systems thinking). It includes not only an organization's *structure* but also how teams are set up and staffed, the style and focus of performance management/metrics, the financial systems and structures, governance (at the project, program, and corporate levels), corporate policies, business process systems (including scaled frameworks), and external realities like government regulation, industry groups, and competitive pressures. Organizational architecture can be seen as an expression of the WE culture but in concrete, observable, and tangible forms.

When we assess our organization from the point of view of the "Organizational Architecture" quadrant, we might ask questions like these: How is the organization designed to support and give visibility to product flow? How Lean are current processes, and how will that impact agility? How will the organization's approach to governance impact the transformation?

In our Agile Transformation experience, organizations often recognize that there is a gap between their existing structure and one that supports agility; we notice that many organizations attempt to bridge this gap by implementing a scaled framework. Scaled frameworks most often, in our experience, re-create the current thinking about structure (a functional matrix) rather than offer a new, adaptive type of structure—one that, for example, flexes with changing market conditions and business needs and is not tied to the normal political hierarchy. In other words, rather than introducing a new way of thinking (as we will see in our later discussion of Evolutionary-Teal development), we are re-creating the existing functional matrix way of thinking (Achievement-Orange).

A popular Agile approach mainly from an ITS perspective is the Scaled Agile Framework (SAFe; both are trademarks of Leffingwell, LLC). SAFe focuses not only on individual processes but also on a *process system* that unites different levels: from the team level, with a product owner and a backlog; to the program level, with a roadmap and a program backlog, and roles such as release train engineer, product management, and release management; to the portfolio or organizational level, with a portfolio backlog, investment themes, and business and architectural epics. When examining any single process in the SAFe framework, we could look at it from an IT perspective. However, for the process *system*—with its interrelationships and synergies, as well as the policies and organizational roles it entails—it is more fitting to see SAFe (or scaled frameworks generally) from a systems point of view (ITS). While SAFe makes references to leadership and culture (I and WE), it does not use the same level of formalization, nor are there specific, implementable "human technologies" (methodologies) that the process system references. The bottom line: Organizations seem to embrace SAFe for the ITS benefits it embodies (scaling an Agile process to an organizational level with role and structural implications) rather than the I or WE practices or methods. Other common approaches incorporating an ITS orientation include Holocracy, Beyond Budgeting, and the theory of constraints.

Insight to Action: Organizational Architecture Success Factors

Several key factors from the ITS quadrant impact a successful Agile enterprise implementation and should be considered for assessment and intervention. Here are a few questions you can reflect on from the ITS quadrant lens view:

- Does the organization structure fit with an Agile philosophy? For instance, does it align around value streams? If not, what is the organizing principle?

- In adopting Agile, what organizational systems and policies will be affected? If they are heavily Amber or Orange—along with the corresponding leadership mindset—what could make change possible?

- How does the organizational structure enable (or constrain) the flow of value? Can the bottlenecks be seen or visualized? What altitude level of thinking did the structure arise from? What issue or perspective does the existing organizational structure create as a point of focus (e.g., political power or manager bonuses rather than value creation)?

- If you want to have an adaptive organization, what organizational structures will enable you to flexibly re-deploy your teams and other assets to adapt to changing market conditions and business strategies? What organizational design options are even available to you?

- How are roles and responsibilities, as well as employee career paths and personal development goals, considered as part of the change effort?

- How does the organization approach scaling Agile?

Organizational leaders inherently know they must scale Agile for agility, yet it is mostly done in a transactional way, through the implementation of an Agile scaled framework, rather than a conscious change initiative that includes both human and business agility aspects of change.

Organizational Culture and Relationships (WE Quadrant)

Fundamental principles of Agile include collaboration, sharing, transparency, and accountability. In turn, it stands to reason that relationships—and how we show up in them—will strongly influence the success of any transformation. The massive shift that needs to take place when moving from a non-Agile environment to an Agile environment usually asks that we change the very DNA of our organization, that our culture undergo a fundamental shift. Transformational leaders must understand how collective beliefs create relationships, culture, and systems (the reverse is also true). They must also understand how people are feeling, and how central emotions are to building the right culture. Thus, the focus of our WE quadrant is *Organizational Culture and Relationships*.

The view from the WE quadrant is of shared meaning, shared values, our experiences of our relationships, and, more generally, organizational culture. In the IATF, this fundamentally includes the altitude of the culture within a team, program, business unit, or organization. Culture in WE is the equivalent to mindset in the I quadrant, but it involves a different type of consciousness—that is, systemic consciousness. Looking from this quadrant, we see whether we have a collaborative and empowering culture, or a predictive, control-oriented one, or a superiority-focused, achievement-driven one. This perspective includes the overall organizational culture as well as the leadership culture (the behaviors and attitudes deemed desirable in leaders). Further, it includes the values we hold together and how we live them (or don't live them), our relationship systems (from the "inside," or how we experience them), and the many nested system configurations of relationships.

What we frequently see in Agile Transformations is a fundamental mismatch between the existing organizational culture (typically Achievement-Orange) and the type of culture where Agile can thrive. Addressing this gap requires focused attention on development of the organization's underlying collective belief structure in a systematic way in the direction of Evolutionary-Teal development.

When we are assessing our organization from the point of view of the "Organizational Culture and Relationships" quadrant, we might ask questions like these: Is the leadership modeling the behavior of the culture we desire? What politics are at play, and how is that showing up in the environment? Who are the collective people who are highly influencing this effort? In what ways does the existing culture align with Agile values? Are people more transactional or more people-oriented in their relationships?

A common Agile approach that incorporates the WE perspective is William Schneider's (1994) culture typology. It distinguishes four culture types:

- Control
- Competence

- Collaboration

- Cultivation

This is fundamentally a WE quadrant perspective (though it also has clear ITS implications), enumerating our shared understanding, beliefs, and approaches to organizational culture, to "how we do things around here in order to succeed" (Schneider's definition of culture). An organization's culture type reflects what people believe together, their shared understanding. For example, in a control-oriented culture, we believe that we must get and keep control if we are to succeed; in a competence-focused culture, we believe that we must be the best in the world at what we do; and in a collaboration-oriented culture, we believe we will only succeed together as a team, not separately. These *shared beliefs* and *mental models* then show up in the way we lead (I quadrant), the characteristics of our process (IT quadrant), and our organizational structure and policies (ITS). Other WE approaches include systems coaching (ORSC), systemic constellations, Virginia Satir's change model, and Dave Logan's Tribal Leadership. Figure 8.2 summarizes these common Agile methods for all four quadrants.

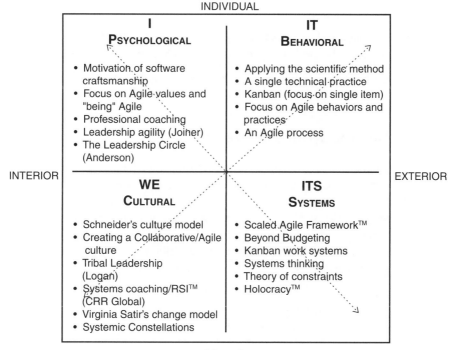

Figure 8.2
Methods used in Agile Transformations mapped to quadrants

Insight to Action: Culture and Relationship Success Factors

Several key factors from the "Organizational Culture and Relationships" quadrant influence the success of Agile enterprise implementation. Here are some reflection questions to ponder as you think about your current organization's culture and the quality of relationships:

- What is the fit between the existing culture and the kind of culture conducive to Agile and organizational agility? How is this culture "carried" (e.g., in the actions and role modeling of leaders, in the permanent structures)?

- What is the level of resiliency of relationships across the organization? More human, people-oriented relationships make for a more Agile environment than do transactional ones. Are relationships even something that can be talked about to make them better? How are relationships different at different holon levels: Between team members? Between middle management? Between senior leaders? Across levels?

- What is the ability to work across organizational boundaries (boundary spanning), moving from an "us versus them" mindset to a shared "we" mindset, achieving synergistic results, and getting beyond the typical "silo wars"?

- Are there transformational leaders who are taking responsibility for designing and helping shift the culture, in part by modeling behaviors consistent with the desired culture?

We will go through each quadrant again, in more depth, as we explore the developmental lines and how evolution or development occurs within each quadrant in Chapter 9 on the Integral Disciplines.

Integrating the Quadrant Perspectives

The very foundation of the IATF is an Integral attitude, so regularly and systematically taking the perspective of all four quadrants is central, both to provide full understanding of a given context and to uncover all the salient approaches to growing a more Agile organization. No method—not Schneider's culture types, the idea of being and doing Agile, software craftsmanship, a focus on individual Agile practices, or a scaling process like SAFe—is the final answer. Being Integral means embracing approaches from each of the quadrants and choosing them depending on how they fit with the change strategy, all to get a comprehensive, balanced effect.

One global comment about organizational change and the quadrants: Bob Anderson, an unparalleled researcher in the field of leadership development, observes in his white paper *The Spirit of Leadership* (2008) that the I and WE quadrants are typically de-emphasized in organizational change initiatives; instead, these efforts are driven primarily by structural and process approaches, leading to failure rates of 85%. This is also what we see in the Agile world, where there is an (over) emphasis on training and implementing Agile practices (IT), and perhaps scaled frameworks and some form of organization design (ITS), with little effective action taken to develop leadership (I) or align culture (WE). Taking Bob's advice to heart, we have emphasized the left-hand quadrants, since we are steeped in multiple effective, scientifically based approaches that develop organizations within those quadrants. Recall that the right-hand quadrants are no less important, but they are more well understood and already more easily focused upon in our industry.

Now that we have explained the quadrant perspective in the IATF, let's consider an example that frequently comes up in an Agile transformation. We'll then put on the lens from each quadrant to examine this situation, providing a sense of integration. Recall a couple of facts about quadrants: They "tetra-arise," meaning they are all available all the time if we just look; one quadrant impacts the others, so how you see a given situation depends on which lens you are looking through; and to be Integral, we need to look from all four perspectives systematically.

This is a scenario we have seen in transformations, and you may also recognize it: *The HR department is not seen as a key player in the Agile Transformation.* Let's look at this scenario from the lens of each quadrant, and consider how it impacts the Agile Transformation effort.

- **Leadership and Mindset:** If we look *at* (from an assessment point of view) the I quadrant, we recognize the need for leadership to develop their own Inner Game, to increase their capacity to support the Agile mindset as well as Agile leadership traits. It might not be obvious to HR or the leadership of the Agile Transformation effort that there is a connection between the type of leadership needed in an Agile environment (typically the purview of Agile coaches) and leadership development (typically within the scope of HR). This is especially true when the transformation is perceived as being an information technology-driven initiative. In contrast, when we look *from* (as the client) the I quadrant, we can see that the HR leader might feel as if their role is being infringed upon if we bring in a leadership development program under the auspices of the Agile Transformation without considering them as a partner in this effort. Taking both perspectives gives us more information to act on. This tendency to divide up the world—the technology organization doing "technology" things, and the HR department doing "people and leadership" things—gets exposed when we take an Integral view.

- **Practices and Behavior:** Looking *at* the IT quadrant, from an HR point of view, we have seen confusion around the new job roles and descriptions that Agile tends to provoke, where there may not be adequate career paths to support the new ways of working and the new practices Agile brings, and where there is a potential mismatch between current skills and needed skills or roles. Looking *from* the IT quadrant, we have seen HR folks struggle to understand Agile, the required skills and competencies, how people's roles will need to evolve, and the fact that a convenient mapping of roles (such as project manager = Scrum Master) often does not do justice to the reality on the ground.

- **Organizational Architecture:** Looking *at* the ITS quadrant, we see HR policies and reward systems—like stack ranking or an emphasis on individual versus team performance—that often don't align with Agile beliefs or values. For instance, such policies often drive individuals to try to stand out rather than focus on team success. Looking *from* the ITS quadrant and the HR person's view, shifting the reward system to be more team oriented will require a big change effort across the entire organization. If HR wasn't given a seat at the table when the Agile Transformation was launched, this may be a difficult and lengthy process later in the game. Bringing HR in early, and trying to see the world from their point of view, can pay big dividends.

- **Organizational Culture and Relationships:** Looking *at* the WE quadrant, we see a culture misaligned with Agile, along with the typical belief that HR is responsible for culture change initiatives. Clearly, these efforts need to be closely integrated. Looking *from* the WE quadrant through the eyes of the HR group, they may not see the connection between culture shift and Agile, which results in a siloed mentality—an "us versus them" mindset instead of a shared "we" mindset about how to drive that culture change.

Development within the Quadrants

Throughout human history, human adaptation has been a dance between external circumstances and internal capacity: As external circumstances became more complex, the internal adaptive capacity had to evolve to be a match for that complexity. Likewise, organizations have evolved out of a need to match the complexity of our world. Right now, we are living in a time of extreme complexity acceleration. All over the world, humanity is asking for authentic leadership, the kind able to solve world problems within the context of wildly varied stakeholder views. In addition, we need new kinds of practices, structures, and cultures to fit the level of complexity we now face. The need to evolve has never been greater.

Agile came about in response to this reality, meeting the world's complexity in the area of software development, an evolutionary adaptation that furthered the ability of groups to collaborate to solve problems and bring products to market that were fit for purpose and met customer needs. This was expressed most commonly as an IT quadrant solution: a series of related practices that got better business results. The trouble is, those practices—designed from the thinking of a higher altitude than previous ways—required corresponding supporting complexity in the other quadrants. For instance, Agile practices (IT) designed from a Pluralistic-Green to Evolutionary-Teal altitude need similarly complex leadership (I) (outcome-creating/self-authoring mind) and culture (Pluralistic-Green culture and human-oriented relationships from a WE perspective). Further evolution of Agile to address large, complex organizations and their need to respond to disruption with their own innovation revealed the need for agility at the organizational level, not just at the team or in the delivery function.

Since Agile is an evolutionary adaptation in a world of ever-increasing complexity, it will help us to have a model of how evolution proceeds *within* each of the quadrants, so as to have a complete picture of organizational transformation (even more specific to organizational transformation than the picture conveyed in Part I). In our Integral map, recall there is a horizontal element—the quadrants, pointing us to different areas of focus and different methodologies and logics. There is also a vertical dimension that represents the level of complexity, whether of practices, culture, leadership, or organizational structures and systems.

We will continue to focus on four primary organizational altitudes—namely, Amber, Orange, Green, and Teal—held in a generic way across all four quadrants. Again, these colors are semi-arbitrary, designed in the Integral Model to match the colors of the rainbow for easy recall. Recall that each successive level is spurred into existence by organizational (or personal, in the case of an individual) challenges and general life conditions that could not be successfully handled by the previous way of organizing. The new level represents a stable way to deal with these new challenges successfully.

Each successive level of organization transcends and includes the previous level. In healthy development, this means culling the adaptive parts of each level for use at the next level. For instance, at the Pluralistic-Green altitude, we still have the ability to utilize Achievement-Orange negotiation skills in an appropriate context. In unhealthy development, in contrast, we often reject everything about the previous level and see it as wrong or naive. Each altitude has *more capacity* to deal with complexity than the previous one, which is generally a good thing, assuming that capacity is actually needed within a given environment (for instance, Traditional-Amber may indeed be the most effective altitude for an organization that needs to manage a simple manufacturing environment in a developing country). As people and organizations realize the need for a new way of being to match the world's complexity, development becomes more possible when we honor what the *current way of being* allows for, while also recognizing what possibilities it closes down. Developing a *new way of being* requires honoring what is healthy in the current way and letting go of what is no longer working, which allows for new capacity to be developed.

Addressing the issue of altitude in the IATF, Figure 8.3 shows the four altitude colors applied to the quadrants. Note that evolution happens within each quadrant somewhat independently of the others.

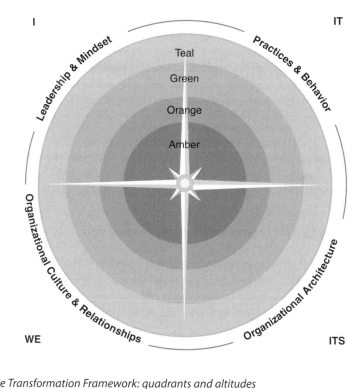

Figure 8.3
The Integral Agile Transformation Framework: quadrants and altitudes

The altitudes used here are highly influenced by *Spiral Dynamics*. However, its levels represent only one or two (of many) developmental lines, specifically within the I and WE quadrants, relating to how the individual, or the culture, "thinks" and values, representing different ways of being human.

The generic altitude colors attempt to abstract the essence of each altitude to give a sense of how it applies across quadrants; the specific ways in which evolution proceeds within each quadrant are explained in Chapter 9. Here, we summarize the altitudes briefly. These summaries are largely based on Laloux's research (2014) on Teal organizations and corroborated by the research of Graves (2005) and Beck and Cowan (1996).

- **Conformist-Amber:** Traditional, process-focused, right way to do things; seeks order, control, and predictability; structured, fixed hierarchy; formal job titles. Planning at the top, execution at the bottom. Conformist-Amber is a good fit for simple work environments and where order is essential (e.g., the military). Certainty-oriented.

- **Achievement-Orange:** Scientific method; effectiveness and efficiency; organization as a machine; management is like engineering. Innovation, accountability, and meritocracy are core concepts. Rational, restrained emotions. Uses goals to control. Budgeting, key performance indicators (KPIs), balanced scorecards, performance appraisals, bonuses, and stock options. Individual freedom. Results-oriented.

- **Pluralistic-Green:** Bottom-up processes, consensus-driven decision making, diversity oriented, servant leadership. Corporate social responsibility; organizational metaphor = family. Vision statements, values-driven cultures, worker empowerment, 360-degree feedback, leaders as teachers. People-oriented.

- **Evolutionary-Teal:** Self-organization; self-actualization, presence, purpose-driven, whole systems–oriented; locus of evaluation = internal satisfaction; has more capacity for perspective taking; minimal rules, maximal empowerment. Organization metaphor = a living system. No (or loose) job titles; peer appraisals; minimal need for hierarchies or consensus. Purpose-oriented.

We will go into considerably more detail with regard to altitudes in Chapter 9 on the Integral Disciplines and lines of development.

How Quadrants Look from Different Holons

Because we are concerned with enterprise-level agility for Agile Transformations, we have largely focused on the organizational holon level. Working at the enterprise level incorporates the people, processes, and views of the levels rolling up to it, but it can also be useful to see the world specifically from the point of view of a team holon (whether a delivery team or a leadership team) or from the program or department holon. Depending on our purpose, it can be helpful to do some scale shifting, looking specifically at an issue from different holon levels (as we would from different quadrants). For instance, if we're working with a program or department, it is helpful to see the world from its point of view, in all four quadrants. Since programs and departments are both holons, they are both parts and wholes. As wholes, we can look at them from each of the four perspectives.

For example, when an Agile team brings up an impediment in the daily Scrum, we would first look at that issue from the team holon view to see if it can be resolved—looking from the I, WE, IT, and ITS points of view. If not, we take another look at it from the program level: What do we see, and what could potentially be solved at that holon level and from any of the four quadrants? Many times, we see issues as organizational impediments that are brought to more senior leadership for intervention. As an alternative, we can think about touring the quadrants, the altitudes, and the different holon levels—of using a new form of systems thinking. In addition to looking at the level of agility in each holon, we also pay attention to how they interact, align, and support the overall organizational goal.

This section takes a tour of each quadrant through the three holon levels of organization, program (or department), and team. We will travel quadrant by quadrant—from the organization to the program to the team holon level.

Leadership and Mindset

In this section, we will tour the organization, program, and team levels within the I quadrant.

Organizational-Level Holon

The "Leadership and Mindset" quadrant, when seen from an organizational perspective, includes the developmental levels of leaders across the organization, from team leaders and first-level managers, to executives, CXOs, and even the board of directors. The developmental level of leaders will set a very definite organizational constraint or ceiling for what can be accomplished in terms of evolving to a more adaptive, complex organization. As Laloux (2014) puts it, "the general rule seems to be that the level of consciousness of an organization cannot exceed the level of consciousness of its leader" (p. 239).

Further, if we are attempting to develop real organizational agility, we will likely need to move into the range of Teal altitude. Citing his extensive research into Teal organizations, Laloux (2014) makes the point: "The CEO must look at the world through an Evolutionary-Teal lens for Teal practices to flourish" (p. 239). But for what, exactly, does the leader's consciousness serve as a constraint? How is the organization structured (hierarchy versus self-organized, functions versus value streams); how does it develop products and services (focused on process, customers, or brand and purpose); what are the attributes of its climate/culture (results-centric versus purpose-centric)? Clearly, development in the "Leadership and Mindset" dimension is essential to our goal.

Program-Level Holon

If we look from the program holon, we see the I quadrant from a bit narrower focus; in essence, we could think of the I quadrant as *Program Member Leadership and Mindset*. At the program level, it is important to pay attention to how people think about their engagement and connection to the overall program vision and goals. Does the program have a mission, similar to the way a product does? Do the members own and identify with that mission? The program should have a strong sense of identity, a differentiation with a compelling vision that teams can rally around (as occurred with the DaVinci program described later in this chapter). If program members do not feel a strong connection to the overall program goals and culture, a sense of identity connecting them to the program or department, the program will be weak as a holon, and people will find connection at the team level instead.

While the most senior leader's level of consciousness sets the constraint on how much the organization can develop, at the team or program level the organization may be able to operate—temporarily—at a higher level than organizational leaders do. Laloux's experience (and ours) makes us quite skeptical of the ability of a group to operate in this fashion in the long term, once more senior leaders understand what is really going on, and how the new way of thinking poses a threat to the current organizational system. Says Laloux (2014): "Ultimately, the pyramid will get its way and reassert control" (p. 238). This is what happens in a bottom-up Agile Transformation approach: It may have limited success, but ultimately it is undermined by the corporate antibodies.

Team-Level Holon

The I quadrant can be seen as *Team Member Values, Mindset, and Engagement*. Team members who feel highly engaged with other team members are more likely to actually *be* a team. Further, to form a strong Agile team, they will need to embrace the values and mindsets of their Agile practices and the pride of software craftsmanship. We can also look at leadership traits in individuals: To what degree are team members able to own the work and hold each other accountable? Can they understand and respect the perspectives of others, both other team members and stakeholders? To what degree can they contain their anxieties when under stress—to come from an outcome-creating stance rather than a problem-reacting one? Do their individual values align with each other, and are they aligned to Agile values? To what degree do team members believe their team mission is connected with, and important to, the overall organization's mission?

Another way to look at this holon is to notice the mindset of leadership at the team level and to determine whether the Agile Transformation effort is solely focused on the team's delivery and results rather than seeing them as part of a bigger effort that rolls up and across the entire organization.

Practices and Behavior

In this section, we tour the three holons within the IT quadrant.

Organizational-Level Holon

At the organization level, we are looking at the "Practices and Behavior" quadrant and how the whole organization develops and measures its products and services, how it uses technology and employs modern technical engineering practices, what level of craftsman behaviors is apparent, and what kinds of interpersonal and communication skills are developed and practiced. To achieve organizational agility, the organization needs to operate as a whole body rather than as a series of silos. This requires boundary-spanning practices and behaviors that bring together leaders, programs, teams, and individuals across the entire organization to collaborate and co-create their future. When we adopt this lens, we look at the overall behavior of the organization and what is blocking it from achieving the results it desires.

Program-Level Holon

The IT quadrant at the program level might be thought of as *Program Practices and Behavior*. This perspective considers how the program develops and measures its product(s), how it employs technical engineering practices (software craftsman behaviors), and the skills and competencies that program members and leaders bring to bear in their communications and interactions and in how they relate with one another. If different practices are used at a program level, your observations could be very different than those made at the organizational level.

When we put on the holon lens of "program," we are not looking at the full organization but only at the program of focus and its relationship—or embeddedness in—the surrounding environment, the organization. From this view, how does our program contribute to the organization's overall results?

Team-Level Holon

The IT quadrant for teams concerns Agile practices and behaviors. For teams, this means how the team engages in Agile practices, what their inspect-and-adapt cycle looks like, how the team employs technical engineering practices, and how (and how well) they communicate and interact with one another. This is largely the purview of the Agile health checks that many people do. An additional aspect is how teams manage dependencies and impacts across teams, including how they manage relationships outside their boundary. Again, the results may be quite different at this level than at either the program or organizational level. In fact, many teams we have worked with had a far greater capacity to employ Pluralistic-Green practices than did their overall organization.

Notice again the behaviors and ways of working between holon levels. If your Agile Transformation is only doing Agile practices with teams, and the way of working doesn't shift between and within each holon, it will not be possible to achieve agility.

Organizational Architecture

In this section, we tour the three holons within the ITS quadrant.

Organizational-Level Holon

The *Organizational Architecture and Environment* quadrant concerns the overall organizational structure, the team staffing philosophy, performance management metrics, the finance and accounting systems and processes, governance, corporate policies, and external realities like government regulation, industry groups, and competitive pressures, as well as the effects they have on the entire organizational body. If we take a numerical perspective on the organization (using various metrics), we can see whether workflows are constrained, efficient, or adding customer value, as well as the overall flow of value in the organization. We can also look at the level of alignment between senior organizational leaders and the organizational goals and strategies, metrics, employee rewards and incentives, policies, and governance. The degree to which senior leaders are *not* aligned on how the organization is architected in these areas will inevitably trickle down to middle management and the program level, which then snowballs down to the team.

Program-Level Holon

For a program, the primary focus is how work flows into and out of the program. We could see this perspective as *Flow Constraints and Enablers*; it concerns the overall environment and the way it supports or inhibits flow, both from and to the program. This includes the surrounding organization in which the program is embedded—for example, how the organizational structure affects the program, how teams are staffed, performance metrics, financing, program governance, and how corporate policies affect the program.

When there is no alignment between program goals and overall organizational goals, the program has too much incentive to remain a silo, its own island. This misalignment is often made evident at the program level, where middle management becomes the "frozen middle" in a transformation effort.

In general, the focus is on how those factors impact the *flow of value* that the program is able to create, either as a constraint (bureaucratic governance) or as an enabler (an organizational policy supporting collaborative workspaces). A program may have varying levels of influence over this external environment. In any case, it is helpful to understand the limitations, and the opportunities, to enhance program functioning.

Team-Level Holon

Finally, ITS is about *Flow Constraints and Enablers* at the team level. The overall environment for a team is the surrounding organization in which the team is embedded, especially any program or department of which it is a part. Issues of concern can include how the team is staffed, who the manager of the team reports to, which performance metrics the team is measured on (or whether different team members are measured differently), and how the team's relationship to the budgeting process, governance, and any corporate policies that affect them unfolds. Again, the focus is on how those factors impact the flow of value that the team is able to create, either as a constraint or as an enabler.

The team is particularly subject to influences from the surrounding ITS environment, especially from the program level. Impediments to the work of Agile teams will show up when no environmental structure supports their ability to do the Agile practices in the way they were intended to be enacted. Some examples follow:

- Team members are all remote, and there are inadequate collaboration tools.
- The team cannot set up physical structures like collaborative workspaces.

- Team members report to different managers who have different goals and use different measurements.

- There are individualistic reward policies that directly undermine the members' incentive to work as a team.

- Policies around the test environment infrastructure or release management thwart the team's flow.

A lack of adequate flexibility in the organization's architecture will greatly impede the team's ability to fully embody the Agile practices and behaviors. In addition, this inattention sends a message that the organization's leadership is not committed to the Agile Transformation; thus, there is no compelling vision for team members to want to enroll in the change.

Organizational Culture and Relationships

Finally, we tour the three holons within the WE quadrant.

Organizational-Level Holon

The *Organizational Culture and Relationships* quadrant is fundamentally about the altitude of the organization's culture—Amber, Orange, Green, or Teal—including leadership, atmosphere, and the mental models and philosophy that drive hiring, rewards and performance, perceptions about failure, learning, accountability, conflict resolution, decision making, organizational values, hierarchy, and authority.

Also of interest is the degree to which different subcultures exist within the organization. Do they harmonize with one another and support the overall organizational mission, or are they a barrier? Does the finance department operate conservatively (Amber) and the technology delivery teams take an inclusive approach with customers (Green), while the senior leadership team focuses on achieving targets at almost any cost (Orange)? Is the Agile Transformation driven purely from IT (practices), or is it truly an organizational transformation?

Michele's Take

Prior to my Agile consulting and coaching days, I was leading a division of a telecom organization that we had formed as part of an acquisition; it was charged with providing solutions for a new base of clients with more complex needs. As occurs in most acquisitions, the partners had very different ways of working and very different cultures. The acquiring organization was centered in Amber; it was very hierarchical with zero tolerance for failure and micro-management/command-and-control leaders but had some pockets of Orange—for example, in the sales and marketing division. The acquired organization was definitely more centered in Green, with some pockets of Orange. It was characterized by little hierarchy, freedom to experiment, a hands-off leadership approach, and an extremely customer-centric attitude. For me to be successful in retaining the clients we had just acquired, I needed to be able to operate in more of a Green culture, which meant that I had to create a subculture within the larger overall culture of our organization. I was able to do this by appealing to the Orange language of the sales group and my direct leadership, who were mostly concerned with results. As long as I achieved results, I was left to run my division mostly in the way I deemed fit.

Program-Level Holon

From a program level, we focus on the culture of the program and the relationships within it, but not necessarily those of the surrounding organization, since they may be different—hence, *Program Culture and Relationships*. The WE quadrant concerns the shared vision of a common product that binds the program together, as well as the program's overall culture. It includes the altitude of the program culture and the values that members hold together. Is there a coherent sense of belongingness across the program, or is it merely a management convenience to join elements into a cost center, calling them by the same name? These two alternatives are clearly different.

Michael's Take

Many years ago, I was the change management consultant for one of the functional teams in a large program going through a major enterprise system implementation. The new system drove the need for many changes, including new job descriptions, many process changes, and the associated training; it also had cultural implications. I and others felt a strong connection to the team, but perhaps even more so to the overall program—named the DaVinci program. There were 250 people on the program, so I didn't know that many of them personally, but we had a very strong sense of identity, mission, and connection with each other; we felt we were going to transform the company. We loved being part of that program together and had a strong shared culture. We essentially had a culture that may have even overridden our relationship to the larger organization. The agency of the program was potentially so great that it undermined the communion of belonging to the company holon. At times, it could have been a question whether we were motivated to complete our program mission, whether the organization wanted it or not.

In an Agile Transformation context, we often see Agile Transformation efforts operated as separate change initiatives rather than being coordinated or consistent in their Agile practices and in their change approach. This causes confusion across the organization, as a common language is lacking that might unite people toward a common goal. Also, you might have experienced programs in various business units competing with each other, vying to be the best, or various programs within a transformation effort competing with each other to "go Agile" first. These behaviors contribute to an us-versus-them culture, which reinforces the status quo and does not bring about transformation.

Team-Level Holon

The WE quadrant at this level could be seen as *Team Culture and Alignment*. For teams, the WE quadrant is about the quality of the team culture—a strong versus a weak culture, Amber versus Orange versus Green versus Teal altitude, and so on—as well as how aligned team members are around a shared vision, their commitment to a shared process, and their mutual accountability toward their common goal. Fundamentally, are they a team, or are they just a collection of individuals?

When beginning an Agile Transformation, it is critical to address the need for team members to understand their new roles and how they will contribute to the team, including what changes and what stays the same. If not, the team members will not have a strong sense of "we," as their sense of identity has not been attended to in bringing in the new way of working. This may trigger resistance to Agile at the team level. At the team level, we are specifically paying attention to healthy relationships that model a culture of Agile values and beliefs.

Summary

In this chapter, we spent a lot of time exploring the quadrants, what they mean in the context of an Agile Transformation, and a few of the developmental altitudes within each level as well as across holon levels. In essence, the IATF functions like an organizational operating system, allowing you to assess, design, and plan a major change initiative within its meta-framework. In the next chapter, we complete our articulation of the framework by honing in on the evolutionary changes that grow a company toward organizational agility, using our Integral Disciplines to tie together the developmental lines within each quadrant.

From Insight to Action

In this chapter, we applied the Integral approach specifically to Agile Transformations. One of the primary uses of the framework is to get the "lay of the land" with respect to a given organization contemplating transformation. The "Insight to Action" sections within the discussions of each of the four quadrants provided a host of potential topics and questions that can form the basis of your customized assessment. And, as you remain in inquiry from a place of genuine curiosity, in awareness of your way of listening, and being grounded in presence, the use of the IATF can be a powerful tool to truly "see" your system and then respond from that place, choosing how you work with what you have become aware of from a systems perspective.

Our recommended action from this chapter is to begin putting together your own *Integral Organizational Assessment*, one that examines the organizational landscape from each quadrant perspective, as well as from any relevant holon levels in your organization. Wherever you currently are with your Agile Transformation (e.g., start, middle, reset) is okay; just capture what you see.

- Start with the reflection questions in the "Insight to Action" sections for each quadrant as inputs to your assessment—which for now will not include altitudes and specific developmental lines.

If those questions aren't useful in your specific context now, then come up with questions that you are curious about and resonate with your current challenges. For each quadrant (and considering the holons), make three columns and jot down relevant questions:

- Column 1: What are the *facts* (observable/known)?

- Column 2: What are the *assumptions* you are making?

- Column 3: What *research* do you want to do to check your assumptions and confirm your facts?

9

The Integral Disciplines: Focusing the Transformation

In part due to the neutrality and meta-framework quality of the IATF, when leaders and coaches understand it, they can almost feel as if there are too many options for its use. From one point of view, this extensibility of the framework is a clear strength; from another, it could be a limitation. Let's examine this issue in some detail to more fully understand how the IATF is constructed. To do so, we need to review the concepts of lines of development (outlined in Chapter 4) and Integral Disciplines (initially covered briefly in Part II).

Integral Disciplines and Developmental Lines

We have worked with *lines of development* in Chapter 4 and in the development of leadership in Part II (Reactive–Creative–Integral). This aspect of Integral thinking is related to our concept of Integral Disciplines. Within each quadrant, evolution happens from less complex consciousness structures (left-hand) or tangible structures (right-hand) to more complex ones—from Amber to Orange to Green to Teal. This evolution does not just happen in a generalized way within the quadrant but rather occurs specifically along one or more lines of development.

Howard Gardner (1983) originally articulated the idea of *multiple intelligences*—the notion that people cannot be adequately measured only in terms of their IQ (which taps into cognitive ability) but also in terms of a series of other types of intelligence (e.g., kinesthetic, spatial, interpersonal, spiritual, moral, cognitive, emotional, musical, logical-mathematical). The lines of development likewise reflect the fact that each of us has different levels of mastery in different areas of life; this is true of organizations as well. In Integral thinking generally, and in the IATF specifically, we take this notion and expand it to all four quadrants. That is, we identify the specific dimensions within that quadrant's domain that reveal what is growing or evolving. These levels are unlikely to match across quadrants or even within the same quadrant. This is similar to how a person can be high in mathematical intelligence but not as advanced in verbal intelligence, though both are I quadrant lines of development.

In an organizational transformation context, we might determine that there is a higher level of development needed in one quadrant or another—or on one line of development *within* a given quadrant rather than another—to achieve our desired outcomes. At this point, we have defined at least eight lines of development across the four quadrants in the IATF (detailed later in this chapter), and lines of development are also extensible: You might discover or define even more in your organizational environment. Thus, it will help to have a more specific focus for our actions rather than attempting to grow all lines equally. That's where the Integral Disciplines come in.

The Integral Disciplines help practitioners focus their use of the framework with a set of directional vectors—one from each quadrant perspective, plus one overarching vector on organizational change—that provides a specific direction and a progress focus to our actions and intentions in moving toward organizational agility. Each Integral Discipline is related to some number of lines of development. However, compared to a line of development, the Integral Discipline is

- Broader in its focus—since there is only one per quadrant

- Not necessarily measurable with a single tool, like a focused questionnaire

- Customizable to the organizational environment, in part by choosing which lines of development will be focused on for your agility goals

- Inherently action-oriented, implying a set of practices, strategies, and goals to make progress toward organizational agility

Integral Disciplines serve the purpose of providing the needed focus for the organizational effort. They also provide a structure in which outcome-creating leaders can stretch themselves into the Integral range of leadership performance, as we outlined in Part II. As when building new muscles, you must exercise them regularly, with a strategic plan for building strengths where you most desire. We introduce the Integral Disciplines as a way to build muscle; over time, these muscles get stronger and stronger until you notice they are developed in an entirely new form. In short, using the Integral Disciplines helps you develop your way of thinking and relate to challenges and life in a whole new way.

By utilizing these disciplines, we have a path to leverage the IATF as an organizational operating system to achieve the goal of organizational agility. We focus on four essential vectors (one within each of the four quadrants) plus the overarching discipline of Conscious Change. The IATF can be used in an infinite number of ways; the Integral Disciplines become a specific, economical way to prioritize and focus its use.

IATF Integral Disciplines

The Integral Disciplines are the handful of key organizational disciplines—that is, sets of Integral practices, perspectives, and goal matrices—that together lead an organization toward overall organizational agility. We have defined these five disciplines based on our transformation experiences, a deep reading of the Integral and organizational change literature, and a prioritization within each quadrant perspective of the highest leverage discipline (related to one or more developmental lines) that can help achieve the goal of organizational agility. Our work in Agile Transformations has highlighted the mismatch between where many organizations currently operate and where Agile intends for them to operate to realize the power of Agile more effectively. It is precisely this gap that we have to bridge to make progress. The Integral Disciplines focus our efforts and provide a kind of yardstick for moving toward our goal.

While each of the five disciplines is specific to a given quadrant, the development of one will likely have both interdependencies and impacts on the others. Thus, working on one discipline will require actions from the other quadrant perspectives and will have beneficial impacts on others. For instance, if I'm working on developing toward a desired culture (WE quadrant discipline), I will also likely need to raise the consciousness of individual people. Similarly, using co-creative practices to innovate will likely require a development or change of the organization's systems. Nevertheless, Evolving Systemic Complexity (to take one example) is a WE quadrant perspective and, with related developmental lines, and can be thought of separately.

The five Integral Disciplines are summarized briefly here:

- **Conscious Change:** A conscious and Integral approach to sustainable change.

- **Evolving Consciousness:** Growing the inner game of leadership.

- **Evolving Product Innovation:** Developing better products through engaging more systemic voices in product creation.

- **Evolving Systemic Complexity:** Maturing collective beliefs and mental models that create culture and relationships.

- **Evolving Adaptive Architectures:** Creating structures and systems that allow for better fit with a changing environment.

These disciplines are depicted graphically in Figure 9.1. Each Integral Discipline is defined in more detail in the following sections, along with its relevant lines of development.

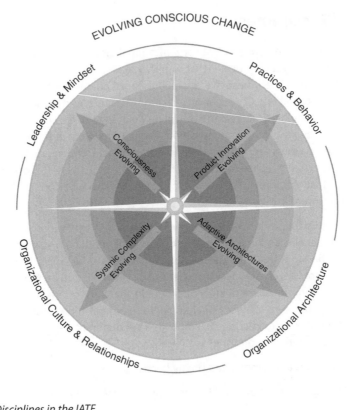

Figure 9.1
The five Integral Disciplines in the IATF

Integral Disciplines Mapped to Developmental Lines

We will now take a deep dive into each Integral Discipline, organized around a specific quadrant focus (except Conscious Change, which crosses all four quadrants); the Integral Disciplines create the singular focus for development within each quadrant in your path toward organizational agility. Based on our experience, we have defined one to three developmental lines as representative cases within each quadrant; these are lines we have found to be relevant to achieving organizational agility. The developmental lines defined within each quadrant help us understand the evolution of that perspective and what you might focus on growing within the relevant quadrant perspective. As we've said, many developmental lines potentially *could be* identified in a given quadrant, each moving from lesser to greater complexity. The IATF is a highly extensible system, so over time community input will likely help us define and articulate more developmental lines within the quadrants, based on experience. Of course, that option is always open to you as a practitioner to match your environment.

Evolving Conscious Change: Developing Your Approach

Agility means becoming so good at the process of change that it becomes your competitive advantage.

The essence of agility is the ability to respond quickly, to adapt to change and to what is emerging. To do this, organizations have to get good at going through change in a healthy way, which means paying attention to the human aspects of change. To that extent, it makes sense for our overarching Integral Discipline to be "Evolving Conscious Change." Conscious Change is brought in from our education, study, and experiences in organizational development (OD) and recognizing a need in the Agile industry to incorporate such thinking and approaches to our organizational transformation work.

The OD field has been evolving since the 1960s. Kurt Lewin established its foundations by providing the theoretical underpinnings that guide OD practice. Lewin's enduring legacy proved to be his innovative blend of science and practice. The practice of OD was built on a philosophy that emphasized collaboration as the pathway to individual and organizational growth. Some of the intervention approaches incorporated into OD work at that time included team building, quality of work life, surveys and feedback, action research, and sociotechnical systems, among other practices.

One classic definition of OD comes from Richard Beckhard's work, published in his book *Organization Development* (2013). Beckhard defined OD as a "planned organizational-wide effort, that is managed from the top to increase organization effectiveness and health through planned interventions in the organization's processes using behavioral-science knowledge" (p. 9).

While that definition and way of working may have been helpful to organizations in the 1960s, we know that it does not work in today's world of complexity. Therefore, we have incorporated updated concepts and approaches of OD in our work on organizational transformation for greater agility using an Integral perspective.

Integral Perspective to OD

Most leaders today recognize the importance of agility or, said another way, the capacity for organizational renewal and development. This is the very reason that agility is not a state that you reach and then are done forever. Organizations need to renew and develop themselves on an ongoing basis; they will go through change as long as the organization exists. Therefore, it is important for Agilists to have a solid understanding of the key forces involved in OD in a world of constant change and uncertainty. From an Integral perspective, we have a different view of change: OD is dynamic, and it does not work to take a linear "playbook approach" to move from your current state to your desired state. This approach works cyclically, responding to the complex adaptive behaviors and systems that emerge in organizations.

To summarize, the Integral Discipline of Evolving Conscious Change is an OD-based approach that helps us go beyond seeing Agile as "any change" to improve a part of the organization. Rather, Agile is an integrated holistic approach that addresses mindsets, culture, behaviors, skills, systems, structures, strategies, and tactics; interventions are formulated at an appropriate altitude level and apply behavioral science to how we consciously plan the development of our organizations. This conscious Integral approach to change considers how all parts of an organization relate to and impact each other, based on systems awareness, systems thinking, self-organization, social interactions, and tactical interventions.

> **Evolving Conscious Change:** To do this requires leaders to take a proactive (conscious), disciplined, and sustainable approach to organizational change, while holding the system as the client and working at all holon levels. Many organizations have multiple transformational or large change initiatives going on at once, using an uncoordinated or nonstrategic approach. The capacity for change in any organization is an important factor in the success of a transformation. Agile Transformations have largely been approached in a siloed fashion, driven by information technology, and lacking in co-creative partnerships with key parts of the organization, such as the business users, HR, change management, and others. Taking such a holistic and leader-driven approach to change pushes us to grow in multiple ways. The Conscious Change discipline moves us away from an autopilot, prescriptive change process, and toward a process that uses conscious thinking and planning, incorporating factors from all four quadrants and any relevant altitudes, using an intentional, structured, and disciplined approach.

> Many of the barriers to change that we encounter in our work with organizations result from the failure to take a conscious approach to the human elements of the change. For example, many organizations impose change on people, without considering their input, clarity about new roles, or capacity for change, given the other change initiatives currently under way. In doing so, they create a culture where employees feel as if the change was done "to them." By contrast, when an organization gets "really good at the process of change," the culture shifts toward co-creation in the change, and the change is experienced as coming "through them," rather than being done "to them."

This is the overarching Integral Discipline of evolving our approach to change to be conscious (rather than occurring as if on autopilot), disciplined, from an Integral OD perspective, addressing both the human and organizational aspects of change, and acknowledging the complexity of organizations to allow for emergence.

Michele's Take

I recently worked with leadership in a division of a large organization in the health care industry that had a wake-up call after a few instances where key products failed in the marketplace. Their ability to respond to their critical issues swiftly, safely, and effectively was paramount to their business. They needed to be able to move people around to where the work was needed and for people to develop capabilities in other product areas. They also needed more cross-functionality and less redundancy in business processes that spanned multiple products.

With the realization that they needed to change their way of working, they went about a big change effort; however, this was not an Agile Transformation in their minds: They didn't have enough exposure to Agile to know to do that, they just knew they needed some big changes. The overarching barrier to their change was the lack of a conscious approach to the transformational type of change they had to undergo. What they didn't understand, or know to address, were the human aspects of change and the conscious, intentional way to approach it. They were on autopilot, going about change in a formal corporate way that resulted in a new structure that was still not cross-functional: It was not aligned to a common goal, lacked clarity of roles, and led to unbalanced workloads, low employee morale, a decline in employee retention, and lack of engagement.

I tell my clients, the key to agility is to get really great at going through change. As an organization, learn to go through the process of change effectively, because that's what agility is all about.

Michael's Take

In my first Agile Transformation in a large telecom company, the approach to change was not a conscious one and led to both some useful learning and some regrettable consequences. In an organization of tens of thousands of people—and hundreds of development projects—there was a CIO-imposed mandate for all teams to move from year-plus release cycles to 90-day releases, virtually overnight. There was a lot of enthusiasm from some players, but no change team was formed, no real change strategy was developed, and no attempt was made to understand what it meant for the thousands of affected workers. Just the CIO's persistence drove the change. He made efforts to enlist his top lieutenants in making the change, but these vice presidents were not successful in further enrolling their direct reports in a meaningful way. The result was a general inability to make this transition (due to software architectural issues, in part), which led to rampant resistance, mostly in the form of whispers in private meetings and passive-aggressive compliance of most of the middle management ranks. That was combined with chaos among the teams, who did not truly know how to use the Agile practices; likewise, the managers did not understand how to manage self-organized teams. The task of leading the change was essentially delegated to a lower-level manager who understood Agile very well, but not organizational change. The bottom line: Out of a rather chaotic environment, there were some success stories of teams that adopted Agile but far more that struggled mightily. After the CIO left, the rest of the organization dropped Agile.

Evolving Consciousness: Developing Leadership and Mindset

One of the most foundational issues underlying many Agile Transformation failures is the mindset of organizational leaders and their ability to work with complexity within their complex adaptive systems. The ability to achieve organizational agility requires a higher level of leadership capacity than what the world has called for previously, one that works with leaders' internal meaning-making system. It is no longer enough to focus on horizontal development, such as training in strategy, business operations, domain expertise, and technical skills. Rather, leaders must consciously focus their attention on developing their internal capacity to meet external demands and to match the environment's complexity. Therefore, we have defined the I quadrant Integral Discipline as follows:

> **Evolving Consciousness:** Goes beyond training leaders and employees to work with the Outer Game and to provide skills and competencies that optimize how people function. That is, developing the Inner Game helps leaders become aware of and question their deeply held assumptions, beliefs, and values; how they got to where they are; and how they could change their way of thinking or making meaning as human adults. These ways of thinking and acting guide everyday actions but may also limit leaders, keeping them stuck in the status quo. For example, an arrogant, critical inner state is much more likely to trigger resistance or defensiveness in others; it will not serve to change the situation at all. In fact, it may even make matters worse. To move from the status quo to change, we must evolve the consciousness of individuals in the organization; that is, we must change the way they make meaning. We can go about this in a conscious, strategic, disciplined way, by utilizing vertical leadership developmental approaches (like 360-degree assessments, peer feedback, and leadership cohorts) to raise the average individual's order of consciousness across the organization.

As we saw in Part II, the internal operating system that most leaders have installed (problem-reacting tending toward outcome-creating) is not designed to lead change but rather to maintain the status quo. If we are to be successful in our transformation, raising the average level of consciousness is key. For this reason, we focus on only one line of development in the I quadrant, *orders of consciousness* (Figure 9.2). This distinction is primarily based on the work of Robert Kegan.

INTEGRAL AGILE TRANSFORMATION FRAMEWORK™

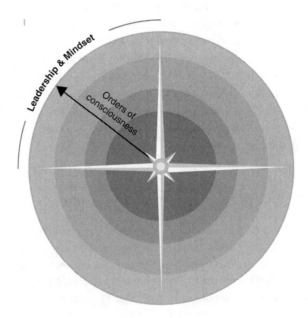

Figure 9.2
The Integral Agile Transformation Framework: development in the Leadership and Mindset quadrant

Developmental Line: Orders of Consciousness

The developmental line known as "orders of consciousness" does not map exactly to the Integral altitude colors; however, there is a strong directional correlation. Let's review three levels on the continuum, corresponding to each of the three major levels for adults (detailed in Part II).

- **Socialized mind:** Relationships with (and approval of) others are critical at the socialized mind level. At this level, one tends to be guided, or even controlled, by what others think, and how one is expected to fit in with peers, the team, profession, organization, family, and others. A major fear of the socialized mind is losing favor with the tribe. The socialized mind is found in the Amber altitude and in some stages of Orange thinking and even into the Green level. Almost 60% of adults are centered at this order of mind (or below). This is the internal operating system of maintaining the status quo (problem-reacting) rather than driving change. Therefore, if we are interested in catalyzing transformation, we need to help leaders develop beyond this order of mind.

- **Self-authoring mind:** Individuals with a self-authoring mind can consider the opinions and expectations of others, then decide what to do for themselves, working from an *internal locus of control*. They have their own internal compass and are self-directed, independent thinkers. At this level, I can choose how to lead or respond, based on circumstances and what I am trying to achieve rather than on whether people will like me or whether I can stay in control. People at this order of mind are subject to their own personal philosophy or ideology: They cannot see it as object but rather see through it (like the proverbial fish in water). A leader operating at this level can drive change and is therefore the minimal level for success in an organizational transformation. Self-authoring is most associated with the more mature Orange into Green levels.

- **Self-transforming mind:** Individuals with a self-transforming mind are able to take a step back from authoring their own thinking and question their own and others' ideologies: considering them, critiquing them, questioning them. What am I missing? What am I assuming that may not be true? and other self-challenging questions are asked when we develop to this level. This is the thinking exhibited by *catalyst* leaders (Joiner & Josephs, 2007), who begin to focus not just on getting results but also on creating environments—cultures—that generate results, aligned around a common vision. A very small percentage (approximately 5%) of the population is stably functioning at this self-transforming level and is in the Teal range. A leader at this level is an ideal choice to lead an Agile Transformation.

Implications   The implications should by now be clear. Simply put, if your goal is organizational agility, you will not be able to do this from a socialized mind foundation. We have seen this mismatch over and over again in our transformation work. Navigating your organization through the waters of transformational change requires an upgrade to your internal operating system or your order of mind, as we saw in Part II. Transformational change can only be led with capacities that come from both the self-authoring and self-transforming minds. For example, I may have a clear vision in my mind for the transformation strategy (self-authoring), but I don't just stop there and tell people to implement my vision. Instead, I take on aspects of a self-transforming mindset, share this vision with others, and then inquire as to how others see this. This process of advocacy and inquiry leads to a new shared, unified vision—which most likely is different from the original. With this self-transforming mindset, I had the ability to step back and objectively look at my vision, fully aware that my thinking is limited or partial and that it is actually co-creation that produces a compelling organizational vision for transformation. This is true for us as transformational leaders and for the overall leadership culture out of which leaders in the transformation operate.

A further implication is the need for taking an Integral perspective—for looking from all four quadrants' points of view. A socialized mind is unable (and not even aware of the need) to consider multiple perspectives. All challenges we see in Agile Transformations are more fully addressed by taking an Integral perspective, since solving for something in only one quadrant doesn't fully address the problem at its root. Looking at all four quadrants is a kind of systems thinking competency that gets to the underlying dynamics and mental models—and the shifting of mental models is how transformation can actually occur.

We must start this journey by becoming aware of our own leadership effectiveness and our impact and then develop ourselves to grow our effectiveness. We aren't able to help others if our level of thinking lacks the capability to see where the "other" is coming from and if we are unable to take their perspective. In essence, if we don't work on ourselves first and upgrade our thinking, it is likely that we will hold others back and hinder the change that needs to happen. When we do work with others to develop, we can inspire them to grow themselves, and maybe even guide them, depending on our experience and training.

Insight to Action: Evolving Consciousness

Turning now to action, we note that the singular focus of the Integral Discipline of Evolving Consciousness is assessing and growing the level of mind prevalent in the organization generally, within the senior leadership of the organization being transformed, and within the change team established to lead the transformation. From our discussion in Part II, recall that the transformational leader role is one that requires a significant level of development. The most effective expression of the transformational leader role (including enterprise Agile coaches) is achieved from the Teal altitude, where all other altitudes are valued and respected. This self-transformational person is able to work at all levels, in all four quadrants, in a conscious way. Such leaders do not force things that are not ready to happen; they are able to talk within the value frames of people and organizations at whatever level they find themselves. Using some of the practices in Part II—getting feedback on your leadership, mindfulness/meditation/prayer, shadow work, journaling, awareness practices, and specific practices for developmental lines such as emotional, spiritual, and moral—will grow your own leadership. You can, of course, also use these practices to help others develop.

- What might you do to grow the collective level of consciousness in your organization? For example, might you establish leadership cohorts, where leaders provide each other support, peer coaching, and accountability for growth? Or perhaps a full-blown leadership development program that involves multiple methods (360-degree assessments, detailed feedback, workshops) that make vertical development an organizational focus?

- What do you believe your current "order of consciousness" is, generally speaking? Where do you believe you are on the Reactive–Creative–Integral spectrum? What about your boss? The transformation sponsor?

Evolving Product Innovation: Developing Practices and Behaviors

Developing products (and services) is a fundamental focus of an Agile Transformation. Growing or maturing this function is the core of the IT quadrant Integral Discipline, which we define as follows:

> **Evolving Product Innovation:** When an organization moves to using Agile practices, that shift requires moving from goal-centric practices (such as waterfall programming) to customer-centric ones; this shift is more or less built naturally into Agile thinking and practices. If you are not there, you must move to this customer-centric position. But if the goal is not just doing Agile well but attaining organizational agility, then an organization must go beyond a customer-centric focus to an organization-centric approach to product creation, which involves transcending and including. In an organization-centric approach, all voices of the system need to be represented. A brand-driven organization is an example of an organization-centric approach. With a brand-driven approach, you include all stakeholders, such as marketing, product development, the customer, and the organization's purpose/original brand. When the organization believes in its brand and joins together in a co-creative process, using solid Lean and design thinking methods and Agile practices, then dramatic improvements in business results, customer satisfaction, and innovative designs become possible. Using this orientation stretches us as leaders, pushing us to work across organizational boundaries, to *see as* those different groups if we are to become effective in creating synergies with the natural diversity of an organizational system.
>
> For example, in the current COVID-19 pandemic, businesses in all industries and of all sizes have had to quickly respond to challenges never before experienced. The only way to achieve a successful response was to let go of the attachment to bureaucracy, strict regulations, wasteful processes, internal politics, and divisive mindsets and come together to collaborate and co-create the solutions needed.

Although Agile implementations have focused most heavily in this quadrant, we have seen there is a developmental mismatch between existing organizational practices and genuine Agile practices, even for those already "doing" Agile. From this viewpoint, to truly achieve organizational agility requires that we evolve the thinking and doing behind our innovation practices, moving from process- or goal-focused, through customer-focused, and into organization-focused innovation. Here's what we see happening in our Agile Transformation experience:

- Practices are typically "installed." As a consequence, we don't see the intended behaviors but something that might resemble them (e.g., going through the motions or even performing them dysfunctionally).

- When the intended behaviors don't show up, the desired results aren't achieved (and people declare, "Agile doesn't work!"). This problem can appear in many places, perhaps being most glaringly obvious in the area of collaboration skills, where people often don't have the underlying EQ capacity to make collaboration work (you have to *want* to know another person's point of view before you can use good listening skills).

- Technical practices are often seen as optional or something the organization will get to later ("after we conquer this whole Scrum thing!"), but they are essential for a strong product innovation function.

- Organizations are moving from waterfall programming to Agile approaches (we call this a *goal-centric* to *customer-centric* movement), yet still are not fully able to make the customer a central focus or integrated with the Agile teams.

- Achieving true organizational agility requires moving from just a team-level and delivery-level focus to an organization-centric approach, where all voices are included and part of the Agile Transformation.

In the "Practices and Behaviors" area, we will define three developmental lines (of many possible) that can be worked on to help us evolve product innovation. As shown in Figure 9.3, these three lines focus on (1) *technical craftsmanship competency*, related to effective engineering practices; (2) *product development practices*, related to creating products and services valued by customers; and (3) *human relating* behaviors and skills, which reflect the ability to demonstrate social–emotional intelligence (EQ) and engage in effective human interactions, especially collaboration. Notice that the IT quadrant includes three developmental lines, while only one appears in the I quadrant. For us, the *orders of consciousness* line is rather all encompassing; growing it enables a great deal in the "Leadership and Mindset" domain. By comparison, the "Practices and Behaviors" domain is more heterogeneous; to do justice to the subject matter of product innovation requires a focus on multiple lines, from innovation to technical to people skills.

INTEGRAL AGILE TRANSFORMATION FRAMEWORK™

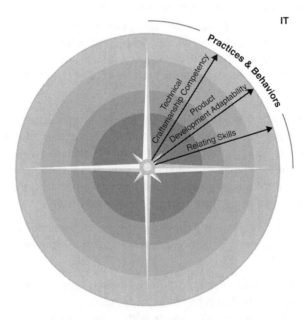

Figure 9.3
The Integral Agile Transformation Framework: development in the Practices and Behaviors quadrant

Developmental Line: Product Development Adaptability

The *Product Development Adaptability* line refers to the process for developing products and services and their fitness for use by customers, their responsiveness to environmental conditions (such as markets—whether internal or external), and their adaptability for future change. Rather than attempt a definitive mapping (which would be somewhat subjective) of attributes at each altitude, we will provide a directionality and sequence to the line, anchoring what is at the Amber (lower complexity) end of the spectrum, what is somewhere in the middle, and what is toward the Teal end.

At one extreme of Product Development Adaptability—the Amber end—product development follows a phased process and relies on process direction rather than customer input, often beginning with a high-level requirements specification that is obtained by a customer proxy (like a business analyst); if you are a developer or tester, you likely never talk to a customer. As a member of a team, you largely work with members of your own function and are not truly cross-functional. You fulfill your part of the process and give the results to your manager. Your project manager may be called a Scrum Master or Agile coach, but they're still a project manager.

In the middle of the continuum—between Orange and Green—we are moving from being focused on the product as a goal (schedule, cost, scope) to being focused on the customer and hearing their voice. *Lean Start-up* (Ries, 2011) is a method firmly in the customer-centric band, centered on build–measure–learn feedback loops informed by interactions with real (or potential) customers. Instead of developing fully realized products or services, product management determines a *minimum viable product (MVP)*—the bare minimum needed to determine the viability of a product—and builds upon that. Just as a fully functioning Agile team will release small pieces of potentially shippable product increments at the end of any given iteration, so product management releases small pieces of potentially viable product increments to customers, or potential customers, to test that viability. This is what the *Agile Fluency* model calls the Optimizing level (Larsen & Shore, 2018).

At the other end of the continuum—toward the Teal end—product creation is an organization-centric activity. To achieve true organizational agility, we are moving beyond the team and program delivery aspect of Agile to an organization-wide view of how products are co-created by all the players in the organization, including customers. Here we are concerned with the customer, but we also focus on our organization's mission and purpose, its brand, and how all stakeholder views contribute to the products and services produced. Boundary-spanning practices that extend beyond the delivery function to other areas in the organization are essential in this new paradigm.

Michael's Take

A transformation client I worked with in the financial services industry had quite a sophisticated product development process that included how the portfolio was managed. Two specific practices were used: (1) a *product council* that weighed in on overall priorities for a major system with lots of internal customers and (2) the way in which the vice president of product development performed *portfolio rebalancing*, optimized for the whole organization.

Before the transformation initiative, the product council was really a committee, where different internal customer groups came to argue for their share of development bandwidth, so as to make the changes they wanted for their users (classic "us versus them" thinking prevailed). By introducing a new practice and a neutral facilitator, the overriding question to each person on the council became "What are the most important changes to make for the good of the organization overall?" This question had an elevating effect on the discussions, leaving people unable (with a straight face) to argue for their own parochial interests against what clearly made sense for the whole business. This outcome would not have occurred if we had used a different practice—for instance, if not all the groups had been present at the same time, which made sure the social conscience of everyone was evoked; or if the question were asked in a way that attacked a given proposal (perhaps to promote a competing proposal), rather than from a neutral point of view by a facilitator.

The second practice—portfolio rebalancing—was done by the chief product owner (a business vice president) and his staff, who put together and regularly updated business cases for products in flight. Rather than just allow products that were a success to continue with their annual funding allotment, he continued to look at what was the best use of the money for the business as a whole, which meant at times rebalancing the portfolio in unexpected ways. Funds were moved to the product that could have the greatest benefit to the business right now rather than when the products were originally funded. Since the delivery teams had prioritized the most important work first, that meant that value creation was front-loaded on projects, and the organization overall won out.

Developmental Line: Relating Skills

The *Relating Skills* line refers to the degree to which individuals are skillful in social interactions and communication, including collaborating together, treating each other with respect, and being able to work on teams in a productive manner. The emotional intelligence (EQ) aspect relevant here is not the internal capacity (an I quadrant perspective) that enables seeing and managing emotions but rather the behavioral skills, or competencies, that represent enacting that internal capacity through actual behaviors. Ideally, we will have both the internal capacity *and* the behavioral competence. Such skills can be taught in various kinds of collaboration and interpersonal skill training. These competencies parallel the related sense of self in the I quadrant—and, in fact, require I quadrant development to be able to successfully enact them.

For instance, we can enact the behavior as best we can, the way that we've been taught. Perhaps we are achieving consensus on our team and enacting the behaviors involved in the practice of consensus, while not actually having the fully corresponding internal awareness and maturity that supports this practice: truly valuing other people's perspective and being willing to give up our own opinion at times. In the process of enacting the behaviors as best we can, we may actually experience an "aha moment"; this becomes the spark that ignites us to embrace a different level of thinking. And the same is true in reverse: We may have the requisite internal complexity (i.e., valuing others' perspectives) without having the behavioral skills to actually be good at collaborating, such as asking good questions, making "yes, and" moves, and so forth.

Let's define the continuum of this dimension in the Relating Skills area. Think about some relating skills that are critical for Agile to be successful, such as conversation/dialogue, caring connection with others, interpersonal intelligence, and mentoring and developing others. At one extreme— toward the Amber end—individuals tend to have conversations that are oriented toward role con- formance rather than being authentic or personal. Crucial conversations may be either avoided or unskillful, as people are unable to fully articulate difficult messages in a meaningful way. Mentoring and developing would look more like teaching or training someone in the process (as opposed to coaching, for instance). Having caring connections would likely be out of the scope of the person's role or need: "I'm not here to make friends," the person might say. The level of interpersonal intel- ligence lacks skill in eliciting, or even recognizing, the perspectives of others, especially when these differ from the authority-sanctioned perspective of the Amber believer. You can clearly see how this Relating Skills developmental line would pose challenges on Agile teams and why there is quite a bit of developmental coaching needed here.

In the middle of the continuum—more in the Orange area—conversation tends to be positional: One person advocates for their view, and the other person advocates for their position. We would experience rushed conversations and multitasking in meetings—in short, a whole lot of talking but not a lot of listening. The mindset is that there is something you need to get accomplished, and "collaborating" with people is the only way in which to get it done. This creates a competitive envi- ronment that lends itself to siloes across the organization, with people protecting their positions. Interpersonal intelligence is again instrumental. We know how to influence people to achieve our goal but don't really take their perspective fully. We mentor and develop others to propagate our way of doing things and to extend our reputation. Generally speaking, we don't have fine-tuned relating skills at this level, because that's not what is important to us.

At the other end of the continuum—the Teal end—individuals engage in more skillful communica- tion and interaction. Among the skills we recognize on this line is an individual's ability to (1) skill- fully *inquire*—to genuinely seek out the thoughts and feelings of others; (2) skillfully *advocate*—to state one's views in ways that allow others to both understand and then question them; (3) balance *advocacy* and *inquiry*—to have the right balance of inquiry and advocacy; and (d) skillfully *frame* a given conversation—that is, to make the context or background of the conversation explicit for oth- ers. More advanced skills involve sensing group dynamics and energy and being able to respond effectively to what one is sensing (what CRR refers to as *Relationship Systems Intelligence*). We recog- nize the need to extend our reach to include more voices in the system, with keen awareness that it is the entire body of the organization co-creating its products and services.

Developmental Line: Technical Craftsmanship Competency

The *Technical Craftsmanship Competency* line refers to the degree to which organizations effectively adopt and integrate the most advanced technical practices, principles, and management strategies in the service of technical agility, including technical engineering practices such as dev-ops, con- tinuous delivery, management of technical debt, continuous integration, test-driven development

(TDD), the latest design thinking practices, and emergent architecture and software and tools. The degree to which technical craftsmanship is developed is highly correlated to the level of agility an organization can achieve. Keep in mind that each developmental line within a quadrant is assessed and then given priority for developmental interventions based on your ultimate goal as an organization. Too often we have seen technical practices seen as the "next step" in the Agile Transformation but not given the same priority as adhering to Scrum practices, for instance.

At one end of this continuum—toward the Amber end—the process is designed so that developers get a design specification before coding starts. Emergent design is not a concept but rather a design spec, expecting full detail on both requirements and design before coding begins. Process means "following the rules" of the department or the boss. Procedures are written to protect the specialty, not cross-functional responsibilities, since mixing different job roles becomes confusing. The practices convey more of an "expert" mindset. Coding and testing are clearly separated, since that is the fault line between the respective departments. Testing happens as a rigid, formal hand-off process, with clear sign-offs holding people responsible before marking the transition.

As the continuum moves into the Orange range, the process becomes less procedural and more individualistic. Developers have more latitude to give their best efforts, which leads to competition and, at worst, showboating. However, it allows for developers to tap into their creativity and come up with innovative solutions. Agile practices that ask developers to work with testers during the process of developing the code are not readily accepted, since this may expose a developer's weaknesses or mistakes. Developers are more apt to want to perfect their code before sharing it. This causes problems for Agile teams when they are attempting to limit their work in progress by carrying one story to completion (swarming stories). The end result is a bottleneck that arises when testing is done at the very end of the sprint. Worse yet, stories are carried over to the next sprint. Add to that the fact that there are typically many more developers than testers. At this level, shared code ownership, code reviews, and pair programming are not popular practices. Technical agility requires development and operations teams to work together, and at this level it is not practical because they are more concerned with their own achievement and not crossing boundaries.

At the other side of the continuum—toward the Green to Teal[1] end—technical practices tend to favor collaboration and emergent design:

- There is not such a focus on role specialization, so that testers (if there are any) learn to code and coders learn to test (this results in what are sometimes referred to as T-shaped individuals, who are broad and deep).

- An architectural runway is considered before coding begins to create an emergent architecture that is not too much to constrain current work and not too little.

- Design thinking work is shared with teams on an ongoing basis, not just at the end of the design team's work.

- Code is considered a shared resource, not an individual one, so the team follows coding standards because code is owned by the community, not by individuals.

- Developers share code early in the sprint, in transparency and in collaboration with testing, rather than "perfecting the code" before allowing others to see it.

- Pair and mob programming are viable practices owing to the realization that crowd-sourced ideas are often the best ideas.

- The long-term and systemic effects of the code are considered, such as involving the operations group early in the process (dev-ops), so that operations and development are in collaboration rather than waiting for a hand-off at the end.

- Refactoring is done regularly and as a matter of craftsman's pride; it's what creates quality.

- Testing is done in a production-like environment early in the process—during the sprints, for example.

- Release management practices are fitted to the organization's culture and to the needs of the stakeholders and are not tied to a rigid cadence or bureaucratic procedures.

A powerful model for understanding how organizations can mature in their use of Agile is the *Agile Fluency* model developed by James Shore and Diana Larsen (2018).

Michael's Take

I worked with a client in the publishing industry who had really strong technical craftsmanship practices and values. Delivery teams adhered to all the technical practices with almost a religious fervor, such that people felt strong confidence in the quality of their products, and this was borne out by their results. When developers were hired, the interviewing and selection practices were carried out primarily by technical people, not managers, assembled by the tech lead and his or her best developers. This sent a strong message culturally as well as in terms of the value of craftsmanship. It also created a strong daily focus for the delivery teams, who had a healthy sense of agency since they were not mere order takers for the product owner but rather were true technical craftsmen.

Insight to Action: Evolving Product Innovation

Let's quickly examine how you might begin thinking about these issues in your organization. The three developmental lines come together in the overall discipline of Evolving Product Innovation. Recall the definition of this discipline: To achieve organizational agility, we must go beyond a customer-centric focus to an organization-centric approach in such a way that all voices of the system are represented in service of product creation. A brand-driven organization is an example of an organization-centric philosophy. With a brand-driven approach, you include all stakeholders.

- The overarching intent is to get better at product innovation, with Product Development, Relating Skills, and Technical Craftsmanship being three critical ways to attain more adaptive innovation. The reason for deciding to focus on any one of the three over the others is the projected impact on your innovation adaptability. It will help to begin considering what is true in your organization. What would likely be the impact on innovation if you emphasize enhancing technical practices in your organization? This is particularly likely if the code is brittle and there is a high total cost of ownership.

- How about the impact of working on developing collaboration skills and practices? This will especially be relevant if there is a heavy silo mentality and a lack of boundary-spanning activity in your organization.

- Or is the biggest lever in developing the product development process itself? This may especially be true if you have not fully landed at a customer-centric level—the focus of Agile frameworks. In any case, the overall focus is on enhancing innovation.

Evolving Adaptive Architectures: Developing Organizational Architecture

Agile is about delivering real value to the customer. To deliver value while using Agile practices as a means of product creation, we need to have visibility of our value streams and the flow of value. This includes both the way communication and human processes create process cycle inefficiency, or waste, and the way in which bottlenecks in the workflow have a negative impact on the human system. Further, the greater the adaptability of an organization's structures and systems, the greater the likelihood of achieving organizational agility. Thus, we have defined the ITS-oriented Integral Discipline as follows:

> **Evolving Adaptive Architectures:** Designing and implementing organizational structures, governance, and policies that optimize flow, value creation, and human well-being is the direction of this discipline. Using design thinking skills, understanding and recognizing systemic effects in bottlenecks and governance logjams, and reorganizing in a way that creates changeable structures that adapt to changing market conditions all enable organizational agility. A company unable to organize around value streams will have a significant impediment toward realizing efficient flow. The Achievement-Orange level tends to make organizational structure and "reorgs" into a political game of territory acquisition rather than a rational, structural design activity to enable legitimate business goals, like flow. We must navigate around these reactive tendencies to enable greater adaptability in our policies and structures. Achieving this goal is highly dependent on our shared mental models and beliefs (WE quadrant).

We will focus on two key points of development within the "Organizational Architecture" (ITS) quadrant that drive the creation of adaptive architectures. *Structural Adaptability* relates to the flexibility and ability to change organizational structures, and *Flow-ability* focuses on how work and processes flow within the organization. These are depicted in Figure 9.4.

INTEGRAL AGILE TRANSFORMATION FRAMEWORK™

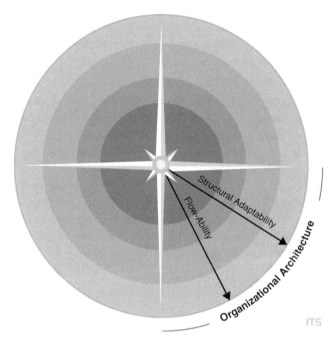

Figure 9.4

The Integral Agile Transformation Framework: development in the Organizational Architecture quadrant

First, let's define what we mean by the term *organizational structure*. It includes the concept of an organizational chart and whether it is hierarchical, matrix, circular, flat, or a lattice. In addition, it includes how teams are staffed (e.g., from a functional pool, through managers' recruitment of members, based on seniority, by individuals choosing their team from job postings); how projects, programs, and other organizational units are governed; how business units are divided (e.g., by product, by territory, by historical acquisition); whether they are product or project structured; how funding happens (e.g., annually, quarterly, at what level of the organization); and related topics that manifest the social structure of the organization. Given this broadened definition, we can describe the developmental line related to organizational structure.

Developmental Line: Structural Adaptability

Structural Adaptability refers to ways in which a given organization tends to organize the structures and systems by which things actually get done and how adaptable those structures are to changing business conditions. It considers the needs of people in the system, changes in the market, innovations in technology, the changing governmental regulation landscape, and any other pertinent environmental conditions.

On one extreme—toward the Amber end of the scale—structures and systems are organized in ways that emphasize the preservation of organizational functions in a pyramid-style hierarchy. Budgeting is done on a function-by-function basis; employees report up through a single functional reporting chain; workflows that cross boundaries encounter (often lengthy) hand-offs and negotiations; functional priorities trump the priorities of the work itself. Structures and systems also tend to be relatively static and immutable. Decision making happens at the top and goes through the process chain, usually involving long delays. The structure is rigid and does not take into account the importance of customers and products.

At the middle of the developmental scale, structural changes are based on the project or on who is in charge, with frequent reorgs occurring when a new leader wants to put his or her stamp on things. As there is a greater focus on customer needs, projects and customer-oriented structures are empowered, leading to competition between them and the functions—for budgeting, for resources, and for governance control. Organizations at the Orange level will hire based on candidates' skill set, expertise, and competence to best fulfill customer needs, so hiring is typically decided by a combination of HR (as the competency experts) and the hiring manager. Decision making is a bit more pragmatic and happens in a more business-oriented way, considering who owns the customer. Even so, there are still fairly lengthy delays involved. The structure is less rigid—it is more flexible in responding to big changes in market conditions—but remains tied to individual executives maintaining control.

In the context of an Agile Transformation, this is the place where scaled frameworks often show up, as a way to map the existing organizational structure to the Agile implementation. The structure of Scrum, by design, has no real mechanism for the components of a modern company outside the delivery team, whereas scaled frameworks provide a sort of on-ramp to the company's existing structure. The downside can be the muting of internal pressure to help the organization become more adaptive and to truly reach organizational agility.

In the Green to Teal range, the organizational structure is more flexible and better able to change regularly as needed, adapting to business circumstances as well as the needs of the people doing the work. Structures and systems are organized in ways that strengthen and emphasize broader systemic interrelations and local needs—in other words, they are systemic. Budgeting is designed to support broader institutional initiatives and tends to follow business processes and local decision making rather than hierarchical position. Employees are mobile, in terms of reporting structure and functional affiliation: They go where their own inspiration as well as the needs of the work lie. Interfunctional boundaries are far more porous, requiring minimal hand-offs and ceremonies. There are no structures or policies that prevent people from directly interacting with the person most relevant to the needs of their work. Hiring more often includes the people directly impacted (the team), who may even be empowered to make the decision. Generally speaking, structures and systems favor broader organizational *adaptability*, responding to both business and human needs. Organizational structures and systems are designed such that they can be changed or adjusted with relative ease. This creates conditions that permit greater decision-making flexibility and strategic malleability.

Developmental Line: Flow-ability

The second developmental line is about processes and the flow of customer-valuable work throughout the organization. *Flow-ability* refers to ways in which a given organization organizes and manages workflows and processes, and how value flows and is created. By "flow," we mean the ability of work, decisions, communication, and other business process components to move throughout the organization with minimal levels of friction or waste (in the Lean sense).

At one extreme of flow-ability—the Amber to Orange end—workflows are based on a push model. Products and services originate internally. That is, budgets are established, release dates are defined, and product design is set internally and then pushed along the value stream until the product or service eventually reaches its end-goal, whether that is an external customer or an internal stakeholder; customers are almost an afterthought. Individual workflows are optimized, often along functional or lines of business, apart from the greater, institutional flow, often leading to more hand-offs and bottlenecks. One outcome is that organizations tend to manage a great number of flows in parallel, creating the need for human behaviors (IT quadrant) and organizational structures to be optimized (or sub-optimized) to deal with the resultant multitasking—which also results in an enormous number of sources of waste and thrashing. Generally speaking, lots of projects are typically in progress at one time to accommodate the needs of stakeholders all vying for top priority for their project.

At the other extreme—Teal end—optimizing flow (Leaning out waste) is the top priority. Thus, workflows are visualized, cycle time is measured, the flow is experimented with, and bottlenecks are addressed, all in the service of optimizing flow. A great deal of management attention is given to managing the overall flow, which is favored over locally optimized flows. Principles like those in Lean start-up and customer development (Eric Ries and Steve Blank) inform management's relationship to matching internal capacity to the customer's real wants. A governance structure like Holacracy is consistent with this type of decentralized, local decision making and monitoring, based on interests and expertise, rather than on organizational position. In a Teal organization, there is a heightened awareness of and attention to what is blocking the flow of value, such that Leaning out waste is a conscious and habitual activity. In contrast, at lower levels on this line of development, the focus is often too strongly on politics or other organizational distractions to fully pay attention to value flow.

Insight to Action: Evolving Adaptive Architectures

As we consider how to put this Integral Discipline into action, we recall the definition of adaptive architectures: designing and implementing organizational structures, governance, and policies that optimize flow, value creation, and human well-being. This single discipline allows us to determine where optimization is most needed—the flexibility and fit-for-purpose attributes of structures and governance, or the focus on flow attributes, or both.

- Within your organization, how visible is the flow of value? Are there measurements around bottlenecks? Are value streams mapped with performance data? Is throughput measured?

- How adaptable are organizational structures, systems, policies, and governance? What triggers a change—a dire crisis, a new vice president, or a business opportunity? Are such structures rigid, or do they allow flexibility?

- Clearly, flow and adaptability affect each other, and there is a tight correlation with culture (WE), as the structures of an organization are, generally speaking, a manifestation of the collective mindset of leadership. How can you leverage this interconnection?

Evolving Systemic Complexity: Developing Organizational Culture and Relationships

Perhaps the biggest mismatch that shows up when Agile is introduced is the discrepancy between a culture in which Agile thrives and the organizational culture into which it is actually introduced. When you undertake an Agile Transformation, there isn't always a realization that your existing culture likely has to change, but that issue becomes painfully visible if it's not addressed at the outset. We therefore defined the WE-oriented Integral Discipline as follows:

> **Evolving Systemic Complexity:** Designing, shifting, and shaping the organization's collective set of beliefs, mores, mental models, and so forth in the direction of—and to create a hospitable environment for—organizational agility, in terms of both culture and interpersonal relationships. For instance, a solidly Achievement-Orange culture is unlikely to tolerate the authentic use of Agile methods. Evolving systemic complexity here would mean growing from Achievement-Orange to Pluralistic-Green thinking and acting. A related notion is the complexity of relationships, from transactional to fully human ones. Treating people as people, rather than as "resources," is an evolution of systemic complexity.

Catalyzing systemic complexity frequently requires shifting the overall organizational vision, business goals, and way of being. As a leadership team examines their own mental models and the effectiveness of their relationship systems, they are pushed into more Integral ways of relating: taking the perspective of others, seeing their own meaning making, confronting the group shadow, and seeing the systemic effects of the group conscience. As leaders help evolve the culture, they naturally come up against the inside of their meaning making and are forced to confront their assumptions, cherished beliefs, and jointly held mental models about the world and what the system needs to do culturally to exist. At this point, we have the opportunity to create a deliberately developmental culture, where evolving consciousness—on both an individual level and a collective level—is valued in the organization alongside achieving business results.

We have identified two developmental lines from the WE perspective: *Cultural Complexity* and *Systemic Consciousness*.

Culture is an issue that senior leadership will need to own at some point, or organizational agility will not be realized; you can't get there only with the practices and the frameworks. Due to the centrality of this issue, the first developmental line in WE is *Cultural Complexity*, which refers to the predominant values, belief structures, and mental models that constitute an organization's culture (essentially, the Laloux/Spiral Dynamics distinctions of Amber, Orange, Green, and Teal).

The second developmental line, *Systemic Consciousness*, is a bit more complex to explain. Agile is all about relationships. Consequently, for Agile to be successful, the quality of relationships is a critical factor. Low trust, high competition, lack of respect, an us-versus-them mentality, and a culture of fear all create barriers to collaborating across organizational boundaries. Since these modes of being-in-relationship are not, in fact, natural to us as humans but rather an artifact of the way our society and organizations have evolved, there's an awakening that needs to happen. Ensuring that Agile is fully effective requires developmental work around relationships and the way that we collectively create culture in the first place; this developmental work requires an expansion of consciousness, which we call *systemic consciousness*.

Depicted in Figure 9.5 are these two focal points of development within the "Organizational Culture and Relationships" (WE) quadrant: cultural complexity (related to its values structure) and the level of systemic consciousness (related to consciousness of the collective at different holon levels).

INTEGRAL AGILE TRANSFORMATION FRAMEWORK™

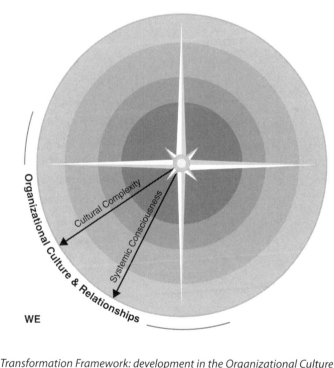

Figure 9.5
The Integral Agile Transformation Framework: development in the Organizational Culture and Relationships quadrant

Developmental Line: Cultural Complexity

Cultural complexity refers to the predominant values, belief structures, and mental models that constitute an organization's culture. In Spiral Dynamics, the term *value meme* is used to describe an organization's collective mindset, which acts as a kind of attractor (in the chaos sense) that helps create specific value-laden artifacts, symbols, and habits. These can include everything from the style of corporate space (cool cafes with couches), to the corporate cuisine (from healthy chef-prepared meals to cafeteria style), to how remote working is addressed (the latest technology tools), to how talent is acquired. When we are looking at an organization's existing culture, there are many indicators that can help us understand its current way as an organization and how that will impact the transformational work—for example, the decision-making processes, the ways in which conflict is managed, the corporate atmosphere and how politics are at play, and more. (We also discussed the leader's role in culture in Part II.)

Rather than just providing a range of what this developmental line looks like, here we have specific research documenting each level. Table 9.1 shows what this developmental line looks like at each of the four altitudes, from a cultural, WE point of view, distilling the material from Chapter 3.

Table 9.1   The Integral Agile Transformation Framework: Cultural Complexity Summary

Altitude	Core Values	Patterns	Beliefs/Mental Models
Amber	Certainty	Hierarchical organizing	We know absolute truth; it's our duty to follow it.
	Order	Authority-centric	Right action is following the rules.
	Duty	Absolutistic (even rigid)	People work best within clear structures.
Orange	Achievement	Strategic organizing	The most deserving are given the most rewards.
	Autonomy	Results-centric	Right action is pragmatic.
	Empiricism	Exploiting opportunities	People must be given freedom to achieve.
Green	Pluralism	Egalitarian organizing	The best answers come from a diversity of views.
	Affiliation	Relationship-centric	Right action is based on our values.
	Harmony	Bottom-up action	Everyone deserves the right to be heard.
Teal	Respect for systems	Self-organizing	We balance what we do with the environment.
	Interdependence	Purpose-centric	Right action is for the common good.
	Emergent	Wisdom beyond ego	People must follow their inner compass.

When our goal is to move an organization to achieve agility, its culture must evolve more toward the Green or Teal range. If we manage to move to the Teal perspective, the culture looks highly independent but with an underlying desire to collaborate and learn from others, particularly in the interest of finding the best ideas. There is strong satisfaction in solving complex problems, a drive to come up with elegant solutions that satisfy multiple stakeholders, and an unwillingness to conform to traditional forms of governance, organizational structure, or management practices throughout the enterprise.

Developmental Line: Systemic Consciousness

Recall how in the I quadrant perspective, the primary mode is consciousness; we can further qualify that this is consciousness from an individual level. In WE—which is about the collective—there is also a form of consciousness, but it is on the group level, the next holon up from an individual. Because this consciousness is centered on various systems—teams, departments, organizations—we refer to the second developmental line in this quadrant as *Systemic Consciousness*. This line is related to left-hand systems thinking. Systemic consciousness could be described as how the system—team, group, or organization—makes sense of its world: what its rules are, how one remains in good standing within the community, what it values, and what it believes.

What does it mean to experience consciousness at the system level? Here's an example many of us have experienced: We join a meeting late, and we sense that there is a tension in the room, even if we weren't there to witness what created the tension originally. Have you had that feeling? This kind of perception happens when we tap into the systemic consciousness present in the meeting, the consciousness of the group holon, rather than of a specific individual. The tension is in the room; you could "cut it with a knife," as the saying goes.

Systemic consciousness also shows up as the unspoken rules of behavior—even though no one has explicitly made something a rule, "everyone knows" you wouldn't do it. It encompasses the group-held beliefs or mental models out of which decisions are made, policies are formed, and organizational structures are created. Patterns of behavior get created from these often unconscious group norms, which in turn create our culture. In turn, changing culture is not just about changing our behaviors but also about changing our group consciousness. Another example: At the beginning of a meeting, everyone opens their laptop and works through the meeting. Conversely, suppose the norm is that no one opens their laptop. If one person then decides to do so, the rest of the room would give "signals" that this is not acceptable behavior in their system.

What is important for us to know about development in the *Systemic Consciousness* line? To achieve lasting change, we have to develop awareness (consciousness) of our current norms and ways of being before change will even become possible. Further, if we are unconscious, these tendencies will degrade our current performance and trap us in unintended habitual patterns of behavior. We can improve our access to systemic consciousness by, for instance, developing our Relationship Systems Intelligence (RSI), which is a further evolution of emotional intelligence and social intelligence. The higher a person's RSI, the more skillfully that individual is able to work with groups. Naming the emotional field, helping to reveal a system to itself, making unconscious agreements explicit—all of these efforts give more access to systemic consciousness and higher group functioning. Systemic constellations are an advanced form of directly tapping into systemic consciousness to understand the underlying dynamics within a system, whether that system is a team, a business unit, or an organization (Regojo, 2016).

At the lower (Amber) end of this dimension, people are totally unaware of systemic consciousness or actively ignore or repress awareness. They are not consciously aware of themselves or others and how they are creating their environment together, and they do not "see" the system at play.

In the middle of the range, people have some access to systemic consciousness—someone may name the elephant in the room, for instance. Nevertheless, they do not take responsibility for their part in creating the group consciousness, nor do they believe they have the ability to collectively change that consciousness, and therefore the things that consciousness creates (e.g., norms, policies, structures). They don't necessarily see that a specific behavior is a "voice in the system" that needs to be heard but rather something that needs to be managed. Managing that voice would not change the consciousness of the system.

Michele's Take

Several years ago, I had a client (and I've had several since) who came to me and asked me if they should "fire" a certain person on the team. They were asking this question because they perceived this person as "negative" and always stirring something up within their own team, as well as in other teams they interacted with. They had already tried moving this person to another team. As I observed this person, I realized that the perceived "negative" behavior was actually a voice in the system that was acknowledging frustration with the bureaucracy and politics—the difficulties the person was having while trying to use the Agile practices being learned. Others simply did not speak up or did so only with a trusted friend or colleague, for fear of retribution. When the client asked me that question, my response was "Well, you could, and you could hire someone else who might behave the same way, or you could listen to the voice of your system trying to speak and inform you of something to pay attention to and to inquire about."

Toward the upper Green and Teal end, we start to take the idea of systemic consciousness seriously. We are able to articulate emotional fields. For example, when coming into the aforementioned meeting, we might say, "Wow, it feels kind of tense in here. What happened?" We start sensing the systemic dynamics at play, and how it is impacting the meeting and the sense with which people are "in the meeting." We are able to do this from a place of presence—being with what is happening not only within ourselves but also within the context of the group. From this place, the observation would not be one of blame but rather of seeing this from a third entity—the system. Further, we begin to take responsibility for the systemic consciousness and see how we can collectively use it as a lever point in changing or shifting culture or the relationship atmosphere within a team or department.

Sometimes, we can "fake it until we make it" (the quadrants influencing each other). At other times, we are in over our heads.

Insight to Action: Evolving Systemic Complexity

To begin taking action, recall the definition of this discipline: designing, shifting, and shaping the organization's collective set of beliefs, mores, and mental models in the direction of organizational agility. Doing this is likely to require a combination of cultural complexity and systemic consciousness. In addition, leadership development—and evolving individual consciousness—is likely to be necessary.

- Where are there openings for doing this type of work first? On a leadership team level, creating greater systemic consciousness may be the place to start, including creating greater awareness of the way leaders' relationships affect their performance, and how together they carry the culture.

- If the whole organization is largely aligned with the transformation intent, working directly on cultural complexity may become more possible. For instance, the values of the next higher level (e.g., Pluralistic-Green) could be seeded into internal communications and activities.

Summary

We have now concluded our discussion of the Integral Disciplines and their related developmental lines in each of the quadrants. There are two points to remember.

First, each Integral Discipline is a way to focus work from that quadrant perspective and will likely require growth in at least one of the developmental lines identified (or some of your own). Collectively working the Integral Disciplines assures you are taking an Integral approach to your transformation.

Second, the quadrants are not truly separate, discrete things but rather perspectives on a common thing (be it an individual, team, program, or organization). The quadrants influence each other developmentally but do not operate in lockstep. So, on the one hand, if a leader becomes more complex in his or her order of consciousness (I quadrant), the leader's behavior (IT quadrant) will *tend* to follow suit—but that's not for certain. On the other hand, we frequently see people espousing Agile process ideas (IT quadrant, Green to Teal altitude) without having the ability to act at the same level of complexity in the I quadrant—for instance, not actually being able to work as a servant leader because the person has not achieved the requisite level of personal development, which requires a self-authoring or higher altitude. Look for the synergies across Integral Disciplines.

From Insight to Action

Having now reviewed all the Integral Disciplines and related developmental lines, including the "Insight to Action" sections within each discussion, it's time to look at the big picture. It is ideal to begin with the results of the Integral organizational assessment from Chapter 8 as inputs to this task. That assessment helped you identify the major areas in your organization that require development. The point of the Integral Disciplines is to focus our use of the IATF in service of moving toward organizational agility. So let's consider each quadrant, as well as Conscious Change, and at least one set of activities or practices to engage each of the disciplines. It will also be helpful to choose a measure related to that discipline, so you can have a sense of whether you are making progress.

Chapter Notes

1. Using the Teal altitude here is potentially misleading. On the one hand, it points us to the fact that this is a more sophisticated level of development within the IT quadrant. On the other hand, it does not necessarily require people to be functioning at the Teal level (or self-transforming mind) from an I quadrant perspective. We can "be" at different altitudes in different quadrants. There may be a question whether, to sustainably act from this level in the IT quadrant, we must also evolve to a comparable level in the I quadrant.

10

Leading an Agile Transformation

This final chapter coalesces the IATF and supporting theories, approaches, and concepts to provide practical guidance for leading an Agile Transformation—an organization's journey to greater levels of agility. There are many titles for those who lead Agile Transformations. Whatever your title—Agile Transformational Leader, Sponsor of a Transformation, Agile Change Champion, or Enterprise Agile Coach—this chapter is written to help you, as an "Integral conscious change leader," co-create and partner with your organization (or your client) to achieve a greater level of agility.

We have made the case throughout this book that transformation starts with leadership, that it requires an Integral conscious approach to change, and that we must evolve the consciousness of leaders and those engaged in the transformational journey. Using the overall *Integral Discipline* of Evolving Conscious Change as our orienting principle—plus industry work on the competencies required for coaching a transformation—we will now more fully explore the journey involved in leading an Agile Transformation.

How to Get Started

If you do not have Agile experience and skill within your existing organization, it is important to find the right people to help you from the beginning. Whether you decide to hire skilled Agile coaches as full-time employees, or whether you choose to bring in a vendor/partner to help you get started, keep in mind that this is one of the most important beginning decisions you will make. Here is some guidance that you may find helpful however you choose to move forward:

- Use an intentional, strategic approach for this process, and make it a high priority.

- Be clear on your purpose for the transformation and what's important to you (the remainder of this chapter will help with that).

- If using a vendor/partner, can they specifically speak to how they will approach and "staff" the engagement? Consistency within the coaches' approach is important.

- If you are planning to use external coaches to start with, make sure you bring in coaches who are aligned in their approach; otherwise, their differing approaches will confuse your organization. Do they truly share a common approach beyond the basic Agile process frameworks?

- Hire Agile coaches who have varied competencies, such as *technical* (Agile engineering/technical practices), *business* (product management), *transformational* (organizational development [OD]/change background), and *leadership* (able to coach leadership at all levels of the organization) masteries.

- Who will be involved during the discover/assessment phase? Will the same people be involved doing the work?

- Can the coaches speak to their change approach? That information should include their approach to handling conflict, resistance to change, developing or growing your existing culture and mindsets, working with your organizational barriers to change, and partnering with other parts of the organization for boundary spanning. Other factors that can help you decide if this coach is a good fit for your organization include their willingness to transfer their knowledge to internal people (if they are external consultants) and whether they have the overall depth of skill and experience needed.

These are a few key things to pay attention to in the initial stages. There is more guidance you can gain from using a highly experienced and skilled consultant/coach to guide you through this beginning process, and even throughout the engagement. One of the most important elements in getting started is to find the right transformational leader. We assume that person to be you, dear reader, and the rest of this chapter speaks directly to you.

Transformational Leader Role and Competencies

Whether your transformational leader role is as an internal or external enterprise coach, or a leader in your organization tasked with leading the transformation effort, the competencies we share here apply across the spectrum of Agile transformational leadership. The following competencies are from work we did with a small group of fellow contributors in partnership with ICAgile over the last couple of years to define competencies for the Enterprise Coaching with Agility track (part of the Business Agility Roadmap) required for a practitioner to be designated an "expert" in enterprise coaching. While the competencies were defined for such coaches, we believe that anyone involved in leading an Agile Transformation will greatly benefit from using this information as a developmental roadmap.

While writing this book, we deepened our thinking about each of these competencies and their alignment with the outcome-creating competencies of leaders, as well as the competencies defined in the OD space for leading organizational change. With that said, we first briefly define each competency, then provide our perspective and recommendations for each in turn:

- **Developing self as leader (instrument of change):** Is self-aware of strengths, weaknesses, and belief systems; incorporates self-development practices to address the gap between intent and outcomes; and sees and manages oneself as an agent of transformation.

- **Developing leadership in organizations:** Invites leadership development at all levels; coaches and develops transformational leaders; and creates or influences leadership development initiatives.

- **Coaching range:** Coaches individuals and systems; coaches as a professional coach; facilitates groups across organizational boundaries; mentors and advises at the enterprise level; able to create training programs for enterprise agility; coaches at different levels within the organization and across multiple domains (e.g., technical, business).

- **Guiding organizational agility:** Works with complex adaptive systems; designs organizational structures; applies adaptive patterns and principles for organizational design and scaling; understands the whole value stream; works with business process and improvements; guides the direction of product creation practices, processes, and behaviors; engages leadership in working with organizational culture; and measures business outcomes.

- **Guiding the change process:** Understands organizational and human processes of change; conducts organizational systems entry; assesses organizational systems; designs the change strategy; guides organizations in implementing and sustaining the change; and communicates, educates, and facilitates at an organizational level.

As we elaborate further on each competency, hold lightly in your mind how you relate to each, and how you might further develop in that area in a way that could offer a greater impact in your work with change. It's not surprising that we start with "developing self as leader"!

Developing Self as Leader

As a transformational leader, your most important tool or instrument in the change is *you*. The journey of "self as leader" helps us more clearly see our limitations and how they show up in the most difficult challenges we face. It is said that leaders cannot take anyone further than they themselves are able to go; this becomes particularly poignant when the topic is transformational change, where the stakes are high and anxiety is easily triggered. Often, we feel "stuck" when working with an individual or a particular organizational challenge, especially when that challenge involves the human elements in change. A pattern that we have frequently observed is that we as transformational leaders are often drawn to (entangled with) issues in clients that we are working on in our own lives. Further, it is not uncommon for us to be unaware of our biases, autopilot approaches, quadrant orientations, and development levels; therefore, we may be unaware that our recommendations are coming from our own way of seeing and doing things and our own ego needs, which may not be what is needed by the client. This is a key reason why one leader can have success, whereas another was unable to make progress. Our ability to facilitate development in others absolutely depends on the *presence* we offer in the relationship. Doing our own inner work as leaders—developing awareness and presence—is the most important work we can do as a human being. Taking a "coaching stance" can be extremely powerful, as we practice working with our inner state, making the experience of presence more accessible. In short, this happens when we practice what we have been preaching in Part II.

How, exactly, does presence make a difference in working with others? When we are present, we invite the other into this same presence. This creates a different energy in the space within the relationship. It invites both partners into a deeper connection, a deeper search for meaning and understanding, a letting go of resistance and fear. We rise to a greater place of resourcefulness and responsiveness to the conversation, seeing and hearing more deeply. We "hear" from our inner core rather than with just our ears. We begin to make more and deeper connections to the other's circumstances. In this way, our presence-based way of leading helps to naturally evoke change in others.

As a transformational leader, engaging in self-awareness and development practices is the key to building presence and to becoming more impactful and effective in our work with others. In addition to presence, our self-awareness helps us take as object our own triggers, altitude and quadrant biases, and limitations, so that they do not become obstacles for others. The path of development covered in Part II for leaders is the same path for Agile Transformation leaders. Some specific competencies associated with "developing self as leader" are as follows:

- Able to maintain awareness of their own emotions and use this to guide how they act in emotionally charged situations.

- able to demonstrate self-control and recognize their own stress points.

- Regularly able to see themselves and their way of being in the moment and notice the impact of this on others.

- Able to articulate and fully accept their own story and how it creates strengths and liabilities in their work.

- Able to adapt their approach to others' needs without compromising their own integrity.

To develop any one of these competencies requires becoming aware of your current level of ability in that area and then engaging in practices that help you strengthen your capability. As humans, we all have different strengths; what's important here is that you develop in the areas necessary to achieve the transformation level appropriate to the complexity of your work. As an example, to be able to maintain awareness of their own emotions to guide their actions when emotions are running high, a person requires a relatively high altitude of development in their "emotional developmental line." At the same time, many people have little access to their emotions and are sometimes unable to name them or recall when they felt "emotional" about something. So, the appropriate work for someone with a low emotional line is to develop a plan, with specific practices, that increases the capability to not only get in touch with their emotions but also "be with" difficult or uncomfortable emotions.

Michael's Take

The following specific example highlights a more general issue that I have seen literally hundreds of times in Agile coaches, where the coach's "ambition" for the client starts running the relationship to the detriment of both parties. An enterprise coaching client team had developed an ambitious Agile Transformation plan with a client, but the plan was not progressing. To be fair to the coaches, the client was attracted by the Agile Transformation buzzwords and willingly went along with the plan. By doing some really great personal work, the coaching team realized that they had helped the client to, in essence, envision a Pluralistic-Green (or even Teal) transformation vision, but the culture and leadership of the client were clearly Traditional-Amber to Achievement-Orange. There was essentially no hope that such a plan could work, which explained why no progress was being made. The group—humbled and open to what might come next—went back to the drawing board. Their courage to see the reality clearly was an example of both ethical action and how the need to do our own inner work helps us to truly help our clients. This is such an important lesson: As coaches, we have the best of intentions to help our clients, but if our clients are not currently capable of certain levels of development, to push them just becomes "our idea," rather than meeting them where they are.

Michele's Take

One of the members of my Enterprise Coaching Cohort Program, Kerri, shared with me how her development of self as leader has impacted her life:

> It has opened my eyes to see leaders as the humans we all are. What I mean by this is that in the past, I might have been quick to assess someone based on outward actions. For the past year, I've practiced engaging with leaders and seeing them through an Integral lens. In the process of doing my own Self as Instrument work, I have softer eyes and a more empathetic heart for others, being curious and less biased during our interactions. The result has been humbling. Leaders have shared with me their appreciation for being heard and being seen by me.

Coaching Range

Whether you are a leader in an organization or a coach, you are guiding people's growth and development. Just as Agile Transformation must start with the leader, so it is the same with coaching. If we are not doing our own work, we limit the territory we can help others explore. Our self-development expands the range of coaching we have access to at any given moment (including both vertical and horizontal development, like learning new coaching techniques). When we expand our coaching range, we become better able to help others discover more powerful ways they can move through their obstacles and generate new insights and possibilities for themselves. Your expanded range of coaching helps you, as a leader, work more effectively with groups and address system conflict across organizational boundaries, thereby helping members engage in new and effective behaviors. Coaching range also refers to our ability to be with a full range of emotions, to be fully present in deep listening with others, to be able to advance their growth.

As a transformational leader, your ability to take on a coaching stance, when the situation calls for it, opens up a very different relational space between you and the other.

The idea of an Agile *coaching stance* (Spayd & Adkins, 2011), as first articulated in the context of Agile coaching, initially had four core competency areas from which to draw to fully occupy this stance: two process-oriented ones (*professional coaching* and *professional facilitation*) and two content-oriented ones (*teaching* and *mentoring*). The former two are about holding space for others to work and develop, whereas the latter two deal with providing direction and constraints for action. As the notion of a coaching stance developed in its use, and as various professional coaching methods have been brought in to the Agile coaching space, a much finer set of distinctions emerged beyond the four core stances to include the metaskills—that is, the "come from" place we use when working with people. Thus, in certain instances a group might require "muscular" facilitation, while in others more "spacious" facilitation would be appropriate. The ability to bring different metaskills (e.g., authenticity, warmth, compassion, fearlessness) reflects our own development and emotional range and must fit the needs of the situation.

All leaders and coaches, whether leading a transformation or not, can greatly benefit from using these techniques in their leadership style. Sometimes the leader adopts a stance of training, or mentoring and advising, especially when a situation is first forming, when the team is new, or when the situation is chaotic. At other times, a leader needs to encourage people and groups to self-organize, to make their own decisions, or to fully buy into the solution; in these cases, neutral facilitating, or individual or group coaching, will prove more effective. Sometimes the switch between stances can be quite fluid in the moment, even moving back and forth between a couple of stances during the same conversation. (When you make these switches, it is often useful to "signal your turns.") Overall, it is helpful to have some training and development in these various competencies. When your moves to different stances occur fluidly, the transitions are seamless to the other person.

One way to think about your own coaching range is by using three key dimensions: (1) the *appropriateness* of the stance you choose in a given moment; (2) the *fluidity* with which you are able to move between stances and ways of being; and (3) the *number or range* of stances you have available to you. The last point reflects being skilled in the four competency areas (coaching, facilitating, mentoring/advising, teaching); working at different holon levels (since coaching an individual is quite different from coaching a team as a system or an organization as a complex adaptive system); and being able to tolerate a range of emotions in yourself and others, as well as a range of altitudes or levels in the hierarchy. For example, working with a team member centered in Green versus a middle manager centered in Orange versus a senior leader centered in any number of altitudes requires very different skills and way of being. Having access to this range is no less important for a transformational leader who is a line manager than it is for an enterprise coach.

Many leaders primarily take a training or advising (directive) stance. When introducing something new, this can be quite helpful. However, for people to find their own path of development and fully embrace the intention of new skills and practices, you do not want to stay in this stance for too long or adopt it too frequently. True facilitation is a skill that requires you to be able to step out of the content, detach from the outcome, listen intently, and stay focused on helping the group achieve their desired outcome through knowledge of collaborative and other group practices. If you find that you need to continually contribute to the content in your sessions, it is wise to bring in a facilitator who can keep your group on track for achieving their desired goals.

A coaching stance is primarily dedicated to serving the development of others, to helping them find their fulfillment. In a business context, the "leader as coach" intention is to help people develop capabilities in areas that will help them achieve their goals and develop competence in behaviors that are authentic, are effective, and produce the desired business results. This looks very different from training or directing (though those stances can certainly be worthwhile). As a transformational leader, your competence and capacity to coach people across and at all levels of the organization will have a major impact on your ability to influence and inspire change. This is the essence of the *coaching range* competency.

Developing Leadership in Organizations

We've said a lot about developing leadership in self and others. We mention it here to reinforce that having an approach to developing leaders at all levels is an important competency needed by an enterprise coach (or any transformational leader). By developing leaders, we don't just mean horizontally in the outer game, through skill or competency training (though such training can certainly be needed), but also vertically in the inner game, raising the level of consciousness. One of the difficulties we have found with this endeavor is that leadership development frequently falls within the scope of HR or a change management area within companies, where at times the distinction between horizontal and vertical development is not clearly understood or prioritized. We're not saying that an enterprise coach necessarily needs to "own" the leadership development initiative, but at the least the coach needs to partner with HR (more on this topic later).

Since the beginning, Agilists have tended to work primarily within the IT quadrant, where leadership development was not seen as an activity that was in scope for an Agile Transformation. (That is an untenable approach, as we have emphasized throughout this book.) In fact, leadership in general has often received far less focus or help, in part because engagement with leaders has been limited to an IT quadrant focus (e.g., processes). Leadership training has typically been a half-day (or less) event that gave leaders a high-level view of Agile activities but ignored the deep changes needed within those leaders. The training may have included Agile leadership traits like being a "servant leader," encouraging "empowering teams" rather than "command and control," and having a basic understanding of Scrum. Most leaders we've encountered did not deeply grasp the concept of servant leadership, much less become able to magically turn into this kind of leader.

It's far past the time to change this situation. It is absolutely crucial that we help leaders make the connection between leadership effectiveness and Agile Transformations and their success. This link seems to be missing in most organizations. Creating it requires us to focus our efforts on building partnerships with HR and the change office or areas where leadership development is owned. At the very least, we should be educating our clients on this link between vertical development and Agile success. At the same time, if it is HR's responsibility to create programs intended to foster the development of the organization's leaders, and we do not respect their boundaries, we will trigger resistance. The HR professionals will feel threatened, since their identity is at stake. Along with their sense of purpose, their basic need for individuality gets stomped on, and they will undoubtedly react in a manner that protects themselves. More often than not, the enterprise coach then takes a reactive stance as well, blaming HR or the leadership for the lack of progress or success. This is an example of why conscious change leadership is so important. On autopilot we make habitual moves. When they don't work, we make ourselves the "victim."

Another key differentiator for an enterprise coach is that such a coach is capable and competent to work with all levels of leadership (part of their coaching range). If you are directly involved in leadership development, see if this is a limitation for you: Many enterprise coaches started out as Agile team coaches, and possibly in the ScrumMaster role at first, so they are not always comfortable, experienced, or skilled enough to work in a coaching/developmental way with executive leaders (though they may be skillful executive advisers). Making the transition to coaching executives requires that you have the necessary capabilities, developed as part of the "self as instrument" and "coaching range" competencies:

- You have a confident sense of self, operating most often in high creative mode. You are not intimidated by people in a position of authority but are able to "speak truth to power" with kindness and respect, overcoming your own fear.

- You are able to hold a systems perspective, which is the way senior leaders tend to see their world.

- You can give immediate and concrete feedback.

- You are able to both challenge and support the leader.

- You are able to tie the coaching to business results and maintain that focus.

- You can make connections and links to situations and circumstances and follow a thread closely.

- You can work with a full range of emotion, including the leader's anxiety (even when the leader is uncomfortable with that anxiety).

- You allow others to take ownership of their goals, successes, and mistakes.

- You are, of course, an excellent listener, holding the connection to the client and still sensing the space.

You may be an enterprise coach currently working in an organization where you haven't been asked to coach the leaders, nor are you contracted to do so. Sometimes, the opposite happens: You aren't contracted to coach leaders, and you find yourself in the position of doing so. In either case, having an open and transparent conversation with the leaders about your role and your desire and ability to coach them, and then designing an alliance with them, is important. It takes presence and skill to get into the right conversation about you filling a coaching role with executives or senior-level leaders. How do they see you now, and what do you need to do to have them see you differently? If you are playing the role of "rescuing" them, and they are giving you "work" to do, they are likely not seeing you as a strategic-level coach or thinker.

It will take conscious unlocking moves to see transformational-type changes in leadership. Unlocking moves come from our presence-based coaching stance. They occur when we become radically curious with others; when we seek to listen and understand more than we speak; when we come from a place of compassion and empathy; when we speak from our inner being (center or core) rather than from our head space, to their center; and when we are able to look *as* them (seeing as they see), instead of only looking *at* them. We help others "wake up" by modeling the behavior of a conscious change leader and by engaging in authentic dialogue with them about mindset and how our inner self drives our outer behavior.

Insight to Action: Self as Instrument

In the previous sections, we covered aspects of conscious change that are focused on your own development as a transformational leader, as well as your ability to develop leadership in others. Take a few moments to reflect on the following:

- How are you currently engaged in practices that develop your self-awareness and work with your limitations?

- What do you believe is your biggest personal challenge as a transformational leader? We don't mean a challenge with someone else, but rather *your* challenge, the thing that keeps you "stuck" in your work with people.

- As you think about your ability and range to move into a coaching stance as a leader, what is one thing you could practice?

- How can you influence your organization to place more importance on vertical development for leaders?

Guiding Organizational Agility

The competency of guiding organizational agility encompasses many of the core reasons that organizations want an Agile Transformation, especially those reasons associated with the right-hand quadrants (though the left-hand quadrants are certainly needed as well). An Agile Transformation is specifically intended to reshape your organization's way of working, its organization structure, its adaptability and flow of value (such as value streams), and the business processes and practices associated with value creation and innovation, as well as the culture and mental models that underlie those right-hand results. Basically, it works with whatever is necessary to enable the level of agility needed.

When you decide you need transformational results, you are looking for a complete change or orientation in how you are fundamentally doing business, resulting in an entirely different level of effectiveness. In this sense, a transformation is unlike a "turnaround" or a "transition," as both of these terms imply incremental progress on the same plane as you currently operate. For you as a transformational leader to be helpful in this process, you must have some understanding of topics like complex adaptive systems, how to apply adaptive patterns to organizational design and structure issues, how to map and work with value streams, how innovation and product development work, and how to help leaders work with changing the organization's culture.

The intention of an Agile Transformation is not to merely "implement" Agile as a new way of delivering software products. Here's the reality check: If the actual organizational intention is merely to adopt Scrum or Kanban, then you will achieve greater organizational clarity by acknowledging the type of change you are seeking is tactical or transitional, not transformational, and by adjusting your approach to accommodate that type of change. Continuing to refer to it as an "Agile Transformation" is confusing and potentially demoralizing, despite the fact that "Agile Transformation" has become a buzzword for anyone implementing Agile practices.

Here's one more example to illustrate what a transformation is like: If you've ever gone back and visited a city, maybe one you grew up in or lived in for a while, and the city had reconstructed different highways and roadways and developed new housing and shopping centers since you left, you likely did not recognize it. You may have even gotten lost! When an organization wants to transform itself, to do business differently, and have different results, it requires this same level of change. So as a transformational leader, start by asking yourself questions such as the following:

- What results do I want, different from the results I am getting today?

- How do I radically increase the results from this change?

- How does innovation play a part in our company?

- How am I linking our Agile Transformation to my drivers of change and desired outcomes?

Let's take one business driver as an example to follow the logic. We know from years of practice with clients that organizations turn to Agile for the following kinds of reasons, among many possibilities: improved time to market, improved customer satisfaction, enhanced product innovation, earlier return on investment (ROI), greater collaboration, better quality, building the right products, and higher team morale. If you stop and take apart even just one of those benefits, you will begin to see how the four quadrants come into play as the organization seeks to fully achieve that benefit.

Let's consider the first possible reason: improved time to market. If Agile practices are brought in only at the software delivery team level, teams typically face the following obstacles:

- Lack of real product ownership

- Significant delays in approvals

- Missing information

- Lack of a clear vision from the business

- The business mindset that Agile is an information technology process

- Competing priorities across the business

- Team members reporting to different people with different and competing performance metrics

- Lack of testing environments

- Lack of excellent technical engineering practices

- Metrics that drive the wrong behavior

- Pressure to deliver more and more each sprint, resulting in technical debt or poor code quality, as well as burnout and decreased team morale

- A culture where experimentation and failure is not welcomed, leading to a lack of transparency

- Leadership delegating rather than leading

If time to market is a real business driver, the business must be a key leader and stakeholder in the Agile Transformation. The business and IT areas, as well as the entire organization, need to address all of the obstacles mentioned to improve time to market. Mindset, culture, behavior, processes, systems, structures—all play a part in the obstacles that teams are facing. And the truth is that most leaders are trying to solve those problems in the same manner they have always solved them, which results in the status quo rather than transformational change. In this scenario, Agile can become the scapegoat. Whatever your business drivers are, take a closer look and see how the internal and external dynamics of change are impacting your results.

In summary, transformation is about innovation, disruption, ideas, possibilities, and creativity. This is how your organization will not only survive but also thrive in a world of constant change. Agile Transformation is *organizational change* requiring both the entire organization to participate and commit to the change and you to give attention to all four quadrants in making the transformation.

Guiding the Change Process

An Agile Transformation leader or an enterprise Agile coach (whether internal or external) has a key role in guiding the organization in the change process. Notice the use of the word "guiding" rather than "being responsible for." The change process is a co-created process with the client and especially with members of the Agile Transformation Community. We've already established the importance of leadership not mandating and delegating the leading of the transformation to others. The ability to co-create can only happen from an outcome-creating stance, from a mindset and thinking that welcomes learning, that embraces other perspectives, that holds compassion for others, and that is less concerned with one's own needs and wants and more concerned with the organization as a whole.

In Chapter 8, we made the case for using an Integral OD approach and consciously attending to the internal and external dynamics of change—this is how you build the change capability in your organization. So what does that look like?

The Human Aspects of Change

From the moment of the leader's wake-up call, the human element of change is there. When leaders recognize that a change is needed in how they are leading their organization, when they recognize the need for a big shift in their way of working and solving challenges, and when they begin to feel in over their heads, then their emotions, feelings, fears, anxieties, and excitement—in short, their humanness—have already entered the process of change. They may not recognize it or be in tune with it, but those human aspects are ever present and at the forefront of whatever actions they will take and how they will be with, and in, the change. Having awareness of their humanness in this change will help them see more clearly how the changes will impact the rest of the organization. It will also help them design their change plan with elements that consider how humans react to change and the importance of building in ways of attending to this need every step of the way. Not doing this will always trigger resistance, which will impact the ability to actually make the change successfully, in addition to making the process more painful.

Many different models address how people go through change, whether that change involves grief, death, divorce, job loss, job change, or something else. Some of these models talk about the human reaction to change in a very linear way. In our experience working with organizational change, people do not necessarily go through the changes in the same way or in a linear fashion. To the extent that you consciously design your change with this understanding, you have the ability to get ahead of many of the barriers to change that keep organizations stuck. Let's take a look at one change model that speaks to the human process of change, the Virginia Satir change model, depicted in Figure 10.1.

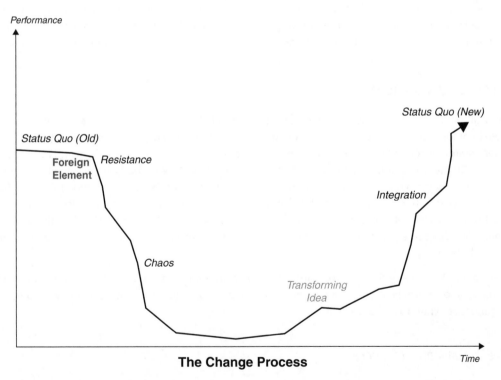

Figure 10.1
Virginia Satir change model (Image credit: https://10minutehr.com/2013/11/11/chaos-in-the-organisational-change-process-dont-try-to-avoid-it-manage-it/)

In the typical change management "to do" approach, the change is planned behind closed doors, and then a formal corporate communication is issued about the change (designed to "spin" the change rather than authentically communicate it), with little to no input from the people doing the work and without co-creation of the solutions designed. Naturally, this approach tends to produce a high amount of resistance. What actually triggers this resistance is people's perception that the change is being done *to* them rather than *by* or *through* them. But what if, instead, at the very start, where a foreign element triggers or reveals the need for a change to the status quo, you inserted an Integral OD approach from a conscious stance? What does the situation look like then? The resistance is likely to be much less.

Contrary to popular belief, humans do not naturally resist change, though they do resist change imposed on them. Here are some other reasons people resist change:

- Risk: Loss of status or security in the company. They believe they will be harmed by the change.

- Non-reinforcing reward systems: They see no rewards with this change. "What's in it for me?"

- Surprise and fear of the unknown: They have insufficient information. For example, they do not understand how it will impact their work, their day-to-day interactions, or their future.

- Peer pressure: They want to protect "the group."

- Climate of mistrust: There's too much unaddressed bad history.

- Organizational politics: They have personal motives. They believe leadership has personal motives.

- Fear of failure: They doubt their capability.

- Lack of tact or poor timing: They resent the leader's implementation approach.

To truly evolve change, to use a more conscious and human-centered approach, would mean considering those barriers to change and attending to the needs of people at the start of the change effort. We know that this will require leadership that is self-aware (seeing the seer) and giving attention to their own development and way of working with others (taking the perspective of others).

The Organizational Aspects of Change

The organizational aspects of change typically attract the most attention, and a number of organizational change models have been around for many years. Among these well-known models are John Kotter's approach (1996) and Prosci's ADKAR model. As with any framework or model, how you use them is key. Just as the human process of change is not a linear and predictable model, so the same holds true for organizational models of change. While some elements of change are linear, in an Agile context we take an adaptive approach, building in frequent feedback loops and course corrections, and we engage the whole system in an intentional process, including all quadrant and altitude perspectives. We should also begin building sustainability early and throughout the change process.

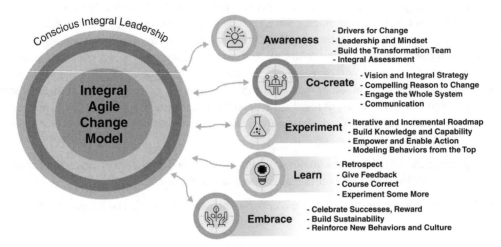

Figure 10.2
The Integral Agile Change Model

We call our approach to change the *Integral Agile (IA) Change Model*. At the highest level of this model, conscious Integral leadership is the overarching element, as it is involved at every step of the change (Figure 10.2). Following are the five big stages:

1. **Awareness:** This stage includes a deeper, multilayered meaning of awareness. It includes awareness of why you are embarking on this change (such as business drivers), what transformation means in your context, what it requires in terms of leadership and commitment, self-awareness of leadership and mindset, awareness of your organizational effectiveness in leading change, building awareness within your leadership and transformation community, and awareness of where you are starting now, through an organizational assessment. The awareness piece doesn't stop after the first steps—it continues throughout within the context of your activity and work at hand.

2. **Co-create:** Our intentional use of this word shines a light on how co-creation is a critical "come from" place for making people feel they are engaged in the change enough to feel ownership and for ensuring the high quality and effectiveness of your solutions. This dimension includes articulating the compelling reason for change, co-creating a change vision, and beginning to engage the whole system.

3. **Experiment:** Experimentation is the Agile way of working and being in change. It requires taking on an adaptive (probe–sense–respond) mindset, rather than a predict-and-plan approach (which comes from a Reactive mind). Experimenting means trying new ways of doing things, and doing them iteratively and incrementally and at different scales. It may mean creating action roadmaps and evaluating them frequently. People will need to understand more about the new way of working so that they will be able to actually experiment—this addresses some of the barriers to change listed earlier. When you empower people so they can experiment, you will be taken back to your own leadership development and your ability to take a step

back and work with your underlying emotions of anxiety and fear and the need to control the situation. When you decide to undertake an Agile Transformation, experimentation is critical, as is having awareness of your current culture and tolerance for risk and failure. Thus, it is key to have dialogues about this topic early on. When you choose to do a transformation, you will likely have to shift your current way of working, and leadership will have to model the behaviors they are expecting of their people. This takes some practice, some experimenting, and both patience and compassion.

4. **Learn:** We experiment to learn and to grow. We think retrospectively about how we did, then keep doing what's working, and learn and correct our course when it's not. We must be willing to give and receive feedback to learn and grow, both individually and organizationally. Learning leads to new experiments and, in turn, new learning. It requires a conscious intentional effort to create a culture characterized by experimentation and learning—and depending on your existing culture, you will need to think about how you build this into your change strategy.

5. **Embrace:** When you are embracing change, you are celebrating successes; you are not wondering whether you should keep doing this but rather how you can reinforce your learning and your success. This dimension exemplifies why the IA Change Model is not a linear model.

Each of these steps should be happening all the time in cycles, as things emerge and unfold, as change happens in the middle of a change effort. Most importantly, leadership should *embrace change*.

Let's explore some of the key elements of our IA Change Model in a bit more detail to understand more about the practical steps.

Systems Entry

With the awareness of the human and organizational aspects of change just described, the way in which you, as the change leader, begin to work with the system that will be changing is vital. From the first conversation about the change, you begin to be a part of the system. In OD, this critical time is known as *systems entry*. It is the part of the change process where things can start to go right or to seriously veer off course. If you are an external enterprise coach, the idea of entering a system likely makes sense; if you are an internal employee, however, it may seem an odd thought. Our experience is that this phase can be more challenging for an internal person, but it is an equally vital time.

The main tasks of systems entry are to determine who the client really is, to establish rapport with key players, to understand the overall "what" and "why" of the change, and to agree on the scope of your role and how you will work together. Systems entry traditionally ends with a form of social contract with the sponsor and other key players that articulates this understanding. This process, and especially the notion of how to "contract" with your client (internal or external), is beautifully articulated in Peter Block's book *Flawless Consulting* (2011). Critically for our purposes, he distinguishes three ways consultants are asked to work: as *experts* (with delegated authority), as a *pair of hands* (just taking care of a leader's "to do" list), or in a *collaborative* way (our preferred approach, and what we call co-creation). Block points out the leverage for how you work together with your client system is highest at the beginning. In particular, if you act overly agreeably and lack integrity, from personal experience, we have found that you will come to regret it.

This is where the work of self-as-instrument in leading change from a place of conscious intention is so important. We must recognize that we create our own experience of reality and that we are responsible for our own actions, behaviors, and results. When we aren't consciously creating the outcomes we desire, we are *letting things happen*. It then becomes easy to fall into the "victim" mentality, blaming others when things aren't going as expected. Getting clear on our own wants and needs as a transformational leader is an essential task during this time.

Here are some important elements to consider at the entry point of the system's change:

- **Identifying who the client really is.** This may seem to be a strange task, but it is actually a bit tricky. For instance, from some point of view, the client is logically the person who is the *change sponsor*, and who you may even report to; from another perspective, it might be the *change team or transformation community*; while from still another viewpoint, it is the *system* itself, the one that aligns with the organizational scope of the change. Each of these perspectives has its validity. Adding to the complexity, they are nested systems. Becoming clear on how to think about who/what the client is—both for yourself and for articulating and aligning with others—will create greater clarity and make the change process go better. When we have failed to clarify who the client really is, we have regretted it.

- **Identifying the change sponsor.** This is a very critical determination, especially if someone has already been designated as the sponsor but is not really appropriate for that role. Two things are essential in a sponsor: commitment and influence. Sponsors must be committed enough to give the initiative their all, even investing part of their own reputation in its success; lacking this, a transformation will struggle. The second notion—appropriate influence and organizational power—is best fulfilled by the person with ultimate authority for the organizational scope of the change. In other words, if the change scope is truly the whole enterprise, the sponsor should be the CEO; in contrast, if the scope is a business unit, the sponsor should be the general manager (or other title) responsible for that business unit.

- **Identifying all of the stakeholders.** Some of the stakeholders will be obvious, whereas others will be a bit harder to identify. Ask a variety of people, from different roles and at all levels of the organization, who will be impacted by the change. This will cast a wide net and also begin the process of building rapport.

- **Contracting.** As we've mentioned, systems entry is an important time for the contracting (social contract, not necessarily a legal one) discussion about your role as transformational leader. Whether you are an internal person given this responsibility or an external Agile coach entering the system, there are some common misconceptions about this role, and without an overt contracting discussion, many (potentially erroneous) assumptions will be made. A contracting discussion, held before assumptions start to cause issues, is a conscious way to go about entering the system. If you are an external coach entering the system, and you weren't a part of the original "sales and solution" process, it is even more important to sit down and develop a mutual understanding of your role, giving the client insight into your own way of working and your values and guiding principles. In this way, you are co-creating the partnership from an intentional space.

- **Building rapport and designing an alliance with the transformation team and all stakeholders involved.** This activity seeks to develop a shared understanding and expectations of your ways of working together—being very clear about roles, responsibilities, expected commitments, how you will handle conflict, how they will offer feedback, and the overall guiding principles and values for collaborating.

- **Clarifying the business case.** It is critical to work with the client to identify the business case for change, the expected outcomes, and the scope of the effort. When this step is not done, or when it is done in a perfunctory way using common jargon, an understanding of what success looks like and how you will know (measures) when you have achieved it is lacking. Therefore, leadership will not have an understanding of whether their Agile Transformation is successful and the data to support it.

- **Clarifying the coaching role.** It is also important to be clear on your coaching role when working with leadership. This can be considered part of contracting, and you should establish a designed alliance with any leader you do coach. In most instances, organizational leaders are not really expecting individual leadership coaching from an enterprise Agile coach, though they likely will seek advice about "being more Agile." Working with different levels of leadership requires a different set of coaching skills and a greater understanding of each leader's business context and challenges. Being clear about what the coaching relationship will look like upfront is critical. When assumptions are left unchecked, we find ourselves not standing fully in our power, because we aren't sure if we are on the right track, overstepping, not stepping up enough, and so forth.

Knowing Your Drivers for the Change

It is critical to understand the factors that are driving your change—to know them from more than a "head space" of knowing, in a way that concretely lays out for people the organization's challenges and the reasons why your Agile Transformation is needed. Drivers of change can come from many places, such as organizational, marketplace, environmental, technological, cultural, leadership, and mindset factors. Much of the time, we see organizational, marketplace, and especially technological factors as business reasons for driving a change. What is often missed by leaders is the reality that even a large technology change, for instance, may also require a transformation in culture and mindset—and not just in leaders but in employees as well. The following example illustrates how a company believed it was just changing a technology and completely missed that there were also cultural, mindset, and environmental change drivers.

Michele's Take

A number of years ago, my mother worked part-time for a large pharmaceutical company. Her job was to deliver critical medications to nursing homes and other critical care facilities across the entire state. The company employed hundreds, if not thousands, of employees in this role. There were, of course, managers, pharmacists, and a large staff supporting this service.

Over time, things changed in this industry, with government and state regulations tightening, changes occurring in delivery methods, and enactment of other regulations on types of medications available to administer, the Health Insurance Portability and Accountability Act (HIPAA), and laws that mandated electronic data capture and filing. In turn, the company was forced to change the way it had fundamentally worked with its clients. The organization's top leaders went about making the changes behind closed doors and then "rolled out" massive changes to the entire company with some tight deadlines and mandates. The leaders did not think about culture or mindset, or basic human respect, or the unintended consequences that might result.

Almost all of the company's drivers were older, retired, or part-time workers. These drivers had built solid reputations with the nursing homes and critical care facilities and their staff, but they were not technologically savvy. Many of the drivers quit their jobs because they were afraid, frustrated, and unable to learn the new technology, or they were fired if they couldn't conform to the new rules. While the company did offer them some training, it wasn't enough, and it wasn't expected.

The care facilities were also not ready for the changes; indeed, they were not even aware of them until after the fact. They became disgruntled, unhappy clients when their drivers quit or were fired. The critical medicines began to be delayed, causing the nurses to have to take shortcuts. The nurses also had guidelines about giving medications to patients, so this had consequences for them as well.

This case is an example of how leaders can miss the impact of what is believed to be just a "technology change." This change actually required attention to all four quadrants and development of a conscious and strategic approach to be successful. You might say, in the end the changes were eventually made. Maybe so, but the costs to the organization, to the leaders, to the employees, to the clients, and to both client retention and employee retention were great. You might be able to get something accomplished through a reactive mindset, but there will always be a high cost associated with it. Moreover, you will not get transformational, breakthrough-type results.

Knowing your business drivers for change is an intentional exercise, requiring seeing the impacts, interdependencies, and deeper aspects of what the changes will entail. It cannot be done on autopilot. In an Agile Transformation, many of the aforementioned drivers of change will come into play, and it will be important to work through each one to create a clear picture of what changes are involved, what outcomes you desire, what measurements and metrics are important to track, what existing data you will use, which new behaviors are needed, what siloes are contributing, and what success will look like. This information will help you in building a change story that will *mean* something to your organization.

Assessing the Organization

Organizational assessments, sometimes in our context referred to as Agile readiness assessments, are intended to make visible the current state of the organizational system, looking at various perspectives, and using a structured Integral approach that considers all four quadrants, as well as the altitude and developmental lines of the organization. We suggested that you informally start formulating questions for your own assessment at the end of Chapter 8. Even if you are well into your transformation effort, now that you have read this book and begun to internalize our Integral approach, we suggest that you seriously consider performing such an assessment. If nothing else, you will be making explicit what you have already taken to be the case implicitly (and likely unconsciously).

An Integral organizational assessment includes looking at the client and their collective beliefs, the level of psychological safety, behaviors and attitudes contributing to the quality of outputs and deliverables, business practices and processes and their degree of alignment with Agile practices, organizational systems and structures and their level of adaptability and flow of value, governance, decision making, tolerance for experimentation, HR performance systems, mindset and effectiveness of leadership, and so forth. This will help you as the transformational leader to see more clearly where the organization is and in turn take appropriate actions and meet the client where they are currently. The assessment should address the gap between the current state and the desired state and provide clarity to guide the next steps.

Consulting companies and independent coaches alike have various approaches to how and when they do assessments and whether they charge for them. We have often been asked to give a full-blown proposal with a clearly identified approach for the transformation early on in the sales process, before we have done an assessment with the organization. Without an assessment, proposing a solution suggests that there is a "one-size-fits-all" approach to an Agile Transformation. If the organization is looking for a true partner, who will develop a solution and an approach that will take its organizational context, challenges, and vision into account in the design of the solution, the proposed approach/solution needs to come *after* the assessment. Of course, assessments need not go on for many weeks or months. The enterprise coach who will be engaged with the client should lead the assessment, with help from other members of the change team, then sharing the findings and recommendations with the senior leadership team. For this reason, we believe it is generally preferable that organizations pay for assessments, as they receive a valuable output as a deliverable. This assessment time gives the client an opportunity to witness the coach/consultant in action and to get a sense for their work quality as well as their personal dynamics.

Building Your Agile Transformation Community

When you've heard the call to change, both for you personally and for your organization, and you understand what is required for this change to become real, you must then determine how the transformation will be led. You will not be surprised to hear us say that this step also requires your conscious intention. In fact, throughout the entire transformation, conscious change leadership is needed at each step along the way.

Your Agile Transformation Community includes the group of leaders at all levels who come together to guide the change; they are all change leaders. This role is not an "extra" responsibility added onto what they are already responsible for but is a key responsibility valued by the organization. We have seen a pattern where various formal Agile roles—such as Product Owner, Change Sponsor, Agile Transformational Leader, Agile Champion, and the like—are "chosen" by management, and then assigned either to people who have more available time (but not necessarily the right skill set) or to busy people as an add-on to their current role (so they then become *too* busy). These are huge mistakes. If the outcome of this change effort is one of the highest priorities of your company, then you have to ask yourself if you are setting the effort up for success.

When building your Agile Transformation Community, consider a variety of factors, such as passion and vision for the change, people who *genuinely want* the role, the competency and skill sets needed, diversity, influence in the organization, high achievers known for getting things accomplished, well-respected leaders, open-minded leaders, great listeners, great communicators, inspirational leaders, leaders who mentor and develop their people versus micro-managers, leaders who aren't afraid to experiment, great collaborators, leaders who balance work and personal life, and so forth. While this list seems a bit idealistic, your careful and thoughtful way of building this team will be well worth the time and effort devoted to it. Start with a leader who possesses many of the characteristics just outlined to help build this community.

Your Agile Transformation Community should include representation from all areas (not just IT). Specifically, it should include the following people:

- The sponsor of the change
- The executive leadership team (the one appropriate to the organizational scope of the change)
- The transformational leader
- The Agile Transformation or change team
- Enterprise- and team-level Agile coaches

Michael's Take

An outstanding example of an Agile Transformation Community occurred in a midsize client in the financial services industry. The group's foundation was the strong partnership between the vice president of engineering (Mac) and a vice president of the business organization (Stacey), who was Mac's client. The two truly had a common vision, and they provided a stellar example of the business–IT partnership that many Agile coaches find lacking in their transformation clients. The group added the vice president of the project management office (PMO; Angie), who owned corporate governance, to the team, which created a center of gravity from a leadership point of view and was an example of a leader-first approach.

I recommended that the group begin working organizational change issues before we started launching Agile teams; though it was not what they were expecting, they took my advice seriously. The result was the leaders really knew what to expect organizationally before the teams they led were confronted with the change issues. They were perceived as truly leading the change. We later added a Scrum Master, a tech lead, and a first-level team manager to balance out the levels organizationally. This Agile Transformation Community guided a successful transformation of at least some aspects of the company.

Guiding the Change Strategy

The enterprise coach plays a critical role in helping the client to co-create the change strategy for the transformation. Your change strategy (strategic transformation design) is a high-level plan of what it will take for the vision to become a reality. The change strategy should include the following elements:

- A structured approach for designing the change strategy in co-creation with the client rather than from an expert-led approach. This makes the client the owner of the change—with your guidance—which reinforces, aligns, and increases the likelihood of the client moving closer to the goals.

- The human and business systems' agility aspects (the internal and external dynamics of the change). Using the IATF as a compass and a map, the enterprise coach is able to see clearly what key strategies are needed in each quadrant and so can design the strategy more effectively.

- How you will communicate your transformation and change story to the organization.

- A structured, designed approach to work with the mismatch between the current culture and the desired culture.

- How decisions will be made, including the flow of decision making and change governance.

- A courageous, authentic conversation with the client, when the espoused change efforts are not reachable with the imposed constraints (e.g., values, culture, capacity, leadership, willingness).

- Principles that the organization will abide by in the change (e.g., purpose, organizational values).

- An iterative and adaptive, rather than deterministic, approach, with built-in feedback loops based on an empirical "inspect and adapt" model.

- A course correction model, in which positive feedback strengthens the existing direction from the current reality to the envisioned state, and in which negative feedback makes transparent the need for learning and course correction. Course correction—pausing to learn and move in a new direction—requires people to be aware of their reactive tendencies that could come online here, given that this is a challenging space for most. It requires people to lean into the ambiguity of not knowing, to admit mistakes and failures, to acknowledge feelings of vulnerability, and to understand that competencies or capabilities may potentially need to be developed. If we aren't operating from an outcome-creating mindset, we can become highly reactive and allow confusion, self-doubt, emotion, and our underlying fear of failure to take over. Alternatively (but still reactively), we may overpower that uncertainty by strong-arming a decision that is not yet ready to be made, but that needs to be held internally to work with the polarity to allow it to clarify itself.

Co-creating a Compelling Change Story

After you have understood your change drivers and created a vision for the change, it is time to communicate that information more broadly and get organizational buy-in. Here is where you need your "change story." The co-creation of your story needs to articulate your drivers of change and your vision in a way that people can understand and feel why the change is needed.

All too often, change is communicated using a formal corporate-style communication method—possibly an email or some formal "announcement." Your organization has likely undergone many types of change initiatives in the past, but it is surprising how many employees in organizations cannot articulate the reason for any particular change. The average employee in a medium-size to large organization seems to be far removed from the vision for the Agile Transformation. We've heard all kinds of answers when we've asked team members and even middle- and senior-level management about why a change was being undertaken, including "I don't know why"—but they generally make assumptions about the rationale.

If you have gone about prior transformations (of any kind), if you have tried an Agile Transformation in the past and it failed, or even if you are doing your first real transformational type of change, it is absolutely imperative to create a compelling reason for people to enroll in this change. They will need to see that it will be different from past failed efforts, and the communication effort will need to involve more than words from leadership. Employees will need to see the authenticity and observed modeling of different ways of behaving and thinking from the leadership. This is also where collective leadership effectiveness comes in. If there are dissention and divisiveness among and across the horizontal boundaries in an organization, the employees will also be divided, siloed, resistant, and so on. To truly be enrolled in the change, those employees will need to be a part of the process and provide input; they will need to feel and see the benefits and to see that leadership is actually leading and embodying the changes they want to see.

Leaders frequently ask us how to create a compelling story for the change. There is no set practice or magical formula, although having an approach that is engaging and comprehensive, and that includes the right people, is important. The first, most critical factor in establishing a compelling story for the change is to make it an intentional co-creative process. Collective conscious awareness is important in going about the task of creating this inviting and compelling change story. Your organization has a story about where it's been, how it got there, what worked, and what's no longer working. There is much to be proud of and to appreciate, and there are things to now let go of because they are no longer helping the organization move toward its envisioned state. Now, you are adding to the organization's story.

Considering Your Capacity for Change

The capacity for change is not typically discussed in the Agile space. So let's get out of Agile land for a minute.

We said earlier that organizations need to get really good at change, because change will always be there. Take a minute and think about all the changes you have had to go through in all the organizations you have worked in. There's likely a mix of small process-type changes and larger transitional or even transformational changes. Lately, organizations are having to go through more transformational changes just to survive.

Now, think about how many of the changes you've experienced were coordinated with the other change initiatives happening in the organization. Was any thought given to prioritization of the changes, impacts, interdependencies, or change fatigue? In all the organizations we have worked with, "organizational change" has not been a conscious and intentional effort. In most organizations, there is no umbrella group that holds the responsibility for all change efforts. People can only sustain so much change, and there is not always sufficient capacity for people to work on many or large initiatives simultaneously. Burnout, employee morale, and employee turnover are inevitable in an organization that does not go about change in a strategic, disciplined, conscious way. And you cannot expect to get creativity and inspiration from exhausted employees.

When we step out of Agile land, we consider other change initiatives, we ask about them, and we seek to discover how the other change efforts will impact the Agile Transformation and how they overlap, in terms of the people, the process, and the technologies. We think about how we will coordinate efforts, align them toward common organizational goals, communicate consistent messaging, and so forth. We also begin to educate the organization about how to approach change, in general, in an entirely different way.

Your organization needs a mechanism for managing change, for prioritizing, and for considering the capacity for more change. Think about this question: If your organization got really good at change, what would your competitive advantage look like? What if getting good at change was a top priority? When you think about change, do you feel frustration, does anxiety kick in, or do you feel resistance? Feel into this, and discover what you can learn about change and your mindset and approach to it. Think about how your employees might feel the same way, when another change comes down from the top, piled onto their already full workloads. You might be hearing things like "Great, here we go again—another change, something else to add to my existing workload!" This is a sign of change fatigue. There are many reasons why we feel resistance to change, and this is one of them.

An outcome-creating leader, in using the Integral Disciplines, looks at all four quadrants in the assessment of the organization's capacity for change. If I'm reacting to pressures, I'm just driving my people; I'm making decisions and I'm mandating change. It takes a purposeful vision, strategic focus, systems awareness and systems thinking (beyond the immediate pressures), sustainable productivity, and genuine concern for the people of your organization to thoughtfully go about enacting organizational change.

Implementing and Sustaining the Change

Once you have developed your change strategy, you are ready to put it into action. An enterprise coach will have a keen eye for identifying all of the factors that will impact the organization's ability to move from the current state to the desired state. The coach will see what currently exists that is supportive, what is missing that needs to be created, and what is there that will block or hinder success. Taking a deliberate and structured approach to identifying these factors, and discovering more about the necessary actions, including what questions need to be answered and what support is needed, begins to create the transformation backlog and inform the roadmap. It is important to prioritize these issues and focus on the things that might block or derail the transformation efforts, making them completely transparent. While we promote transparency in Agile, it is not unusual for people to hold back on delivering some hard facts or asking some difficult questions, depending on the culture and the transformational leader's own reactive tendencies.

Your roadmap/implementation plan should include the following key elements:

- Prioritized work items (actions)

- An owner for each action item

- Individuals/teams working on items

- Timeline: A roadmap that is a living document, looking at shorter time frames, allowing for inspecting and adapting and course correction actions

- Impacts, dependencies, interdependencies: Areas of the organization impacted by or involved in the change

- Staff/resources: Time, materials, and budget needed for the work

If your organization is hiring outside consultants and coaches, an important early step is to build into your strategy how you will sustain the change. This isn't limited just to how you will sustain your Agile Transformation once the external coaches are gone. Rather, it is important to have an intentional strategy early on in the transformation for the outside Agile coaches to mentor and develop people who are moving into this role. In addition, it is critical to create strategies and actions that will sustain people's motivation and keep the momentum going, especially for an Agile Transformation that is likely to take quite a long time. The enterprise coaches and transformational leaders should work with the energy of people, sensing and responding to it. More importantly, they should proactively build energy-sustaining strategies all along the way of the transformation journey.

Working with the Barriers to Change

Organizational impediments are often revealed during the change process. At the organizational level, these impediments can become major barriers that compromise your ability to achieve agility. These types of barriers typically involve strategic misalignments in areas such as the drivers for the change, the vision, and the change strategy; they affect all quadrants of culture, mindset, structure, and practices. If leaders are not aligned on the problem they are solving, the solutions, and the execution, obstacles will show up in many different forms within the process of the change.

Many times, you can identify some of the barriers to change in the upfront assessment, and we recommend that your change process include ways to resolve these impediments in your change strategy. Notably, when organizations are unwilling to begin the transformation with an approach that targets culture change, the challenges will expose themselves and then will need to be addressed. Many of these challenges were described earlier in the discussion of the human and organizational aspects of change.

When working with your organization's barriers to change, your leadership stance will be a key factor in your ability to be collaborative and co-creative in solving these challenges. One way to approach these issues is to set up an organizational structure that is cross-functional and cross-level, where you instill a culture of curiosity rather than one of fear or anxiety, that follows practices stemming come from a "sense and respond" mindset, and that facilitates a process that distinguishes between facts, feelings, and assumptions in an objective way.

Insight to Action: Guiding the Change Process

We have just covered quite a bit of material on the elements involved in guiding the change process—from consciously considering the human and organizational aspects of change all the way through implementing and sustaining the change. There are many possible actions you can take, which will vary within the context of your organization's change. Here are some actions you might try:

- Observe how you are paying attention to the human aspects of the change and how this might be contributing to some of your barriers to change. How are you reacting personally?

- Assess the approach you are using for your change and whether your change model incorporates all aspects of the Integral quadrants. If you aren't currently using a change model, how can you influence and modify your current approach?

- Take some time to go through each element in "Guiding the Change Process" section and make notes about actions you might take to address a current barrier to your change.

- As you take these actions, and in conversations with others, maintain a stance of curiosity and inquiry with them. Notice what is needed to meet them where they are and to be helpful in generating new insights. When you feel "stuck," pause, breathe, challenge your thinking, and choose your next move from a conscious stance.

- Remember the "transcend and include" approach. When you feel frustrated or "stuck," notice what is healthy or partially true about the other person's thoughts or ideas, acknowledge those positive aspects, and include them in your approach. When you can more consistently do this, you will be able to move into a collaborative discussion. A good way to think about this is the improv approach of using "yes, and. . . ." When you adopt this approach, you don't deny the other's inspiration.

Activating the Integral Disciplines

As we wrap up the book, let's take stock of where we're at. You might feel as if we've just hit you with a bewildering array of perspectives, reflections, practices, and potential actions to consider. Actually, putting the IATF into action at this point could seem a daunting task: There are, after all, an infinite number of options. To help focus your thinking, here are just one or two actions within each Integral Discipline that we believe will jump-start your effort. You might consider it a list of "the things you could begin tomorrow" to apply the IATF to your transformation.

Using the Integral Disciplines as an Organizational Compass

The most salient effects we can have proceed through focused action. The Integral Disciplines provide a structure for that focused action when engaging an Agile Transformation. We'll offer a personal example to introduce this way of thinking with an analogy.

If a person wishes to be as healthy and high functioning as possible in every respect, some forms of training and discipline are better than others. If we want a well-functioning life—physically, emotionally, mentally, and spiritually—a random program simply will not cut it. The latest diet, or the most highly rated exercise program, will not get us to *all* of our goals. Rather, we need to design a focused program that economizes our effort and has the synergistic benefits of "cross-training," where working on one component of the program (say, weight training) is complementary and synergistic to another component of the training (say, yoga or Pilates). In the end, doing both together gets us more quickly to our overall goal (in this example, perhaps increasing core body strength).

This principle of a multidisciplinary, cross-training program was used by some advanced Integral practitioners in collaboration with Ken Wilber to develop *Integral Life Practice* to fulfill the goal of having the highest functioning life in every key dimension. There are four core modules in Integral Life Practice: Mind, Body, Spirit, and Shadow. We can understand intuitively that it makes sense to create a feeling of wholeness and balance in our lives. The experience of the Integral Life Practice's creators—and ours—is that taking just one practice from each module, when done regularly in a disciplined way, creates stunning results. The Integral Coaching process uses the same principle with different lines of development across the four quadrants to help clients grow. We have used this underlying design principle to develop the Integral Disciplines.

By taking some regular action in each of the five areas defined by the Integral Disciplines, you will dramatically increase your chances of success. Rather than employing an IT quadrant–focused approach of "teaching, tooling, and enacting" the Agile practices—and rationalizing that we'll get around to leadership and culture issues after we have Agile "installed"—we take a balanced approach right out of the gate. This does not necessarily mean our efforts are equal in each discipline—but we don't ignore any of them, either. The amount of effort within each discipline does not have to be great, but it does need to be consistent and substantive.

The five Integral Disciplines become a kind of compass for the transformation, setting the direction and allowing us to check where we are at, as we go along. To help you move in this direction, we conclude the book by considering what you might do to put each of the five Integral Disciplines into action.

Actions for Evolving Conscious Change

Assess your current change process

- What is your current change process and in what way are you consciously and intentionally incorporating both the human and organizational aspects of change?

- Try experimenting with the Integral Model. Notice what elements might be missing from your overall approach (e.g., organizational assessment and contracting). Try implementing some of the missing key elements that are having a big impact on your results.

- Does your organization consciously pay attention to all change initiatives in the organization and have an approach for prioritizing and coordinating all change efforts under one umbrella? You might consider experimenting with establishing a small change office to begin with. Discover all of the change efforts currently under way and learn as much as you can about them, including how people are feeling. Once you have this data, you will have a better understanding of the organization's current capacity for change, including adding the Agile Transformation as another large change initiative.

Actions for Evolving Consciousness

Vertically develop your organization's leaders   Leading an organization through transformation requires you to develop the internal and external capabilities needed to navigate this type of complexity, which requires vertical leadership development. Given the likelihood that many leaders are "in over their heads" in regard to the transformation, the first step is to get valid 360-degree feedback for all leadership involved, and then follow it up with a structured leadership development program based on which competencies need further development. In setting this up, we recommend checking in with and perhaps partnering with your HR group, since they will likely manage the use of leadership coaches and 360-degree assessment instruments. It is important to link the development of leadership within the context of the Agile Transformation to the leadership development efforts of HR.

Develop your collective leadership effectiveness   An additional (but complementary) way of supporting vertical development is through the use of peer leadership coaching cohorts. In these groups, leaders support each other in their leadership development goals, learn to give feedback, and hold each other accountable to their individual and collective development goals.

Actions for Evolving Product Innovation

Determine your current level of product development maturity   You first need to assess your organization's current altitude in regard to its product development practices. If senior management still sets deadlines, rather than the product owner deciding that the product is ready for release, your organization likely has a more goal-oriented approach to development. As we said in Chapter 9, this middle range of altitudes (Orange moving into Green) is about moving from being focused on the product as a *goal* (schedule, cost, scope) to focusing on the *customer* and hearing their voice. If your organization is too focused on meeting the project management goal for the product, moving to *customer-centric* development is a strong move. All Agile methods inherently incorporate a customer-centric approach, though they may not be practiced in that way within a given organization. Conversely, if your organization is already operating from this customer-centric place, bravo! The next step is to move to a more organization-centric approach, in which all voices in the system—not just customers' voices—are heard and considered.

Take on a small handful of new practices geared toward organization-driven product development   Which practices you use, and how you use them, will depend on your starting point (from the assessment action). If you're starting from a *goal-centric* place, it will likely be quite difficult to reach an *organization-centric* level, so instead aim for the *customer-centric* middle ground. In part, we favor this incremental approach because it is easier for an Orange culture to make sense of focusing on the customer rather than the whole organization. If you are already a solid *customer-centric* organization, take steps to move toward the *organization-centric* level by defining a broader product owner team function, using transformational facilitation techniques such as deep democracy, and implementing boundary-spanning practices. For instance:

- See everyone as a voice of the system.
- Create and facilitate transformational containers.
- Practice deep democracy.
- Adopt boundary-spanning practices (particularly buffering, reflecting, connecting, and mobilizing).
- Establish a product owner council.

Actions for Evolving Adaptive Architectures

Determine your current adaptive architecture performance   Again, this action is a kind of assessment piece that is addressed before you launch into an intervention. There are multiple possible places to start working on organizational structures, policies, and/or governance. Try to determine the highest leverage points to increase the adaptability of the organizational structure and its fit with Agile philosophy, such as through alignment around value streams. We might ask questions like these:

- Is the organization designed to support and give visibility to product flow? Is it aligned around value streams?
- In what ways does the organizational structure enable—or constrain—the flow of value?
- How capable is the organizational structure of shifting and flexing in response to changing environmental conditions?
- How Lean are the current processes, and how will that impact agility?
- How does the organization's approach to governance impact the transformation adaptivity?

Next, choose a target area to focus on, based on your assessment, and try some experiments. We suggest you pick one area first: either organizational structure within a given area, policy alignment around Agile philosophy (performance management and funding are two likely valuable targets), or governance regarding some organizational set of the product portfolio. Some possible interventions include the following:

- Reorganize a given area around natural *value streams*.

- Redesign the *governance* process and structure in a sufficiently large part of the portfolio to see the effect.

- Launch a *policy alignment* initiative for some key policies in a substantially sized business unit.

Actions for Evolving Systemic Complexity

Assess the current culture   The first step, from a WE point of view, is to assess the fit between the existing culture and the kind of culture conducive to Agile and organizational agility and in line with your vision. Without a basic sense of your organizational culture's *meme stack* (e.g., Amber-ORANGE, or ORANGE-Green, or Orange-GREEN), it will be difficult to know what is possible and what to focus on first. This assessment could be done within the change team, within the Agile Transformation Community, and/or with other key stakeholders.

A simple card sort technique can be used with perhaps 10–30 participants. Each card represents an altitude value (with the same number of cards provided for each altitude, such as 5). Those values are ranked by participants, who place the cards individually into piles (which can be assigned numeric values to create a way to score them). For instance, this value applies to our organization: Almost always (5)—Sometimes (3)—Rarely (1). Table 10.1 provides an example of the words that might be used at each altitude for the cards.

Table 10.1   Keyword Concepts That Describe Each Altitude

Altitude	Keywords
Traditional-Amber	Tradition
	Conservative
	Predictability/structured
	In control
	Hierarchical
Achievement-Orange	Freedom/self-reliance
	Goal-driven
	Innovation
	Accountability
	Rationality
	Achievement

Altitude	Keywords
Pluralistic-Green	Equality
	Hearing from everyone
	Diversity
	Sensitivity/connection
	Pluralism
Evolutionary-Teal	Creative
	Self-determination
	Systemic
	Self-organization
	Purpose-driven

From this data, we can estimate the culture meme stack in play. For instance, here is a possible scoring with 15 people sorting 5 cards for each altitude:

- Amber card score = 75

- Orange card score = 264

- Green card score = 130

- Teal card score = 67

This scoring suggests a culture that is ORANGE-Green, meaning solidly Achievement-Orange but evolving into Pluralistic-Green. This result will then have implications for how we try to use Agile—perhaps emphasizing time and cost savings, and carefully tapping into the Green elements that are emerging, with an emphasis on relationships, consensus, and diversity of ideas and opinions.

In addition, to understand the culture and relationships better, we might ask questions like these:

- Is the leadership modeling the behavior of the culture they desire?

- What politics are at play, and how is that showing up in the environment?

- Who are the collective of people who are highly influencing this effort?

- In what ways does the existing culture align with Agile values?

- What is the level of resilient relationships: Are people more transactional or people-oriented in their relationships?

- To what extent can we work across organizational boundaries, moving from an "us versus them" mindset to a shared "we" mindset, and getting beyond typical "silo wars"?

Summary

This chapter has fully explored the topic of leading an Agile Transformation, within the framework of a set of competencies defined for transformational leaders, plus the five Integral Disciplines, with an especial emphasis on conscious change.

In Conclusion

At the beginning of this book, we referred to the IATF as a kind of Rosetta stone, translating between different views of what's needed, different contexts, and different approaches to Agile Transformation. This systems-thinking tool is intended to help you see more clearly and act more effectively. We hope this meta-framework has become a viable reality for you and that you will use it in ever-deeper ways.

As we were writing the book, our world was going through perhaps the most complex global challenge we've ever faced. The COVID-19 pandemic has given clarity to the fact that we are all the same in our humanness, in our vulnerability, and in our potential for creating a new vision for our future. Every industry, every country, and all people have been impacted; the decisions we make now will produce consequences and results that no one can be entirely certain about. And yet, in the face of this uncertainty, leaders are called to make decisions and take action. If ever there was a case for raising our consciousness, surely this is it.

Now, it's up to each of us to continue the journey of evolving consciousness in our world—through our organizations, through our practices, through our leaders, and with the people who devote their lives to the organizations in which they work. This endeavor can only start with us, individually and collectively, for transformation is always an inside job.

And that is how we change the game.

References and Relevant Readings

Anderson, Robert J. (2006). *The Leadership Circle™ and Organizational Performance.* The Leadership Circle. https://jp-ja. leadershipcircle.com/wp-content/uploads/2018/03/The-Leadership-Circle-and-Organizational-Performance.pdf

Anderson, Robert J. (2008). *The Spirit of Leadership,* Position Paper, theleadershipcircle.com.

Anderson, Robert J., & Adams, William A. (2016). *Mastering Leadership: An Integrated Framework for Breakthrough Performance and Extraordinary Business Results.* Hoboken, NJ: John Wiley & Sons.

Anderson, Robert J., & Adams, William A. (2019). *Scaling Leadership: Building Organizational Capability and Capacity to Create Outcomes That Matter Most.* Hoboken, NJ: John Wiley & Sons.

Anderson, R., & Garvey-Berger, J. (2019). *Integral Self Informed by Grace.* Coaches Rising Seminar.

Bánáthy, B. H. (1997). *A Taste of Systemics.* The Primer Project. http://www.newciv.org/ISSS_Primer/asem04bb.html

Bateson, Gregory. (1979). *Mind and Nature: A Necessary Unity.* New York: Ballantine.

Beck, Don Edward, & Cowan, Christopher C. (1996). *Spiral Dynamics: Mastering Values, Leadership and Change.* Oxford, UK: Blackwell Publishing.

Beckhard, Richard. (2013). *Organization Development: Strategies and Models.* Reading, MA: Addison-Wesley.

Bertalanffy, Ludwig Von. (1968). *General System Theory: Foundations, Development, Applications.* New York: George Braziller.

Bertalanffy, Ludwig Von. (1974). *Perspectives on General System Theory.* Edgar Taschdjian, ed. New York: George Braziller.

Block, Peter. (2011). *Flawless Consulting: A Guide to Getting Your Expertise Used.* 3rd ed. San Francisco: Wiley.

Bradden, Gregg. (2019, November 7). *The Language That Will Change Our Future* [Video]. https://www.youtube.com/ watch?v=8Y4K6TJoPUk

Burns, James MacGregor. (1978). *Leadership.* New York: Harper & Row.

Capra, Fritz. (1997). *The Web of Life: A New Scientific Understanding of Living Systems.* New York: Anchor.

Davidson, Mark. (1983). *Uncommon Sense: The Life and Thought of Ludwig von Bertalanffy, Father of General Systems Theory.* Los Angeles: J. P. Tarcher, Inc.

Ernst, Chris, & Chrobot-Mason, Donna. (2010). *Boundary Spanning Leadership: Six Practices for Solving Problems, Driving Innovation, and Transforming Organizations.* New York: McGraw-Hill Education.

Esbjörn-Hargens, Sean. (2010). *Integral Theory in Action: Applied, Theoretical, and Constructive Perspectives on the AQAL Model.* New York: SUNY Press.

Gardner, Howard. (1983). *Frames of Mind: The Theory of Multiple Intelligences.* Needham Heights, MA: Allyn & Bacon.

Goldratt, Eliyahu. (1990). *Theory of Constraints: What Is This Thing Called Theory of Constraints and How Should It Be Implemented?* Great Barrington, MA: North River Press.

Graves, Clare. (1971). *How Should Who Lead Whom to Do What?* http://clarewgraves.com/articles_content/1971_YMCA/1971_YMCA_10.html#fig1

Graves, Clare. (2005). *The Never Ending Quest.* Christopher Cowan & Natasha Todorovic, eds. Santa Barbara, CA: ECLET Publishing.

Hellinger, Bert. (1998). *Love's Hidden Symmetry: What Makes Love Work in Relationships.* Phoenix, AZ: Zeig, Tucker & Co.

ICAgile®. Enterprise Coaching Competencies. www.icagile.com

Integral Coaching Canada. https://www.integralcoachingcanada.com/icc-advantage/coaching-method; https://www.integralcoachingcanada.com/sites/default/files/pdf/jitpintroduction.pdf

Joiner, Bill, & Josephs, Stephen. (2007). *Leadership Agility: Five Levels of Mastery for Anticipating and Initiating Change.* San Francisco: Josey-Bass.

Kegan, Robert. (1982). *The Evolving Self.* Cambridge, MA: Harvard University Press.

Kegan, Robert. (1994). *In Over Our Heads: The Mental Demands of Modern Life.* Cambridge, MA: Harvard University Press.

Kegan, Robert, & Lahey, Lisa. (2009). *Immunity to Change.* Cambridge, MA: Harvard Business Press.

Kotter, John. (1996). *Leading Change.* Boston: Harvard Business Review Press.

Kotter, J., & Heskett, J. (1992). *Corporate Culture and Performance.* New York: Simon and Shuster.

Laloux, Frederic. (2014). *Reinventing Organizations: A Guide to Creating Organizations Inspired by the Next Stage in Human Consciousness.* Brussels: Nelson Parker Publishing.

Larsen, Diana, & Shore, James. (2018). *The Agile Fluency Model* [Ebook]. https://www.agilefluency.org/ebook.php

Laszlo, Ervin. (1996). *The Systems View of the World.* Cresskill, NJ: Hampton Press.

Lavigne, Genevieve. (2011). *Self-Determination Theory.* https://journals.sagepub.com/doi/pdf/10.1177/0146167211405995

Meadows, Donella, & Wright, Diana, eds. (2008). *Seeing Systems: A Primer.* White River Junction, VT: Chelsea Green Publishing.

Organization and Relationship Systems Coaching (ORSC). https://www.crrglobal.com/courses.html

Oshry, Barry. (1995). *Seeing Systems: Unlocking the Mysteries of Organizational Life.* San Francisco: Berrett-Koehler Publishers.

Pruyn, Peter W. (2010, June 9). "An Overview of Constructive Developmental Theory." *Developmental Observer* [Blog]. http://developmentalobserver.blog.com/2010/06/09/an-overview-of-constructive-developmental-theory-cdt/

Regojo, Cecilio Fernández. (2016). *Organizational Constellations.* http://www.nasconnect.org/uploads/1/0/7/4/10746039/systemicmanagement-ebook.pdf

Ries, Eric. (2011). *Lean Startup: How Today's Entrepreneurs Use Continuous Innovation to Create Radically Successful Businesses.* New York: Crown Business.

Rooke, David, & Torbert, William. (2005, April). "Organizational Transformation as a Function of the CEO's Developmental Stage." *Organization Development Journal 26*(3), 86–105.

Schein, E. H. (1980). *Organizational Psychology*. 3rd ed. Upper Saddle River, NJ: Prentice-Hall.

Schneider, William. (1994). *The Reengineering Alternative: A Plan for Making Your Current Culture Work*. Burr Ridge, IL: Irwin Professional Publishing.

Senge, Peter. (1990). *The Fifth Discipline: The Art and Practice of the Learning Organization*. New York: Doubleday.

Senge, Peter, et al. (2004). *Presence: Human Purpose and the Field of the Future*. New York: Society for Organizational Learning.

Snowden, David, & Boone, Mary. (2007, November). "A Leader's Framework for Decision Making." *Harvard Business Review, 85*(11), 68–76, 149.

Spayd, Michael, & Adkins, Lyssa. (2011). *Developing Great Agile Coaches: Towards a Framework of Agile Coaching Competency* [White paper]. Agile Coaching Institute. https://www.agilecoachinginstitute.com/wp-content/uploads/2011/08/Agile-Coaching-Competencies-whitepaper-part-one.pdf

Weinberg, Gerald. (1975). *An Introduction to General Systems Thinking*. New York: Wiley-Interscience. (2001 ed.: Dorset House).

Wiener, N. (1967). *The Human Use of Human Beings: Cybernetics and Society*. New York: Avon.

Wilber, K. (1995). *Sex, Ecology, Spirituality: The Spirit of Evolution*. Boston: Shambhala Publications.

Wilber, K. (1996). *A Brief History of Everything*. Boston: Shambhala Publications.

Wilber, K. (2000a). *A Theory of Everything: An Integral Vision for Business, Politics, Science and Spirituality*. Boston: Shambhala Publications.

Wilber, K. (2000b). *Integral Psychology: Consciousness, Spirit, Psychology, Therapy*. Boston: Shambhala Publications.

Wilber, K. (2006). *Integral Spirituality: A Startling New Role for Religion in the Modern and Postmodern World*. Boston: Integral Books.

Wilber, K., Patten, T., Leonard, A., & Morelli, M. (2008). *Integral Life Practice: A 21st-Century Blueprint for Physical Health, Emotional Balance, Mental Clarity, and Spiritual Awakening*. Boston: Shambhala Publications.

Zenger, John, & Folkman, Joseph. (2009). *Extraordinary Leaders: Turning Good Managers into Great Leaders*. New York: McGraw-Hill.

Index

Photo by izusek/gettyirr

Register Your Product at informit.com/register

Access additional benefits and **save 35%** on your next purchase

- Automatically receive a coupon for 35% off your next purchase, valid for 30 days. Look for your code in your InformIT cart or the Manage Codes section of your account page.

- Download available product updates.

- Access bonus material if available.*

- Check the box to hear from us and receive exclusive offers on new editions and related products.

Registration benefits vary by product. Benefits will be listed on your account page under Registered Products.

InformIT.com—The Trusted Technology Learning Source

InformIT is the online home of information technology brands at Pearson, the world's foremost education company. At InformIT.com, you can:

- Shop our books, eBooks, software, and video training
- Take advantage of our special offers and promotions (informit.com/promotions)
- Sign up for special offers and content newsletter (informit.com/newsletters)
- Access thousands of free chapters and video lessons

Connect with InformIT—Visit informit.com/community

the trusted technology learning source

Addison-Wesley · Adobe Press · Cisco Press · Microsoft Press · Pearson IT Certification · Que · Sams · Peachpit Press

 Pearson